William Samuel Lilly

First Principles in Politics

William Samuel Lilly

First Principles in Politics

ISBN/EAN: 9783337132842

Printed in Europe, USA, Canada, Australia, Japan

Cover: Foto ©ninafisch / pixelio.de

More available books at **www.hansebooks.com**

First Principles
in Politics

WILLIAM SAMUEL LILLY

HONORARY FELLOW OF PETERHOUSE, CAMBRIDGE

"Oh for a statesman—a single one—who
understands the living might inherent in a
principle !"

SAMUEL TAYLOR COLERIDGE.

NEW YORK:
G. P. PUTNAM'S SONS
LONDON:
JOHN MURRAY
1899

The Knickerbocker Press, New York

WILLIAM HARTPOLE LECKY, M.P.

DEAR MR. LECKY,

When your treatise on *Democracy and Liberty* was given to the world, I had the pleasure of receiving a copy from the author. In expressing my thanks for the gift, I told you that I was engaged upon a work dealing, to some extent, with the same topic; and that I should deny myself the gratification of perusing your volumes, until I had finished the task to which I had set myself. I was anxious to guard against the risk of unconsciously appropriating any of your thoughts.

Three years have passed away since then. At last, I have completed my book and have read yours. And I rejoice to find that, although I write from another standpoint, and pursue a different method, there is much in the conclusions reached by me for which I may claim the sanction of your authority. It is, therefore, with a special satisfaction that I avail myself of your kind permission to inscribe these pages with your name; a name which, as I have said elsewhere—and I prefer to repeat the

words, because they were not written *ad hoc*—may
well stand as the symbol of all that is best in the
historic literature of our age: impartial accuracy,
magisterial serenity, sustained self-command, skill in
truly discerning and in logically marshalling facts,
power of ratiocination, severity of taste, and purity
of style.

But it is not merely in conclusions that I have the
happiness of finding myself largely in accord with
you. As I venture to believe, we agree in what is
the cardinal doctrine of this work—the most fundamental of the First Principles upon which it insists.
And my warrant for so thinking is a passage long
familiar to me in your *History of European Morals*—
a book which, as I well remember, came into my
hands when I was an undergraduate at Cambridge,
and took me captive by the charm of its diction and
the cogency of its dialectic. You there rank your-
self among "those moralists who assert that we possess a natural power of distinguishing between the
higher and lower parts of our nature"; and you
proceed to illustrate this point by a very striking
comparison: "Man is like a plant which requires a
favourable soil for the full expansion of its natural
or innate powers: yet those powers, both rational
and moral, are there: and, when quickened into
action, each will discharge its appointed functions."
Here we come to the very root of the difference between the two schools of thought which at present

divide the intellect of the world. I hold, with you, that reason is the characteristic endowment of man; that it is separated by a whole universe from instinct; and that what you admirably term "progressive energy" is a note of it. The capacity for ethical development is possessed by the human race alone. And the root of the capacity lies in this: that man—and man alone—is *animal rationale*.

Hence it is that I believe in the doctrine of Natural Right. And I think one chief cause of the wide-spread disbelief in that doctrine is what you term, with just severity, "a very mischievous equivocation in the word 'natural.'" The notion is common that if we assert a Law of Nature, we imply belief in a state of nature such as Rousseau, and the *philosophes* of the last century, vainly imagined. I suppose the late Sir Henry Maine did more than any one else to popularise this misconception, by lending to it the authority of his great name. It appears to me the chief blemish upon his valuable writings, which have done so much to advance among us the scientific study of jurisprudence, and to which—as I gladly testify—my own personal obligations are considerable. But, assuredly, we must account as utterly unhistoric the remarks in his *Ancient Law:* "The belief gradually prevailed among Roman lawyers that the old *jus gentium* was, in fact, the long-lost code of Nature"; and "the inference from this belief was immediate: that it was

the Prætor's duty to . . . revive, as far as might
be, the institutions by which Nature had governed
man in the primitive state." The Law of Nature,
as understood by the great Roman jurisprudents,
following the teaching of the philosophers of the
Porch, means an objective law of Righteousness,
embodied in, and learnt from, the highest part of
nature—Reason. And they identified this *jus naturale* with the *jus gentium*, because it is found in all
countries, and is applicable to all men, on whose
hearts and consciences it is written. Its dictates are
the body of rights, "the obligatoriness of which," to
quote the words of Kant, "can be recognised by the
rational faculty *a priori*." "No nation," as the Roman orator finely said, "can overthrow or annul it:
neither can a senate nor a whole people relieve us
from its injunctions." It is a law of absolute and
unconditioned authority, ruling throughout the universe, in all spheres of rational existence. It is the
ideal type to which positive law should ever more
and more approximate, though it can never be wholly
realised in human enactments.

It appears to me that if we once lose the conception of this law, we empty life of its true value,
which is ethical : we reduce right and wrong—I do
not mean in their applications, but in their essence—
to a mere question of latitude and longitude, climate and environment, temperament and cuisine.
Hooker's indignant language, when he reprobates

" their brutishness, which imagine that virtue is only
as men will account of it," seems literally accurate.
And the curious thing is that writers of the Utilitarian school, while denying the doctrine of the *lex
naturæ*, really found themselves upon it. They must
appeal to the rational faculty in support of their contention that man ought to pursue happiness, and, as
the more refined of them hold, the higher kinds of
happiness. For their "ought," they allow, is incapable of proof. They may not consent to call it
an intuition of the practical reason. But that is
what it really is, if it is anything more than an arbitrary assumption; it cannot possibly be derived
from sensible experience. Of course, there is a
Utilitarianism to which both you and I would
heartily subscribe: the doctrine that the criterion of
the goodness or badness of actions is their congruity
or incongruity with man's rational nature. Equally
of course, should we agree in rejecting the teaching
that the determinative source of moral quality is the
free volition of Deity. Right and Wrong, in their
nature, are what they are from everlasting to everlasting, and are unchangeable even by the fiat of
Omnipotence.

Considerations such as these were long out of
fashion in this country. But fashions change. Truth
does not. "Truth," in Cudworth's happy phrase,
"is the most unbending and incompliable, the most
firm and adamantine thing in the world." On that

foundation I have endeavoured to build in this work.
However many its defects, of which no one can be
more conscious than myself, I am very sure that, in
offering it to you, I may truly use the words of
Montaigne : *C'est icy un livre de bonne foy.*

I am, dear Mr. Lecky,

Very truly yours,

W. S. LILLY.

ATHENÆUM CLUB,

March 25, 1899.

SUMMARY

CHAPTER I

xi

Summary

CHAPTER II

THE ORIGIN OF THE STATE

CHAPTER III

THE END OF THE STATE

The conception of the State most common in this country is that it is a mere machine, driven by the forces of public and private interest : a sort of huge insurance society, the taxes being the premium. Hence the conclusion, so widely prevalent, that its

CHAPTER IV

THE FUNCTIONS OF THE STATE

Summary

Summary

Summary

And so viewed it is a limitation of a man's freedom : it
is a binding agreement for the diminution of personal liberty 89

There are many things as to which the State does not
permit such freedom ; well-recognised classes of
agreements which it does not and should not
validate and enforce 90

Conspicuous among such agreements should be reckoned
those tainted by usury, in respect of which it is the
function of the State to intervene for the protection
of individual rights and of its own supreme right . 90

Equally justifiable, and indeed necessary, is its intervention, in many cases, for the restriction and
regulation of industrial agreements. In such contracts the action of private interest cannot be
relied upon as all-sufficient. Human labour is not
mere merchandise . . . 92

The contrary doctrine, insisted upon by the old "orthodox" Political Economy issued in the establishment
of a tyranny of capital of the most odious kind,
based upon a fictitious freedom of contract. . 95

This doctrine has now largely fallen into discredit,
chiefly through the influence of the German historical School of Political Economists, which has
laboured successfully to overthrow the old doctrine
of *laissez-faire*, to bring out the insufficiency of
personal interest as the sole rôle of economic action,
to insist upon the principle that the State, as an
organism—and an ethical organism—has a most
important function with regard to the industrial
contracts of its subjects . . . 96

To the apprehension of this principle we owe the long
series of Truck Acts, Mines Acts, Factory and

Summary

CHAPTER V

THE MECHANISM OF THE STATE

Summary

Summary

CHAPTER VI.

THE CORRUPTION OF THE STATE.

It is the constant peril of the State that its authority

nbegin.

By it "a distinct, definite, clearly stated law" may be referred to the judgment of the numerical majority 233

Its success in Switzerland, which is pretty generally admitted, seems due to the extremely peculiar political conditions of that country, where something very like equality of fact prevails among the electors. It is inapplicable to countries where, society being highly complex and artificial, such equality of fact does not prevail 235

Sixth. The Multiple Vote. This is a far more promising device for mitigating the evils of False Democracy, and Mill urged its adoption with much earnestness, 236

His main argument in its favour has never been answered, and seems unanswerable. And the experience of Belgium shows that there is no practical difficulty in working it 236

Seventh. A Strong Upper Chamber. Multiple voting, however carefully and justly organised, would be, at the best, but a palliative for the mischiefs of False Democracy. Hence the necessity for a Second Chamber composed of elements qualifying it to oppose itself to the class interests of the majority, and to raise its voice with authority against their errors and weaknesses 237

In order to possess that authority, it should specially represent those factors in the national life which will never be adequately represented in an assembly due to the accident of popular election. This truth has been more or less recognised in the constitution of the Upper Houses in most European countries, and in the United States of America . . . 239

CHAPTER VII

THE SANCTIONS OF THE STATE

The thought which ended the last chapter may serve
to begin this. It is, indeed, the keynote of the
present volume. Reason, manifesting itself in
ethics, is the right rule of human action, public
or private. And law, which is a function of Reason, is the very soul of a body politic . . 253

PAGE

more vitiated progeny : children born with special
predispositions for crime . . 314

What, then, are the remedies? They would seem to be
chiefly three. First, a transformation of the existing order of rights in the interest of the suffering
working classes. Secondly, the addiction of adult
habitual offenders to industrial servitude. Thirdly,
the modification—to a great extent, the eradication
—of the terrible tendencies transmitted by them to
their offspring through a system of ethical discipline, of training of the will, which alone is education in the true sense . . . 305

The poor in virtue, as in this world's goods, we have
always with us. But only in a society which has
lost, or largely forgotten, " the mighty hopes that
make us men," does poverty degenerate into pauperism, and vice grow rankly into crime . . 306

Without these hopes—our special heritage among the
tribes of animate existence—to lift us above the
self of the appetites and the passions, we do not
rise to the true level of human life, whether individually or collectively 306

This is not, indeed, a first principle in politics. But it
is a first principle underlying all politics. The
known and natural do not suffice for human society.
It requires ideals which point to a life beyond the
phenomenal, where justice shall at length triumph,
where its rewards and penalties shall be adequately
realised, and which witness to a Supreme Moral
Governor who shall bring about that triumph and
realisation 306

That is the direct teaching of the parable of Dives and
Lazarus. On that teaching the poor lived throughout

Summary

*Fragments of this work which have appeared from time to time in
the* Quarterly, Fortnightly, Contemporary, *and* New Reviews, *and in
the* Nineteenth Century, *now find their place in these pages, by the
courtesy of the respective proprietors of those Magazines.*

FIRST PRINCIPLES IN POLITICS

FIRST PRINCIPLES IN POLITICS

CHAPTER I

THE FOUNDATION OF THE STATE

A STRIKING characteristic of the present day is
the well-nigh total effacement from the general mind, of the idea of law. This statement will,
perhaps, seem paradoxical to many of my readers.
" Why," it may be objected, " there never was a time
when law was more talked of; every school-boy,
every school-girl babbles of it : you cannot take up
a newspaper without finding some mention of laws
of conduct, laws of political economy, laws of nature,
laws of all kinds." True; but these so-called laws
are, for the most part, not laws at all, for they do
not possess that character of necessity which is of
the essence of law. What are commonly presented
to us as laws of conduct, are mere corollaries to what
are designated laws of comfort. They are, as a
writer much in vogue tells us, "generalisations from
experiences of utility." But experiences of utility,
however multiplied, cannot do more than counsel.

They can lay no necessity upon us to fulfil what they indicate as desirable. They are devoid of that categorical imperative indicated by the word "ought," which is the very note of an ethical law. Again, the so-called laws of political economy are usually statements, more or less probable, of the course likely to be adopted by free agents in pursuit of their own advantage; and such statements are not laws in the proper sense of the word. Once more. If we keep strictly within the domain of experimental science, we have no right to speak of laws. The notion which we express by the word "must" has no place in pure physics; its place is taken by the word "is." The mere physicist cannot get beyond ascertained sequences and co-ordinations of phenomena. What he calls "laws" are formulas; hypotheses which have won their way into general credit by explaining all the facts known to us, by satisfying every test applied to them. I am far from denying—I strenuously affirm—that there is a sense in which necessity may be predicated of physical laws. But for that sense—nay, for the very notion of necessity—we must quit the proper bounds of physical science; we must go to an order of verities transcending the physical, to what Aristotle called τά μετά τά φυσικά—to metaphysics; that is to say, to supersensuous realities, to the world lying beyond the visible and tangible universe. Only those laws are absolutely or metaphysically necessary which

are stamped upon all that is, and therefore upon the
human intellect; which are the very conditions
of thought, because they are the conditions under which all things, all beings, even the Being of
Beings, the Absolute and Eternal Himself, exist.
I need not pursue that topic further. I have said
enough in elucidation of my present point, which is
this: that every physical truth is necessarily connected with, or rather taken for granted, some metaphysical principle. "That which doth assign unto
each thing the kind, that which doth moderate the
force and power, that which doth appoint the form
and measure of working, the same we term a *Law*,"[1]
says Hooker, summing up, in his judicious way the
Aristotelian and Scholastic teaching on the matter.
Note the words "assign," "moderate," "appoint."
Law is of the will and of the intellect; and the will
and the intellect are not the proper objects of
physical science.

I beg of my readers not to suppose that in insisting so strongly upon this matter I am indulging in
mere logomachy; in unprofitable strife about words.
The question is concerning the true idea of law—an
idea of the utmost practical importance. The doctrine that the universe is governed in all things by
law, "the very least as feeling her care, and the
greatest as not exempted from her power," is no

[1] *Ecclesiastical Polity*, book i., 2.

mere abstract speculation which men may hold or
reject, and be none the better or the worse for holding or rejecting it.   No ; it is a doctrine fraught
with the most momentous consequences in all relations of human life.   Law is not something arbitrary,
the edict of mere will ; it is, in the admirable words
of Aquinas, "a function of reason."   Lose the true
idea of law, and you derationalise the universe.
You reduce the wondrous All to mere senseless
mechanism.   You undo the work of the creative
Logos.   You enthrone Anarchy in its place.

These are not the words of rhetorical declamation.
They are the words of truth and soberness.   And if
we seek an illustration of them, we have but to look
around.   For what—if I may use the German word,
now indeed, naturalised among us—what is the
Zeitgeist of the age in which we live?   I suppose
the first thing that strikes any thoughtful person,
conversant with contemporary speculation as exhibited in current literature, is the perfect babel of
opinions to which expression is given.   All men
who can write grammatically—and many, indeed,
who cannot—seem to think they have a call to express their "views" on all subjects, human and
divine.   And their views will be found, in the
vast majority of cases, to consist of shreds of information, generally distorted and often erroneous,
claptrap phrases, picked up at hazard, and dignified
by the title of "principles," preferences, and predi-

lections, always unreasoned, and not seldom unreasonable. But if we shut our ears to the "hideous hum" of these crude imaginings which fill the newspapers "with voice deceiving," and give heed only to the utterances of those who possess some intelligible claim to be our intellectual guides, what do we usually find? We find exactly the same anarchy of thought. In those sciences, indeed, where we have to deal with phenomena verifiable by sensible experience, order reigns. And there is something majestic in the calm with which they declare, "That is so." But in every region of intellectual activity outside their domain, the minds of men are "clouded with a doubt." It is a doubt which extends to all first principles of thought and action. The temper of the times is anarchical in the proper sense of the word. That is the true account of the *Zeitgeist*. Nor can we doubt that it arises, in great degree, from the intense devotion of the age to physical science—a devotion so astonishingly fruitful in the development of material civilization—and from the use of its methods in departments where they can produce only a negative result, or no result at all. Certitude is naturally intolerant. In the age of faith, theology supplied ample evidence of this truth. In our age of unfaith, physical science supplies as ample. There has arisen among us a dogmatism of physicists, not less oppressive than the old dogmatism of divines. There has been a tendency, and more than a tendency, to assert that outside the boundaries of physical science we can know nothing; that its methods are the only methods of arriving at truth : a tendency to restrict our ideas to generalisations of phenomena ; to treat mental and moral problems as mere questions of physiology ; —in a word. to regard what are called the laws of matter as the sole laws. And the effacement of the true idea of law is directly traceable to the claim made for physical science as the one criterion of reality—a claim made in ignorance or forgetfulness of the unquestionable fact that its foundations are laid in the supersensuous ; that its greatest generalisations are nothing else than the application of primordial ideas of the intellect as psychology reveals them in consciousness.

Such, beyond doubt, is the tendency of the age. And nowhere is it more strikingly exemplified than in the domain of politics. Some time ago I mentioned to an accomplished friend that I had it in intention to write the book upon which I am now engaged, as a sort of sketch of, or introduction to, the laws of human society. He replied, " My dear fellow, you imagine a vain thing. There are no first principles in politics or last principles ; there are no principles at all, and no laws giving expression to principles : it is a mere matter of expediency, of utility, of convention, of self-interest." The voice of the *Zeitgeist* spoke through the mouth of my accomplished friend. And, indeed, the literature of

the age teems with evidence how widely the view
which he expressed is held.   In 1858 Lord Salisbury, then at the beginning of his public career,
noted the significant fact that in English politics
" no one acts on principles or reasons from them." [1]
This is even truer now than it was then.   And it is
true of other countries than our own.   Writing recently in the *Revue des Deux Mondes*, M. Leroy-
Beaulieu declared—and no one ventured to gainsay
him—that in France, and in the Latin races generally, " contemporary politicians of all classes, from
municipal councillors to Ministers, taken on the
whole, and with few exceptions, are the vilest and
the narrowest of sycophants and courtiers that humanity has ever known ; their sole end basely to
flatter and develop all popular prejudices, which, for
the rest, they but vaguely share, never having con-
secrated one minute of their lives to reflection and
observation."   So in the United States of America,
Mr. Brice tells us, " neither party has any principles,
or any distinctive tenets ; . . .   tenets and policies,
points of political doctrine, and points of political
practice, have all vanished : all has been lost except
office and the hope of it." [2]   I need not enlarge upon
a state of things which must be familiar to my readers, and the exact description of which is anarchy
or lawlessness.

[1] In a remarkable article in *Oxford Essays*, 1858.
[2] *The American Commonwealth*, vol. ii., p. 344.

Now, I have been led to write this book by the deep conviction that "nothing is that errs from law"—law issuing from the nature of things, which is rational ; law, the first fact in the universe, though invisible, inpalpable, imponderable : most real, indeed, because most spiritual. I hold that law rules in the province of politics, as in every other segment of human life ; and that to interpret the law, and to bring it into harmony with the varying conditions of human society, is the highest task of the legislator. Properly speaking, politics—the word is here used in its old and only worthy sense, not in its modern acceptation of vote-catching—must be considered a branch of ethics. And by ethics, it may be not unnecessary to add, I mean the science of natural morality indicating what action is right, and what is wrong, as befitting or unbefitting a rational creature. Politics form a chapter, not in physics, but in the Philosophy of Right, by Right being understood, as Krause has admirably defined it, " the organic whole of the outward conditions of a life according to Reason." [1]

The question before us, in this initial Chapter, is, What is the Foundation of the State ? Not, I beg my readers to note, what is the actual genesis of any State in particular, but on what deep underlying principle human society must rest. I start, then,

[1] " Das organische Ganze der äusseren Bedingungen des Vernunftlebens." Quoted by Green, *Works*, vol. ii., p. 341.

with the position that the foundation of the State
is the law of man's moral nature, in virtue of which
he is a *person* invested with rights and encompassed
by duties. The natural rights of man and the
natural duties of man, I say, are the necessary postulates of political science. Let me not be misunderstood. I am very far indeed from holding, with the
sophists of the French Revolution, that these natural
rights and duties are independent of conditioning
circumstances; that they have the empirical deter-
minativeness or the binding force of positive law;
that they can be translated off-hand into fact. I am
merely asserting, to quote the words of Green, that
"there is a system of rights and obligations which
should be maintained by law, whether it is so or
not, and which may properly be called natural," [1]
as issuing from the nature of things. From the
very first dawn of philosophy the conception has
prevailed of an absolute order of right, embracing
and harmonising all public rights. It is, metaphysically considered, the ultimate foundation of
all human justice, and conformity thereto is the
criterion of the moral and rational validity of positive
law. It is binding upon the conscience of the individual as such, for it is, in Butler's phrase, that
"law of virtue under which we are born." It is
binding upon the conscience of the State, as such,
for "the value of the institutions of civil life," Green

[1] *Works*, vol. ii., p. 339.

well observes, "lies in their operation as giving reality to the capacities of will and reason," the possession of which is "the condition of a moral life."[1] And the ideals of right which constitute it are the fundamental principles determinative of the proper construction of a polity. Now, of these ideals, the ideal of justice is the first, and embraces, in some sort, all the others. Hence the dictum, *Justitia fundamentum regni.* Yes ; justice is the true foundation of the State. On justice, assuredly, every commonwealth must be based if it is to endure. Build on any other foundation than that adamantine rock, and your political edifice, however imposing with "cloud-capped towers and gorgeous palaces," will pass away like "an insubstantial pageant." When the rain descends, and the floods come, and the winds blow and beat upon it, fall it must. And great will be the fall of it.

---

[1] *Works*, vol. ii., p. 337, 338. Of course, some eminent writers on political science deny to the *jus naturæ* the name of law (*Recht*) which they restrict to positive law. But they admit the thing, though they reject the name. Thus Lasson, who will not hear of *Naturrecht*, substitutes for it *das Gerechte*, which, he says, "is deduced from universal nature, from the pure expression of reason, and from the historical process. The *Gerechte*," he adds, "forms the ideal standard (*Anforderung*) of *Recht*, a standard to which it never fully attains" (*System der Rechtsphilosophie*, p. 231). But that is precisely the true account of τὸ δίκαιον, *jus naturæ*, or *Naturrecht*.

CHAPTER II

A T the basis, then, of politics lies the question,
What is just? Political philosophy, as I just
now insisted, is a chapter in the Philosophy of
Right, and in it we may proceed either by synthesis
or by analysis. We may take certain rights, and
investigate their ethical source and their primary
principles. But we cannot deduce from a principle
alone—even if it be a true principle—its varying
applications and ramifications, in the varying conditions and needs of human society. In politics
both the *a priori* and the *a posteriori* methods are
equally valid and equally valuable. Neither is sufficient by itself. History teaches us the *how*, metaphysics the *why*. To know anything scientifically,
we must know it in its development; in the process by which it has become what it is. But that is
not enough; we must know it also in its cause.
The *a priori* method has never been popular in
England. And the absurdities and atrocities of
the Jacobin disciples of Rousseau, in the last century,
not unnaturally overwhelmed it with discredit.

11

The mistake of the legislators of the French Revolution did not, however, lie in their belief that there are first principles in politics. It lay in their gross misapprehension of those principles, and in their fond conceit that what would suit the phantoms of their ratiocination—all alike, equal, independent, and entering for the first time into a social contract—would also suit the beings of flesh and blood, so widely differing in character, capacity, and condition, who inhabited eighteenth-century France. I do not know who has written more wisely on this subject than Taine. And it may be worth while here to translate a page which he has devoted to it, although in an English version small justice can be done to the vigour and picturesqueness of the original.

When a statesman who is not altogether unworthy of that great name comes upon an abstract principle—such, for example, as that of the sovereignty of the people—he admits it, if at all, like every other principle, with the necessary qualifications (*sous bénéfice d'inventaire*). For that end he begins by picturing it to himself as applied and working in the world. And so, uniting all his own recollections and all the information he can get together, he imagines some particular village or borough or small town, in the north, or in the south, or in the midlands of the country for which he legislates. Then, to the best of his ability, he represents to himself the people engaged in acting upon his principle—that is to say, voting, mounting guard, collecting their taxes, and carrying on their business. From these ten or twelve groups with which he is familiar, and which he takes as specimens, he draws conclusions by analogy regarding the rest and the whole country. Clearly it is a

difficult and risky operation. In order to be approximately
exact, it needs rare talent for observation, and at every step
exquisite tact ; for the problem is to work out correct results
from quantities imperfectly collected and imperfectly noted.
And when a politician succeeds in this, it is through a delicate
divination which is the fruit of consummate experience united
to genius. Moreover, he proceeds in his innovation or reform
with caution ; almost always he makes preliminary trial of it ;
he applies his law only by instalments, gradually, provision-
ally. He is always ready to correct, to suspend, to thin out
his work, according to the good or bad success of his tenta-
tive application of it ; and the condition of the human
material which he has to handle is apprehended by him,
however superior his intellect may be, only after much man-
ipulation. Just the opposite is it with the Jacobin. His
" principle " is an axiom of political geometry, which is self-
evident ; for, like the axioms of ordinary geometry, it is
formed by the combination of certain ideas, and its evidence
compels the immediate assent of every mind which entertains
together the two terms of which it is the sum. Man in
general, the rights of man, the social contract, liberty,
equality, reason, nature, the people, tyrants,—such are the
elementary notions. Precise or not, they fill the brain of
the new sectary. Frequently they are there only as grandiose and vague words. But that does not matter. As
soon as they are congregated in his mind, they become for
him an axiom, which he applies presently in its entirety
upon every occasion and to all lengths. As to real men,
he is not in the least concerned about them. He does not
see them. He has no wish to see them. With eyes shut, he
casts in his own mould the human material which he handles.
Never does it occur to him to picture to himself beforehand
that manifold, shifting, and complex material of peasants,
artisans, townspeople, clergy, nobles, as actual life presents
them, at their plough, in their lodging, in their place of
business, in their presbytery, in their town-house, with their
inveterate beliefs, their masterful inclinations, their real
wills. Nothing of all this can enter, or find a place in, his
mind. The avenues are blocked by the abstract principle
which puffs itself out and monopolises all the room. If, by

the channel of the eyes or ears, actual experience drives in
by force any inconvenient truth, it cannot find a home there.
Crying and bleeding though it be, he drives it away. Nay, if
need be, he will take it by the throat and strangle it, as a
slanderer, because it gives the lie to a principle sacred from
discussion and true in itself. Surely such a mind is not
sound. Of the two faculties which ought to pull equally
and together, one is smitten with atrophy, the other with
hypertrophy. The counterpoise of facts is not there to
balance the weight of formulas. Overloaded on the one
hand and empty on the other, the intellect is upset with
violence in the direction to which it leans. And this is the
incurable infirmity of the Jacobin mind. [1]

The topic before us in the present chapter is the
Origin of the State. First, let us inquire what
history has to tell us concerning it. The origin
of *humanity* is a subject upon which we need not
enter. Nor is the prehistoric condition of our globe
a matter which need detain us. For speculations
upon the long career of evolution from Protozoa to
Man, I may refer my reader to a great multitude of
capable and copious writers, whose names are in
every one's mouth : speeding him on his way with
Mr. Herbert Spencer's confident assurance that " he
will find no difficulty in understanding how, under
appropriate conditions, a cell may have given origin
to the human race." Whether the race made its
original appearance in one region only of the now
cooled and solid earth, or arose under varying conditions in different countries and at different geological
periods, is also a problem which has much exercised

[1] *La Conquête Jacobine*, p. 18.

ingenious minds, and which—to borrow a phrase from Butler—has "with equal rashness, I fear, been determined contrary ways." We are bidden by *savants* of the greatest authority, or, at all events, of the greatest authoritativeness, to recognise in the negro the primitive type of human kind : not the negro familiar to most of us, with some varnish of the civilisation of higher races forced upon him, but the negro of whom the Takroor Nigritians are now the nearest representatives—a creature in his low intellectual faculties, brute instincts, and physical conformation, approaching very nearly to the mammalian animal. His history is, however, a blank. No monuments, material or mental, witness to him. So that, for our present purpose, we may relegate him to the realm of conjecture, as a mere brutal phantasm, and not *man* at all. Man, as we meet with him in history—historic man, we may say—possesses exactly the same distinctive characteristics in the earliest annals or our race and in the latest; and one of them is, as Aristotle tells us, that he is "a political animal"—a being living in civil society. Professor Max Müller is absolutely well warranted when he writes, " If [savage] means people without a settled form of government, without laws, and without a religion, then, go where you like, you will not find such a race." [1]

So much is certain. Equally certain is it that

[1] *Nineteenth Century*, January, 1885, p. 114.

the polity which earliest history reveals to us is monarchical. Monarchy is, in fact, the one form of government to which the term, "natural" may properly be applied. I need hardly observe how utterly unhistorical is the conception of primitive society so widely popularised through the influence of Rousseau. Not a community of men and citizens all sovereign and equal, but autocracy, is the earliest form of the State known to us. Of civil society the family is the germ. The authority of the father, king over his own children, is, as a mere matter of historical fact, the earliest form of the *jus imperandi.* And the patriarchal state is everywhere the primitive polity. The archaic king, or autocratic chieftain, is, if I may so express it, the artificially extended father. The regal power is but the paternal power in a wider sphere. Most people who have passed through a public school or a university understand, more or less clearly, how far-reaching this *patria potestas* was in ancient Rome. It reached even farther in ancient India, where we find the father as the rajah or absolute sovereign of the family that depends upon him. In the expansion of the patriarchal family to the tribe, to the primitive nation, the attributes of the father remain unchanged. His word is still law; and, what is significant, as Sir Henry Maine points out, "his sentences, or θέμιστες, which is the same word with our Teutonic word

dooms, [though] doubtless drawn from pre-existing
custom or usage," are supposed to "come directly
into his mind by divine dictation from on high, to be
conceived by him spontaneously or through divine
prompting."[1]   It is in connection with the person-
age whom we call the king that law, civil or criminal,
enforced by penalties to be inflicted in this world,
first makes its appearance in the Hindu Sacred
Book.[2] The archaic king is the supreme judge
and legislator, as well as the supreme general, and
is invested also with a distinctly religious character.
It is interesting to observe how these attributes of
kingship, in its earliest form, even now attach, in
theory, to its latest development.   The Queen is still
the source of legislation : statutes are enacted by
Her Most Excellent Majesty.   The judges of the
High Court are her judges, and derive their authority
from her commission.   She is the head of the Army
and Navy : we speak of the troops as Her Majesty's
troops, of the fleet as Her Majesty's fleet.   She is, in
virtue of her ecclesiastical supremacy, the ultimate
arbiter in causes, whether of faith or morals, within
the National Church ; and her decisions of them,
given upon the advice of her Privy Council, are
irreformable.   I merely note this point in passing.
I go on to remark that the whole history of the
progressive races of the world is a moving away,
ever farther and farther, from the patriarchal state.

---

[1] *Dissertations on Early Law and Custom*, p. 163.   [2] *Ibid.* p. 38.

2

The unit of archaic society is not the man, but the family. The individual, as we conceive of him, has been slowly developed during thousands of years. Human history may be not improperly regarded as the history of his evolution.

History, then, shows us the family as the origin of the State, and traces *how* it developed from that rudimentary or embryonic monarchy, into the varied and complex forms in which it now exists. And if we ask *why* it is that men live gregariously, and not in isolation, the answer is that in so doing they merely obey a law of their being. That is the true account of the families of the earth. The extra social man of whom Rousseau fabled, is not man at all. Such a being, Aristotle rightly judged, would be either a wild beast or a god. *Unus homo, nullus homo.* It may be sometimes necessary, for the purposes of argument, to abstract man from the society which is his normal condition. But, as a matter of fact, he is found only in society. He is, in the Aristotelian phrase just now quoted, "a political animal." Here, and not in the theories of contract, of force, of divine right, of utility, is the true explanation of the *why* of the State. I am far from denying that in those theories there are elements of truth. I suppose no one now believes that human society is the outcome of a social contract. Probably Rousseau himself did not believe it. Mani-

festly a contract presupposes the State, not the
State a contract. Without the coercive power of
the State, an agreement would not possess the binding
force of a contract ; it would be merely a nude pact.
But we may say, in the language of the jurisprudents,
that the obligation of obeying the laws regarding
things in themselves indifferent, arises *quasi ex con-
tractu*, or from what we may call a virtual contract.
Again : no doubt force is an essential element in
every regimen. But it is curious that any thoughtful person should have found in it the sufficient
explanation of government. Every polity, however
rude, requires the ideas of right, and of law for the
maintenance of right. Might, without these ideas,
would not give rise to a commonwealth, but to a
gang of robbers; to anarchy plus the sword.
Once more. Utility is, doubtless, a conspicuous
note of civil polity. For civil polity is an instrument of incalculable good to the human race.
It is a condition and a means of man's progress,
both material and ethical. This is the sufficient
justification of the State. But it is no more than
that. And the authors of the American Declaration
of Independence greatly erred when they pronounced
it " self-evident " that " Governments are *instituted*
among men to secure certain inalienable rights."
That is the effect of governments, doubtless. It is
not the reason which causally determined their
institution. Lastly : there is a sense in which

divine right may be truly predicated of the State:
not the absurd sense admirably ridiculed by Pope,
of "the right divine of kings to govern wrong,"
whether the king be a single or a multitudinous
despot; but this, that civil society is natural to man,
and so may, and must, be regarded by all theists as
instituted by the Author of Nature. And now let
us look more closely at the matter.

Man is by no means the only animal that lives
in community. Not to multiply instances, bees
and ants display an instinct analogous to that
which gives rise to human commonwealths. What
is the essential difference between human society
and animal society? To answer that question
we must ask another: What is the essential
difference between men and animals? It is a
question of psychology, of what is called—I know
not whether very happily—comparative psychology. The lower animals unquestionably exhibit
many of man's psychical powers. As unquestionably, they are deficient in others. They have a
kind of self-consciousness, a kind of volition, a
certain feeling of causation, and of the adaption of
means to ends; they are endowed with appetites,
desires, emotions; they can form mental images,
or phantasmata, and can associate them. But
all these things belong to the sensitive faculty.
Can we, without absurdity, ascribe to them acts
of our intellectual faculty? The ancients explained

intellect as *intus legens;* and the explanation undoubtedly indicates a great truth, whatever we may
think of the etymology. Consider for a moment what
human knowledge really implies. And here I may
be permitted to repeat words which I have written
elsewhere, as I do not know how to better them,
though, for my present purpose, I shall a little
compress them.

The images presented to our intellect by the eye, the
ear, the touch—Aristotle and the schoolmen after him called
them phantasmata—are the *direct* results of sensuous experience. But knowledge means something more than that.
We may go on—we do go on—to the reflex act of subjecting
those phantasmata to the judging faculty. Passive sensation does not constitute knowledge, in the true sense. The
instrument of knowledge is thought (*quo cognoscimus*).
Knowledge (*quod cognoscitur*) is what is gained by thought.
There is a perception of sense which is concerned with the
material, the extended, the corporeal. There is an analytical
interpretation of that perception, an intellectual appropria-
tion of it (*das Bewusstwerden*) which has to do with the
immaterial, the unextended, the uncorporeal. The two are
often confused. But there is no great difficulty in distinguishing them. Let us picture to ourselves the intellect at
its actual contact with the presentments of sense. I take
into my hand a stone. I am directly conscious of it as an
otherness, a non-self. Feeling proper (sensation) reveals to
me so much. And I proceed—this is the next step—to interpret the sensation intellectually, to *cognise* the stone as
hard and heavy. Thus does the thinking subject respond to
the stimulating object, and convert the feeling into a felt
thing. Here is something more than sensation ; here is an
interior expression of sensation formulated in words ; here
is intellection. Surely, so much is clear. But we may
advance yet a step further. From the cognition of the
stone as hard and heavy, we may, by comparison and abstrac-

tion, advance to the general concepts of hardness and weight. These are the three steps in our knowledge which Kant distinguishes as Experience, Understanding, Reason, and which, under whatever names, are commonly admitted by metaphysicians.[1]

Now, the lower animals have in common with us this Experience—sensuous experience—of which Kant speaks. We must also attribute to them a power of associating their experience by an exercise of memory and of expectant imagination—*facultas æstimativa* the Schoolmen called it—which undoubtedly presents some analogy with Understanding. But it is not Understanding, for they do not possess that μνῆμη συνθετικῆ, that synthetic memory, of which we make such vast use: it is sensuous reflection proceeding by way of sensuous inference. They do not attain to intellection. They stop short at feeling. Still farther are they removed from the apprehension of general concepts, abstract ideas, universals. And such apprehension is the essential characteristic of Reason, the distinctive faculty of man, in virtue of which he is a *person*, according to the excellent definition of the Schoolmen : *naturæ rationalis individua substantia.*

Whether our race has always *exercised* that faculty of reason is a question unnecessary to be discussed here. Kant apparently thought that it had not. Anticipating in this, as in other instances, the conclusions of certain modern physicists, Kant

[1] *The Great Enigma*, p. 141.

held that "man was not always an *animal rationale*, but was once merely an *animal rationabile*," possessing the germ whence reason developed; and that "he became rational only through his own exertions,"[1] extending, I suppose, over vast periods of prehistoric time. However that may be, certain it is that man, as a matter of fact, exercises this faculty of Reason, and that no other animal exhibits the capacity for it. Equally certain is it that from this faculty spring those endowments which clearly mark man off from the other animals, however acute and subtle their instincts. Marvellously acute and subtle, indeed, those instincts are, as displayed, for example, in their art. But this art is unconscious, or automatic. It is inconceivable that bees, in constructing their hexagonal cells, possess a knowledge of angles. Equally inconceivable is it—to take another striking instance of animal action with a purpose—that the numerous insect tribes which lay up food for their *larvæ* have before them the idea of futurity. They live under the law of instinct. Man lives under a sort of hybrid law, at once instinctive and rational. They have, as their one spring of action, impulse—sensuous impulse; ὄρεξις, Aristotle calls it, and the Schoolmen, *appetitus*. Man has impulse *and* reason: ὄρεξις μετὰ λόγου: *appetitus rationalis;*

---

[1] See his curious discussion, "Vom Charakter der Gattung," in the second part of his "Anthropologie in Pragmatischer Hinsicht:" *Werke*, vol. vii., p. 261 (Rosenkranz and Schubert's ed.).

and that means will. It is from the self-control
exercised by man in virtue of his endowment of
rational will—the phrase is a pleonasm: reason,
pace Schopenhauer, is of the essence of will—that
his activity, as a whole, is distinguished from
animal activity. It is because of this endowment
that we impute to him merit or demerit—words
which, in their proper, or ethical sense, are inapplicable to animals. Morality is of the will.
We do not hold our horses or dogs morally responsible for what they do, or leave undone; we
do not praise or blame them, in the sense in which
we praise or blame even a little child. Man alone
is, as Aristotle defined him, "an ethical animal
having perception of right and wrong, justice and
injustice, and the like." This is the first great
difference arising from man's endowment of reason,
which marks him off from animals, and the State
from animal commonwealths. The State arises,
like those commonwealths, from an original necessity. But, unlike them, it "is shaped and established through the free activity of the rational will,
whose inner nature it reflects." [1] "Man," says
Spinoza, "consists in reason." So does the State.
It is, in Hegel's admirable phrase, "Reason manifesting itself as Right."

Again. It is in virtue of reason that man is
endowed with the attribute of verbal language to

[1] Lasson, *System der Rechtsphilosophie*, p. 297.

represent thought. The voice of the animal world,
even in its most melodious forms—the song of the
nightingale or the lark—is only an expression of
sensuous feeling. The speech of man, however rude
and harsh, is informed by intellection. Hence, no
doubt, it was that the old Greeks employed the
same vocable—λόγος—to denote reason and word.
Human language is the direct outcome of that
apprehension of universal relations to which reason
is essential. Hobbes maintained that man is a
rational animal, because he possesses the endowment of language: *Homo animal rationale quia
orationale;* but this is, if I may employ the
vulgar phrase, to put the cart before the horse.
The true account is that man possesses the endowment of language because he is a rational animal:
" Homo animal orationale quia rationale." It is
reason which generates these general signs, general
names, general propositions, which make up human
language, and which are the indispensable instruments of human thought. As St. Augustine said:
Cogitamus, sed verba cogitamus. Sophocles, cele-
brating in his magnificent choral ode the wond-
rousness of man, notes language as among the
most distinctive and stupendous of human inven-
tions. And rightly. The whole edifice of man's
greatness, in public and in private life, rests upon it.
In particular—for that is the point which specially
concerns us here—it is in words that man embodies

the concepts of Right, and the laws in which those
concepts are formulated for the guidance of ordered
human life in civil society.   The difference between
the murmur of bees and the articulate speech of
men, indicates the measure of the difference between
the State and an animal community.

Once more.   Progress is the result of reason manifesting itself in will and expressing itself in language.
Every thinker stores up his thought in language.
Every generation transmits that treasure to the generations that shall come after.   And thus has arisen
the world's intellectual wealth.   In the words of
Abelard, " Not only is language generated by intellect, but it, too, generates intellect."   *Sermo gen-
eratur ab intellectu et generat intellectum.*[1]   It is
language which enables man to capitalise his gains,
moral, mental, and material.   It is through this endowment that "great things done endure " for our
race, and lead to greater.   This is what progress
means.   And of progress the human race only is
capable.   It is—

> " man's distinctive mark alone :
> Not God's and not the beasts' : God is, they are ;
> Man partly is, and partly hopes to be."

And human society, we must always remember, is
the condition and instrument of this progress, in
which of course it shares.   The ant has not in the
least varied since the day when the writer of the
book of *Proverbs* sent the human sluggard for a les-

[1] Quoted by Max Müller, *Science of Thought*, p. 41.

son of wisdom in her ways. Bees perform now precisely the same complicated and ingenious acts which Virgil described. two thousand years ago in in the *Georgics.* Singly and collectively, they remain as they were at the beginning, while man, singly and collectively, has moved onward and upward. And the reason is that the ant or the bee is a mere *Naturwesen,* bound fast in fate like nature's other products. Because they lack the endowment of rational will, whereby " man is man, and master of his fate," and the endowment of rational language which is the chief instrument of his volition, they abide for ever in the stationary state of instinct. The society of animals, like the art of animals, tends towards no ideal, because the ideal does not exist for animals. The law of progress, rightly considered, is the irresistible attraction for the human will of good, and specially of that highest good which the Schoolmen termed *bonum honestum,* ethical good. The root of progress is the distinctively virile quality which the old Romans aptly called *virtus* : devotion to the true, the just ; to the idea of Right which reason reveals. Advance in knowledge of natural law, and in skill in applying it to the arts of life, is no true *human* progress unless it springs from this root. The real subject of progress is man himself ; the real source of progress is in the idea of Right. And in the ever-expanding application of the principles embodying that idea, as it grows in

the public conscience, is the third great distinction
marking off the State from the animal commonwealth.

Such, then, are the essential differences between
human and animal communities; and they are as
patent as are the analogies. Animal communities,
in their highest forms, are an expression of instinct.
The State, in its lowest form, is an expression of reason : a lasting external work in which that distinctive endowment of man is manifested. We will
conclude this inquiry into the origin of the State
with certain pregnant words of Lasson :

> The external ground for the existence of the State is the
> nature of man. There are no men without continuity of
> social life (*Zusammenleben*). There is no continuity of
> social life without order. There is no order without law.
> There is no law without coercive force. There is no coercive
> force without organization. And this organization is the
> State. The inner ground for the existence of the State is
> man's endowment of Reason, which is the most distinctive
> part of his manhood.[1]

[1] *System der Rechtsphilosophie*, p. 296.

CHAPTER III

THE next step in our inquiry is, What is the
End or Object of the State? And here again
we may well follow the guidance of "the master of
those who know." "The nature of a thing," according to the Aristotelian dictum, "is its final end"
(ἡ δὲ φύσις τέλος ἐστίν). Yes ; the nature of a thing and
its final end are, in some sort, identical. If we would
know its final end, we must know its nature. What,
then, is the nature of the State?

I suppose the conception of the State most current
in this country is the purely Utilitarian one which
regards it as a fortuitous concourse of men bound
by the tie of common advantage ; a mere machine,
driven by the forces of public and private interest ;
a sort of huge insurance society, the taxes being the
premium. Perhaps no one has done more to diffuse
this conception among us than Lord Macaulay. It
is the underlying thought of one of the most popular—and in many respects justly popular—of his
writings, his famous essay on Gladstone's *Church and
State*. And so, in accordance with it, he insists that

"the primary end of Government" is "the protection of the persons and property of men." He thinks "that government should be organised solely with a view to [this] main end." He adds "if a government can, without any sacrifice of its main end, promote any other good work—the encouragement of the fine arts, for example—it ought to do so"; while "it is still more evidently the duty of government to promote, always in subordination to its main end, everything which is useful as a means for the attaining of that main end."[1] Is this a sufficient account of the State ?

I venture to say that it is not, any more than the Utilitarian philosophy, upon which it rests, is a sufficient account of man. The protection, not of persons and property, as Macaulay puts it, but of the *rights* of person and property, which is a very different thing, is, no doubt, the duty of the State. But what is a right? and what is the relation of the State to rights? The answer to these questions may enable us to discern the true nature of the State, and to conclude thence to its end.

A right is commonly defined as a moral power residing in a person, in virtue of which he calls anything his own. It is, in point of fact, the thing so deeply detested by the whole Utilitarian School, "a metaphysical entity," and cannot possibly be other.

---

[1] *Works*, vol. vi., p. 372, 373.

This, after all, need excite no surprise; for every
problem of thought, if we investigate it closely
enough, lands us in metaphysics. "Man," Schopenhauer truly says, "is a metaphysical animal." He
ever asks, and cannot keep from asking, Why? The
other animals only ask, How? A right arises from
the nature of things, according to that excellent
saying of Cicero: *nos ad justitiam natos; neque
opinione, sed natura, constitutum esse jus.*[1] And
so Trendelenburg: "All right, so far as it is right
and not unright (*Unrecht*), issues from the impulse
(*Trieb*) to maintain an ethical existence."[2] And,
therefore, it is only of man that right, in the strict
sense—right with its correlative duty—can be predicated; for man alone is an ethical being. I touched
upon this matter in the last chapter. It will be
proper, in the present connection, to add a few
words to what I there said. In all organic being
there is an internally directive power which is its
chief characteristic. The lower organic natures are
blindly and sensuously influenced by that power
In the higher organic natures it is rationally and
freely exerted; and then we have rights and duties
—that is to say, morality. If the moral ideal is considered in its individual character, as independently
manifested in the pure will, or as human perfection,

---

[1] *De Legibus*, l. i. c. 10. I know of nothing better in Cicero's philosophical works than his argument upon this subject. It is just as
valid now as when it was written.

[2] *Naturrecht auf dem Grunde der Ethik*, p. 46.

it is called virtue; if viewed in the form of the
universal, as a directive rule, winning over and per-
suading the individual will, it is moral obligation.
The two are but different sides or aspects of the
same thing.

There are, as the Scholastics have it, three degrees
in the dynamic evolution of being—*ens, suppositum,
hypostasis:* thing, individual, person. Man alone,
is a *person*, and capable of right (*subjectum juris,
rechtsfähig*). He alone possesses the faculty of re-
cognising, and willing the creative thought of his
being, of discerning the law of virtue, under which
he is born, and of working for his true perfection,
which is ethical. He alone is free, according to
Aristotle's definition of freedom, for he alone exists
for himself and not for another; he alone is self-
determined and an end to himself. It is, I say, from
the ground of his personality that his rights and
their correlative duties spring up. And all his
rights are but aspects of his first aboriginal right to
belong to himself, to develop his personality. Ob-
jectively considered, they all spring from Right—
a great, rational, organic whole, embracing and
harmonising all particular rights; independent of
human volition; known perfectly only to the Absolute and Eternal, in whom it is ever conceived, ever
realised : an ideal, but most actual. It is, as Bluntschli observes—I shall have to return to that point
presently—"this law of nature and reason which

furnishes the foundation and limits of historical formulated law."[1]

As a *person*, then, man has rights—rights which attach to human nature, and may, therefore, properly be called natural. But only in society is personality realised and developed. The human "I" requires for its explication the human "Thou." Personality means not only rights, but rights recognised and allowed. Green well points out that a right is, "on the one hand, a claim of the individual arising out of his rational nature, to the free exercise of some faculty; on the other, a concession of that claim by society, a power given by it to the individual of putting the claim in force."[2] Civil society, as we saw in the last chapter, is man's natural state. The very concept of the person implies intercourse with others, implies reciprocal rights. Of these reciprocal rights positive law is the guarantee and the shield. But what is positive law?

All law, according to the dictum of Aquinas cited in the first chapter, is a function of Reason. Human law, properly considered, is not what Mirabeau called it, "a caprice": it is the rational or ethical will—the two adjectives mean the same —of the commonwealth; or, to quote the well-known dictum of Kant, "the expression of the reason (*Vernunft*) common to all." It is the recogni-

---

[1] *Politik*, p. 31. Cicero calls it, very happily, "ipsa naturæ ratio, quæ est lex divina et humana."—*De Officiis*, lib. iii., c. 6.

[2] *Works*, vol. ii., p. 450.

3

tion and sanction by the State of a portion of that system of correlative rights and duties which Reason itself reveals. It is, in strictness, not made, but apprehended and declared and enforced by man. Heraclitus, two thousand years ago, summed the matter up : "All human laws receive their life from the One Divine Law "—the Law of Nature and Reason. And so Aquinas : "A human law bears the character of law so far as it is in conformity with right reason : and, in that point of view, it is manifestly derived from the Eternal Law. But inasmuch as any human law recedes from reason, it is called a wicked law ; and to that extent it bears not the character of law, but rather of an act of violence." [1]   Or, as he elsewhere puts it, [2] "Laws enacted by men are either just or unjust. If they are just, they have a binding force in the court of conscience from the Eternal Law, whence they are derived. . . . Unjust laws are not binding in the court of conscience, except, perhaps, for the avoiding of scandal and turmoil." [3]

Let us pursue further our inquiry regarding the nature and attributes of the State. We saw in

[1] *Summa Theologica*. 1, 2, q. 93, a. 3, ad. 2.

[2] *Ibid.* q. 96, a. 4.

[3] On this subject Bluntschli writes, "Das Gesetz ist seinem Wesen nach der Ausdruck und die Offenbarung des natürlichen Rechtes und nicht ein willkürliches Product. . . . Auch das ungerechte Gesetz ist, so lange es in äusserer Kraft besteht, von den untergeordneten Organen des Staates als ein gültiges zu handhaben."— *Allgemeines Staatsrecht*, p. 140.

the last chapter that it arises from the nature of
man, of which the tendency to live in civil society
is part and parcel. And, in view of that tendency,
we may say that the State is a natural entity.
But that tendency is not realised by blind unconscious growth, as of the plant. It is realised by the
human will. A man may cut himself off from
society and still live, say as a religious recluse,
a human life. A branch cut off from a tree
perishes. The law of the body politic is other
than the law of the vegetable world. It is in virtue
of human volition that the State is a polity, or
political entity; but it is more than a political
entity. It is a fellowship of *persons*—that is, of
moral beings for moral ends. The necessities of
existence force men into polities. But the end
of civil societies is not mere existence. It is existence in accordance with man's highest and distinctive attribute—Reason. And so Aristotle insists
that the State was formed that men might live, but
exists that they may live nobly : γιγνομένη μὲν οὖν τοῦ
ζῆν ἕνεκεν οὖσα δὲ τοῦ εὖ ζῆν. The State is the realised
order of Right, as the Germans say, *die realisirte
Rechtsordnung*. It is an ethical entity. And as
the organic manifestation of the personality of a
people, it may properly be called an organism or
a person. It is an organism, for it is, in the words
of Bluntschli, "a great body, capable of taking up
into itself the feelings and thoughts of a people, of

uttering them in laws, and of realising them in facts." [1] It is a person, for rights and duties, the distinctive notes of personality, attach to it.

Such, then, is the State. And, being such, its end is *den Rechtszustand zu schaffen und zu sichern* —that is, to define, maintain, amplify, and secure its own rights and the rights of its subjects. Let us consider this a little in detail. And we will begin with the lower order of rights; the rights of individual persons.

Until a century ago, it was well-nigh forgotten, throughout the greater part of the Continent of Europe, that such rights exist. In the New Monarchy, which had arisen on the ruins of mediæval liberties, the old doctrine succinctly formulated by Aquinas, that "the king exists for the people," was contemptuously rejected. It was held that the people exist for the king, whose "right divine to govern wrong" was the favourite theme of a servile clergy. The Parliamentary assemblies, which throughout the Middle Ages had served as the guarantees of individual right were suppressed, or turned into mere machinery for the registration of the royal will. Louis the Fourteenth's doctrine, *L'État, c'est moi*, was accepted as *the* first principle in politics, and was the germ of what Lamennais has well called "that terrible disease of Royalism," which, little by little, ate out all the forces of society. The

[1] *Allegemeine Staatslehre*, p. 22.

drastic remedy of the French Revolution has, after long working, expelled that disease from most European countries.   We may well demur—every scientific jurisprudent must demur—to many propositions of *The Declaration of the Rights of the Man and the Citizen*, which served as its manifesto. But we should, at all events, recognise that it impressed deeply, we may hope ineradicably, upon the popular mind the truth that man does possess certain rights as man—rights which may properly be called natural, as issuing from the nature of things, as attaching to the attribute of personality, which is the very ground of human nature.   It is not necessary that we should here consider the various ways in which these rights have been classified by philosophers and jurisprudents.   But it is of importance to insist that they all spring from what Trendelenburg has happily called "the self-same fount of right," and that they "are governed by the unity of an inherent co-ordinating idea." [1]   It was the apprehension of this truth which led Spinoza to specify as the end of the State *quoad* the individual, liberty: which he explains as meaning that "men should use in security all their endowments, mental and physical, and make free use of their reason." [2]

There are four manifestations of this aboriginal

---

[1] *Naturrecht auf dem Grunde der Ethik*, p. 1.
[2] *Tractatus Theologico-Politicus*, c. xx., 11.

right of man to freedom upon which, for our
present purpose, it will be well to touch. The
first is the right of existence—liberty to live;
the next, the right to the self-determined use of
the human faculties, mental and physical, which
is personal liberty; the third, the right of property, which is realised liberty; the fourth, the
right to be considered in the legislation and
government of the commonwealth, which is political
liberty. But these rights of the individual are not,
of course, absolute. They are conditioned by duties,
without which they can no more exist than can the
three sides of a triangle without the angles. They
are ethical entities—that is to say, they are subject
to the moral law, and are strictly fiduciary in their
character. Again, they are subject to another
limitation. Although, in themselves, they are not
created nor abrogable by positive law, they are held
in subordination to the rights of the State in which
they acquire validity and coerciveness. Let us
dwell a little on both these points.

The aboriginal rights of the individual are conditioned by duties. And if those duties are disdained,
the rights lose their character, and become wrongs.
This is true of all of them. It is true of the right
of existence, which is conditioned by the duty of
labour for the benefit of the community. No one
capable of doing any useful thing has a right to
otiose existence. The Apostolic injunction, that

"if any man would not work, neither should he eat,"
is a moral axiom of universal application. Of course,
it does not hold good when it is not the will, but the
ability to work which is wanting, whether by reason
of immaturity, senescence, disease, or other accident.
Then the right to existence remains; and I may
observe that the recognition of that right is the
foundation of the English Poor Law. The State is
the expanded family ; and no member of that family
should be left, undeservingly, to starve. But it
should be noted that this right is strictly personal.
It does not imply a right to beget offspring for the
community to support. Mill is well warranted when
he observes, "To bring a child into existence without a fair prospect of being able, not only to provide
food for its body, but instruction and training for
its mind, is a moral crime, both against the unfortunate offspring and against society."[1] I add that
there must be something very wrong in any commonwealth where many people have, in fact, no "fair
prospect" of being able to make such provision.
The right to personal freedom, again, and all that it
implies—the right to freedom of conscience, freedom
of the press, freedom of public meeting, and the
large class of rights of personal relations (*Personen-
verbände*)—is conditioned by the duty of respecting
those limits within which right resides: *fines quos
ultraque citraque nequit consistere rectum.* Thus,

[1] *On Liberty*, p. 189.

for example, though "thought is free," as soon as
it manifests itself externally, and is brought in
contact with the environment, it is confronted with
the law grounded in the very faculty of reason
whence thought springs.   No sane person, I suppose
would maintain that every one has an absolute and
unlimited right "to give public utterance, in every
possible shape, by every possible channel, without
any let or hindrance, to all his notions whatsoever."[1]
So, too, the right of public meeting—unquestionably
a part of the right of personal liberty—is not absolute
and unlimited.   It does not mean a right to assemble
tumultuously, or in arms, to the danger of the public
peace; or to block thoroughfares, or places of
general resort, to the detriment of the common
convenience.   And there is clearly a great distinction to be made between meetings in halls or
rooms, and meetings in the open air : a distinction
upon which the Belgian Constitution very properly

---

[1] See Cardinal Newman's *Letter to the Duke of Norfolk*, § 6.   It may
be noted that Spinoza, in Chapter XX. of his *Tractatus Theologico-
Politicus*, the theme of which is " In libera republica unicuique et
sentire quæ velit et quæ sentiat dicere licere," when summing up his
argument, clearly indicates the limitations of the principle for which
he contends :   " His ostendimus : I. impossibile esse, libertatem
hominibus dicendi ea, quæ sentiunt adimere ; II. hanc libertatem
salvo jure et auctoritate summarum potestatum unicuique concedi, et
eandem unumquemque servare posse, *salvo eodem jure, si nullam
inde licentiam sumat ad aliquid in rempublicam tanquam jus
introducendum, vel aliquid contra receptas leges agendum ;* III.
hanc eandem libertatem unumque habere posse *servata reipublicæ
pace,* et nulla ex eadem incommoda oriri quæ facile coerceri
non possint ; IV. eandem *salva etiam pietate* unumquemque habere
posse."

insists.[1] I need hardly observe that in England, of late, this great right has been grossly abused, and has become, in practice, a grave wrong. Such, beyond question, is the true account of those " monster meetings "—the phrase is apt—which, from time to time, disfigure Hyde Park, and which I ventured to describe, some years ago, " mere multitudinous assemblages, taught to yell at the word of command, with no pretence of discussion, no opportunity of hearing the other side of a question, and no capacity of understanding it, if they did hear it; hindrances to the discharge of the lawful business of a law-abiding subject, and a gross infringement of his liberty; overflowings of rascaldom and anarchy; nefarious menaces of brute force, which should be sternly repressed as a public danger."[2]

We cannot say, then, that a man's right to personal liberty implies a licence to do what he likes with his endowments, whether of body or mind.

[1] In Art. 19 : " Les Belges ont le droit de s'assembler paisiblement et sans armes, en se conformant aux lois qui peuvent régler l' exercice de ce droit, sans néanmoins le soumettre à une autorisation préalable. Cette disposition ne s'applique point aux rassemblements en plein air, qui restent entièrement soumis aux lois de police."

M. Giron, commenting upon this Article, writes as follows : " Est donc légal le réglement communal qui interdit tout attroupement de nature à encombrer la voie publique, à diminuer la liberté ou la sécurité du passage, et toute manifestation publique pouvant ou amener les citoyens ou amener du désordre, troubler la paix ou la tranquillité des habitants, soit qu'elle ait lieu par des chants, cris, bruits, tapages, sérénades, illuminations, cortèges, expositions de drapeaux ou d' emblèmes, soit de toute autre manière."—*Le Droit Publique de la Belgique*, p. 464.

[2] *On Shibboleths*, p. 115.

As little can we say that his right to property
implies the same unlimited dominion over it. The
philosophical justification of this right is that
private property is necessary for the explication
of personality in the workaday world. A desire
to appropriate things external to us, to convert
them into lasting instruments of our will, is one
of the elements of our being. We cannot picture
to ourselves a state of existence in which man
does not exclusively possess what is needful for
self-preservation. The ultimate ground of private
property, then, is necessity arising from the nature
of things. Man, alone of all animals an end to himself, has an indefeasible right to live out his own life;
he has an indefeasible right to what is necessary to
enable him to do that. Property is necessary. It
belongs to the moral realm—the realm of rights. It
springs from human personality; from the ethical
idea and psychological being of man. But only in
civil society is this right, like all rights, realised.
Property, in its original idea, is the guarantee to a
man, by the State, of the fruits of his own labour
and abstinence—that is, of the ethical exercise of
his personality, The *ethical* exercise, I say. Possession is one thing : property is quite another. A
thief, by availing himself of possibility and power,
may possess my watch ; but he would have no property in it, for he would have acquired no right to
it through the unethical exercise of his personality

whereby he obtained it. He would have no title to it which the State would protect, title being *justa causa possidendi.* Such is the right to property, which may properly be regarded as being of the nature of a social reward. And the right, like all rights, is indissolubly linked to obligations. Property is fiduciary; it is held for the benefit not merely of the proprietor, but of the commonwealth. Hence it is that the application of a portion of it for the relief of the suffering members of the commonwealth is something more than a duty of charity; it is a duty of strict justice—*debitum legale,* Aquinas calls it. I add that though the right to property may, as we have seen, be properly reckoned among natural rights, it belongs, according to the accurate distinction of the Schoolmen, to the secondary sphere of such rights,[1] and not like the right of existence, to the primary sphere. And so it has to give way to that higher right if the two come into conflict. It is the common teaching of the greatest masters of ethical science and has been for the last thousand years, that extreme necessity makes all things common; and that a man who, through no fault of his own, is in danger of perishing by hunger, may, without culpability, take from another, even against the other's wish, what is necessary for the sustentation of life.

[1] " It is not against the natural law," writes Aquinas, " but is added thereto by the discovery (*ad inventionem*) of human reason."— *Summa Theologica,* 2, 2, q. 66, a. 2, ad. 1.

I suppose this view of property will seem monstrous to that large class, who, as the French say,
mangent leurs rentes, in all good conscience, apparently supposing that they were sent into the
world for that purpose alone.

> " Full to the utmost measure of what bliss
>   Human desires can seek or apprehend,"

they do not even suspect, apparently, that wealth
has any other use than that of ministering to their
own gratification ; that they are called upon to fulfil
any other social function than that of absorbing—
gracefully, if possible—the proceeds of their stocks
and shares.   That duties attach to the possession of
land, is a belief which has never been wholly effaced
from the public mind, though of late years it has
grown dim.   That this holds good of all kinds of
property, seems to be very widely accounted an
amazing, an irrational doctrine.   And yet it is true;
and that opposite doctrine of " the inalienable nature
of purchased beef," which Carlyle thought the one
tenet held with real assent by most Englishmen, is
not true.   As the rights of property cannot subsist
without correlative and commensurate duties, so the
performance of those duties cannot be neglected
without bringing the rights into peril.   We cannot
insist upon the rights if we refuse to discharge the
duties ; or, if we do so insist, we shall find our insistence, in the long run, idle.   More.   A man's *moral*

claim to his rights ceases if he cease to perform the correlative duties. And if it is wrong to deprive him of them—I am speaking from the point of view not of human law, but of ethics, whence, however, all our legislation derives its very life—the wrong lies not in any injustice which would be done to him, but in the tendency of the measures which would have to be employed against him to unloose the bonds of the social order. Private property is a great, an indispensable institution ordained by man for the common good. But the respect due to the form in which it exists, in any given condition of society, depends upon its practical working. If its owners forget the tenure upon which they hold it, if by rapacity, by luxury, by inhumanity they make their ownership a public mischief instead of a public benefit, they are undermining the existing order of proprietary rights, and are preparing the ruin of the present social system. Such are the first principles applicable to this grave matter—principles largely effaced from the public mind by that debased and debasing Utilitarianism which proclaims pleasure as the end of life, self-interest as the rule of life, and money payment as the bond of life: which loses sight of the cardinal truth that society is an organ-ism, a rational organism; that the law of the human race is solidarity governed by the eternal and immu-table principles of Right.

Once more. The right to political liberty—to be

considered in the legislation and administration of a
country—is conditioned and limited by duties. It
is a right which, like the other rights just considered,
springs from the very ground of human nature. A
man is a *person*, not a thing, nor a mere animal; and
his rational co-operation in the commonwealth is
necessary to his ethical development, and to that of
his fellows. I say that he has a right to be considered politically; and in a high state of civilisation
"considered" means directly or indirectly consulted.
This does not imply the absurdity of asking his
opinion on legislative or administrative problems regarding which he is absolutely ignorant. But Mill
is well warranted in writing, "It is a personal injustice to withhold from any one, unless for the prevention of greater evils"—I shall touch upon the
proviso presently—"the ordinary privilege of having
his voice reckoned in the disposal of affairs in which
he has the same interest as other people."[1] To say
that a man has a natural right to a vote is nonsense. To
say that he has a natural right to a share of influence
in the State corresponding with his personality, is the
soundest of sense. And, no doubt, in the existing
order of European society, a vote is the readiest and
simplest way of exercising that influence; which is
not equivalent to saying that is always, or even generally, the best way. But a man's right to political
influence is conditioned by the duty of using it *in*

[1] *Considerations on Representative Government*, p. 159.

debito modo; and gross violation of this duty properly entails the suspension or deprivation of the right. Every one recognises that this is so when a man sells his vote for money. But few people, apparently, comprehend the reason, which is that the electoral franchise is not only a right, but a trust; and a trust because it is a right. To sell a vote for money is not, however, the commonest way of violating the duty which its possession imposes. "A base and mischievous vote is now, I am convinced, much oftener given from the voter's personal interest, or class interest, or some mean feeling in his own mind."[1] I am again quoting Mill; and I go on to express my entire concurrence with his opinion that this evil, which assuredly the law should always discourage, if it can seldom reach, it now actually protects by the foolish function of the ballot. The practical effect of the ballot is to enable a voter to yield himself up to those unworthy and immoral motives "free from all sense of shame or responsibility." Experience amply vindicates the truth of Mill's observation: "People will give dishonest or mean votes from lucre, from malice, from pique, from personal rivalry, or even from the interests or prejudices of class or sect, more readily in secret than in public."[2] It is not too much to say that the introduction into elections of voting by ballot, has done more than

[1] *Ibid.*, p. 195.
[2] *Ibid.*, p. 203.

anything else to obliterate from the public mind the
true conception of the right of the individual to
political power as fiduciary; to diffuse the notion
that it is an absolute possession which a man may
employ as he likes for the gratification of his "own
interest, pleasure, or caprice; the same feelings and
purposes, on a humbler scale, which actuate a despot
and an oppressor."[1]

All the rights, then, which attach to the individual
as a person, have limitations which may be described
as inherent in them, for they arise from the very
idea of right as a moral entity. These rights it is
the office of the State to protect and amplify. "In
society," according to Kant's admirable saying,
"man becomes more a man." The State is the instrument for the development of private right, for
the evolution of the individual. I may remark, in
passing, that the State, in certain cases, is bound to
maintain a right attaching to personality, even when
those invested therewith would sacrifice it. The
maxim of jurisprudence, *Volenti non fit injuria*,
does not always hold good. No woman is at liberty,
for example, to infringe her right to existence by
consenting to "an illegal operation," or to extinguish
her right to personal liberty by selling herself into
meretricious slavery. This by the way. My present point is that the rights attaching to man as a
person are limited, not only in the manner which

[1] *Ibid.*, p. 192.

has just been considered, but also by the rights of
of the State in which they require validity and coerciveness. The State is the nation in its corporate
capacity; and the rights of the organic whole come
before the rights of any constituent part. Or, to
put the matter in another way, the community,
taken collectively as forming a moral body, is
superior to the community taken distributively, in
each of its members. Every one will allow that
the individual may sometimes be justly required to
sacrifice himself for the State. No one would maintain that the State should ever sacrifice itself for the
individual. The State, as a moral body, a person, is
invested with all the great rights of personality—
the right of existence, the right of personal liberty,
the right of property, the right of political power.
These rights, of course, are no more unlimited than
are the corresponding rights of the individual. But
those rights of the individual are held in subordination to them. For a just cause, the State has the
right—the very word "right" implies a just cause
—to take the life of any one of its members, or to
require him to lay down his life for it, and to find
his glory and happiness in the sacrifice: *Dulce et
decorum est pro patria mori.* For a just cause it
has a right to restrict his personal liberty, to take a
portion, or even the whole, of his property, to deprive him, partly or entirely, of political power.
This is not the doctrine preached by the late M.

4

Gambetta when he told the French clergy, "Render
unto Cæsar the things which are Cæsar's, and all is
Cæsar's." All is not Cæsar's, whether the Cæsar be
a single or a many-headed tyrant. And there are
cases when passive resistance to such a claim is per-
missible : cases in which active resistance is permis-
sible and revolution justifiable. The State is an
association of moral beings. To say that, is to say
that its power has moral limits. And grave infringement of those limits invalidates its moral claim to
obedience. But the maxim, *Salus reipublicæ su-
prema lex*, is true. Human society is governed by
the great law of sacrifice.[1] The most sacred of individual rights must give way, in extreme necessity,

[1] It seems difficult to conceive of juster views on the subject of resistance to the civil power than those expressed for it by St. Thomas
Aquinas. He teaches that a tyrannical government is not a lawful
government, and that a general rising against such a government is
not sedition, provided it does not involve evils greater than those
which it seeks to remedy. He also points out that when the ruler
bears sway in virtue of a constitutional pact—and such was the case
in most mediæval governments, as the coronation offices sufficiently
witness—breach of that pact entitles his subjects to depose him. See
the *Summa Theologica*, 2, 2, q, 42, a. 2, ad. 3, and the *De Regimine
Principum*, 1. i. c. 6. This is, of course, a very different doctrine
from " the sacred right of insurrection " proclaimed by French Jacob-
binism. Schiller has admirably summed the matter up in those very
fine lines of *Wilhelm Tell*:

> " Nein, eine Grenze hat Tyrannenmacht :
> Wenn der Gedrückte nirgends Recht kann finden,
> Wenn unerträglich wird die Last—greift er
> Hinauf getrosten Muthes in den Himmel,
> Und holt herunter seine ew'gen Rechte
> Die droben hangen unveräusserlich
> Und unzerbrechlich, wie die Sterne selbst.
> Zum letzten Mittel, wenn kein andres mehr
> Verfangen will, ist ihm das Schwert gegeben."

to the rights of the community; the individual good to the common good.

To sum up, then. We may say that the end of the State, both for itself and its subjects, is what Aristotle calls εὖ ζῆν[1]: noble or worthy life; a com-plete and self-sufficient existence; the development of its own personality, and of the personalities of its subjects, under the law of Right. It exists for itself and for the individual, just as the individual exists for it and for himself. It exists for the well-being of the whole, by means of the constituent parts, and of the constituent parts by means of the whole. And we must understand well-being in the widest sense of the word civilisation. We must take it not only as signifying the kind of improvement which distinguishes a wealthy and prosperous nation from savages and barbarians, but also, and far more, as denoting eminence in the best characteristics of man and society; advance on the road to perfection; happiness, nobleness, wisdom.[2] It is in this emi-nence, this advance, these spiritual goods, that the real greatness of men and nations consists. The roots of human progress—not only the grace and

[1] So Plato, in the Eighth Book of the *Laws:* Δεῖ δὲ αὐτὴν (τὴν πόλιν) καθάπερ ἕνα ἄνθρωπον ζῆν εὖ.

[2] "The word Civilisation is a word of double meaning. We are accustomed to call a country civilised if we think it more improved; more eminent in the best characteristics of Man and Society: further advanced in the road to perfection, happier, nobler, wiser. But, in another sense, it stands for that kind of improvement only, which distinguishes a wealthy and powerful nation from savages and bar-barians."—Mill's *Discussions and Dissertations*, vol. i., p. 160.

beauty of life, but material prosperity and power,
spring from them—are probity, honour, the capacity
of self-sacrifice, the subordination to high ideals.
They are essential to the εὖ ζῆν, the noble or worthy
existence of the State. They are essential to its
security, influence, and dignity, which are the conditions and the means of the security, influence, and
dignity of its subjects. For its subjects are itself.

CHAPTER IV

THE FUNCTIONS OF THE STATE

THE State, then, is the realised order of Right. Its end is not the manufacture of "the greatest happiness of the greatest number," or of any number,[1] but the vindication and development of its own rights and the rights of its subjects. What are its proper functions in promoting that end? It is perfectly clear that those functions will vary vastly in the vastly varying stages of social evolution. They will be quite other in the enormous complexity of modern life from what they were in the utter simplicity of the patriarchal period, or in the comparative simplicity of the mediæval. I am not here writing a historical treatise, or an academical disquisition. I can only indicate what appears to me the general principle which should determine the sphere of the State's action, and then illustrate it by exhibiting some of its applications to the present

---

[1] Lasson remarks, in his trenchant way, " Der Staat hat in keinem Falle die Aufgabe die Menschen glücklich zu machen. Nur ein grober Eudämonismus kann daran denken." (*System der Rechtsphilosophie*, p. 319.)

condition of European society, with especial reference to England.

The primary right of the State, as of the individual, is, to be.   Now, war, not peace, is the law of
life; and the struggle for existence is a universal
fact.   Obviously, the first function of the State is
to maintain, in a condition of the utmost efficiency,
such fleets and armies, and other preparations for
war, as its security against rival States demands.
This is the condition of its external peace, according
to the hackneyed dictum, *Si vis pacem para bellum.*
Equally obvious is its function to maintain its internal
tranquillity by its magistrates and police.   They are
its ministers attending continually upon the application and enforcement of the rational will which finds
expression in its legislation—those dictates of Right,
that Justice, wherein it is rooted and grounded.

Again.   The right of the State, as we have seen,
is not merely to existence, but to complete existence, noble and worthy existence, an existence in
accordance with the dignity of human nature.
Hence, among its functions must be reckoned the
promotion of civilisation in both senses of the word.[1]
It is the guardian of the ideal and of the material
interests of the people whose personalities it incorporates; and upon its efficient and prudent discharge of the trust depend its dignity and greatness

[1] See p. 51.

—*majestas* was the fine old Roman word. I cannot here dwell—nor is it necessary for the present
purpose—upon the many and various ways in which
this function of the State is fulfilled. But I may
observe that clearly it should undertake, or effectively provide for, all strictly public works. Things
of imperial importance it should itself control : for
example the roads of a country, especially what are
now the chief highways, the railways. Matters of
local rather than of general concern, such as light-
ing, drainage, and water-supply, it may properly
entrust to the municipalities, or other corporate
bodies, invested by it with due powers for dealing
with them. But the rivers, the woods, the moun-
tains, and all those gifts of nature which constitute
the amenity of a country, should be under its direct
care, as being among the most precious of a nation's
possessions.

So much seems clear. The real difficulty is to
determine what are the proper limits of the State's
interference with individual action.

The true principle would appear to be that the
State should leave free all interests and faculties
of its subjects—*Kräfte* is the German word, but
"mights" is not an adequate translation—so far as
is consistent with the maintenance of its own rights.
It is no part of its functions to do for them what
they can do for themselves better, or even as well.

It is a part, and a very important part, of its functions to allow them to develop their own personality,
to become more and more men, to make the most
and the best of themselves, for their own and the
common welfare.   And not only to allow, but
prudently to aid, whether by direct encouragement
or by the removal of hindrances.   This is the just
mean of State action in respect of the subject.   It
is equally removed from a false paternalism and a
false individualism.

The false paternal theory of the State's functions
makes it not merely a high, but the only factor of
human development, as the creator and arbiter of
the rights of its subjects.   The sufficient condemnation of this doctrine is that it is utterly unethical :
that it is altogether fatal to that human freedom
which is the essence of personality.   It is expounded,
in different forms, by two very different schools.
The one is what we may call the German school
of political mysticism : a philosophical travesty of
the old very unphilosophical legitimism, which
invests the State—the monarchical State—with
theocratic attributes, and imposes on the subject
the one duty, to obey ; a school of which, I suppose, Stahl is the most considerable writer.   It
would seem from some of his public utterances
that the present German emperor must have
been deeply influenced by the teachings of this
school, which so far as I know is its only title—

whatever that may be worth—to the least consideration.

The other—a far more influential school in contemporary Europe—is the Jacobin or ultra-Radical
school which, consciously or unconsciously, represents the sophisms of Rousseau. This school insists
that man belongs wholly to the State: the falsely
democratic State resting upon a fictitious universal
suffrage—I shall justify this account of it in a subsequent chapter. Statolatry is a barbarous word
which I write with reluctance. It expresses, however, an indubitable fact. The falsely democratic
State, exalting itself "above all that is called God
or that is worshipped," is exhibited by the school of
which I am speaking as an earthly Providence, and
the only real one; the sole object entitled to man's
reverence and awe. The cardinal principle of this
school, as expounded by the late M. Gambetta, is,
*Il vous est défendu d'aller contre l'opinion domi-
nante.* Does any one venture to appeal to the
ancient maxim, "Thou shalt not follow a multitude
to do evil?" The answer is, "A multitude do evil?
What flat blasphemy! It is impossible. What the
people"—the numerical majority—"wishes is just;
their will is the very source and norm of right." It
is merely a revival of ancient Cæsarism, with this
difference—a difference vastly for the worse—that
the new Cæsar is not one, but many. It is a negation of that fundamental truth that human authority

is limited and fiduciary, and subject to the eternal, imprescriptible, and indefeasible laws of ethics. And it is not the less, it is the more dangerous, because it comes to us in the name of liberty. It is a manifestation of that Liberalism which Burke described as not liberal, which in Rivarol's phrase is the diminutive of liberty. Unquestionably, the invasion of human freedom by the falsely democratic State is one of the greatest perils of the age.

The opposite error to this false paternalism is the false individualism professing the doctrine of *laissez-faire*, which sees in civil society nothing more than a struggle for existence among millions of human atoms; which regards the function of the State as nothing more than to keep the ring while they fight. And it is in the same condemnation. It ignores or denies that great truth unfolded in the last chapter, that as man is an ethical animal, so the State is an ethical organism; and that the action of the State should therefore be governed by "the normal laws of nature and of nations."

So much may suffice as to these two manifestations of the "falsehood of extremes." Let us now, in the light of the general principle above laid down, consider seven "burning questions of the day," as they have been called, to which that general principle is applicable.

1. THE STATE AND EDUCATION

First, then, as to education. What is the function of the State regarding it? The claim is made, and has largely prevailed throughout the civilised world, that the education of children is the immediate concern of the State. This claim appears to me, upon the face of it, monstrous. Of all liberties which are bound up with, and flow from, human personality, one of the most sacred [1] is the father's right to educate his children as his conscience dictates. The State, upon the other hand, has the right and the duty to maintain for its subjects the conditions under which a free exercise of their faculties is possible, for their own and the general advantage. And in view of that end it is warranted in insisting that a modicum of instruction be acquired by them all. We live in an age where well-nigh every adult male is directly entrusted with a share of political power. The State may justly require, and ought to require, that he shall receive such training, intellectual and moral, as will enable him to realise, so far as may be possible, the responsibilities involved in its exercise. We live in an age when national prosperity is largely dependent upon individual culture. The State may justly require that in this respect its subjects shall,

[1] Mill writes, " It is one of the most sacred duties of the parents (or as law and usage now stand, the father), after summoning a human being into the world, to give to that being an education fitting him to perform his part well in life towards others and towards himself." —*On Liberty*, p. 189.

at the least, not fall behind the subjects of rival nations.   This, and this only, is its function in respect
of the general education of the country.   And if the
father cannot, or will not, comply with these legitimate requirements, the State is warranted in inter-
fering, directly or indirectly, to supply his default.
This is the principle on which grants in aid of de-
nominational primary education have been given in
this country.   It is the principle of the Act which
originally established School Boards; a measure
sound and just in itself, whatever we may think of
particular provisions of it, and of the application
given to them—questions with which I am not here
concerned.

   That is the function of the State with regard to
the general education of the country, which, of
course, must be of the kind called "primary."   Its
function with regard to education of a higher kind
is similar.   For example, it is bound to see that the
universities and great public schools efficiently discharge the duties entrusted to them, while leaving
them the greatest possible liberty as to methods and
details.   The interference of the British legislature,
in our own day, with these institutions for their improvement and greater utility, is entirely warranted ;
which, of course, is not the same thing as saying
that it has been, in all respects, judicious and beneficial.   But what is always unwarrantable, except,
as Mill remarks, " When society in general is so back-

ward that it could not or would not provide for itself any proper institutions of education unless the government undertook the task," is that the State should "take upon itself the business of schools and universities."[1] It is not the function of the State to be the general schoolmaster of its subjects. And its usurpation of this function, as in France, is a gross infringement of individual right. It is also a deadly blow to that individuality of character which the State is bound to cherish and protect, as an indispensable element of national well-being. Diversity of education is a chief factor of such individuality. In the sagacious words of Mill, "A general State education is a mere contrivance for moulding people to be exactly like one another; and as the mould in which it casts them is that which pleases the predominant power in the government, whether this be a monarch, a priesthood, an aristocracy, or the majority of the existing generation, in proportion as it is efficient and successful, it establishes a despotism over the mind, leading by natural tendency to one over the body."[2]

2. THE STATE AND RELIGION

Next let us inquire what is the function of the State with regard to religion. I speak of the State as it exists *hic et nunc*. It appears to me that the highest *idea* of the State involves the profession of a

[1] *On Liberty*, p. 191.   [2] *Ibid*

common faith by its subjects. Religion is both the greatest bond of political unity, and the most effecttive guardian of public morality. Plato, in the *Republic*, expresses the wisdom of the ancients on this subject when he describes " the erection of temples, and the appointment of sacrifices, and other ceremonies in honour of the gods, and all the observances which we must adopt in order to propitiate the inhabitants of the other world," as " the most momentous, the most august, and the highest acts of legislation." So, in the Age of Faith, the vision of the seer of Patmos was realised ; the " kingdoms of this world "—or, at all events, of the Western world —had " become the kingdoms of our Lord, and of His Christ": and the first note of the State was Christianity.[1] But Christendom is as much a thing of the past as is classic Hellas. We live in an age not of religious unity, but of religious disunity ; in an age, not of faith, but unfaith. And the attitude of the State towards religion in such an age, must be far other than what it was in ancient Greece or in mediæval Europe. The modern State is compelled, by the nature of the case, to profess itself "incompe-

[1] Accordingly, St. Thomas Aquinas writes, *Finis ad quem principaliter rex intendere debet in se ipso et in subditis est æterna beatitudo* (*De Reg. Prin.*, l. iii., c. 4). Hence the severity of mediæval legislation against heresy. " It is much worse," writes Aquinas, " to corrupt the faith which is the life of the soul, than to forge money, which is merely an instrument of temporal good. Therefore, if forgers and other malefactors are justly delivered to death by the secular ruler, so *a fortiori* should be convicted heretics. *Summa Theolgica*, 2, 2, q. 11, a. 3.

tent in the matter of cults;" the essentially modern
principle of toleration is forced upon it. "My dominion ends," said the first Napoleon, "where the
dominion of conscience begins"; expressing, with
his wonted clearness and incisiveness, the principle
which he was, in some sort to translate into fact.

What, then, in such an age as the present, is the
function of the State with regard to religion? It
appears to me admirably indicated in the well-known
words of Adam Smith : "Philosophic good temper
and moderation with regard to every religious creed."
Benevolent neutrality seems to be the true attitude
of the State towards all cults, which do not directly
conflict with its own rights and duties. And this
for a reason, well expressed by an ancient Chinese
emperor, that "the great principle of Eternal
Right" (Tào)—which is the foundation of the State
—"underlies all religions, although it does not always appear in the same form." On no State is this
benevolent neutrality more imperative than on the
British, which is at once a great Protestant, a great
Catholic, a great Mohammedan, and a great Hindu
power. Whether or no the State should accord
pecuniary subventions to the different cults existing
in its territory, as is done in France,[1] is a question
merely of expediency, and involves no point of prin-

[1] It must not be forgotten that the beggarly stipends paid to the
Catholic clergy in France, are in compensation for the secularisation
of their property by one of the most gigantic and flagitious acts of
confiscation which the world has ever witnessed.

ciple.   But certain it is that, as the Western world
at present exists, no State can fairly adopt as its own
any religious profession.

"Adopt," I say.   It does not in the least follow
that where an established church already exists, it
should be disestablished, and its property pillaged.
Such a course is often demanded in respect of the
Church of England, and is supported by arguments
of which some seem to me decidedly dishonest, and
all utterly unconvincing.   The most pretentious of
them is grounded on what is called "the right of
religious equality."   But the pretence is empty.
Such a right does not exist.   It is no part of the *lex
naturæ*, either in the primary or the secondary
sphere.   It is unknown to the common law of this
country, and is not recognised in the statutes.   It is
a mere spurious fabrication.   It illustrates the oblit-
eration of the genuine idea of right from the general
mind, and the prevailing tendency to invest with
that august name any whim, or prejudice, or ebulli-
tion of concupiscence.   The question of the Established Church of England, is an eminently practical
one, and should be viewed not in the mist of a fictitious "right of religious equality," but in the sunlight
of actual facts.   The Established Church belongs to
an order of things which is the outcome of English
history, and into which we have been born.   It is
part of "that prescriptive constitution which," to
use the words of Burke, "has grown out of the

peculiar circumstances, occasions, tempers, dispositions, and moral, civil, and social habitudes of the
people." The point for a publicist to consider is,
not whether, if he were writing a treatise *De Republica,* or excogitating a brand new polity, he would
make provision for such an institution, but whether
the institution, as it exists and works, subserves or
thwarts the true end of the State. I do not believe
any man can honestly declare that any real right,
whether of the body politic or of the individual,
suffers from the Established Church. The attacks
upon it are generally made by those who call themselves Liberals, and even "Advanced" Liberals.
Surely they might well make an examination of
conscience on the matter. I cannot understand how
any mind not blinded by religious or—what is quite
as common a cause of intellectual cecity—irreligious
fanaticism, can fail to discern the vast amount of
good work done by the Anglican Establishment
as a liberalising agency : as a minister of culture,
and that of the best kind, which is ethical ; as an instrument for the idealising of life. And unquestionably all this is achieved without the smallest
infringement of liberty. No man is obliged to profess the doctrines of the Church of England, or to
attend its services, or to subscribe one penny towards
its support. To which I add, that no religious com-
munion so peculiarly liberal as the Anglican Establishment has ever existed among men, or is likely

5

ever to exist. Can Liberalism be carried farther
than in a church—it is best to give concrete instances—wherein Dr. King, the Bishop of Lincoln,
Dr. Ryle, the Bishop of Liverpool, Dean Paget of
Christ Church, and Dean Fremantle of Ripon, Canon
Fleming of York, and Canon Newbolt of St. Paul's,
dwell together in the unity originally created, and
still maintained, by Queen Elizabeth's *Act of Uniformity?* Dr. Arnold, in his *Lectures on Modern
History*, observes that "we may consent to act together, but we cannot consent to believe together,"
and argues that the bond of a church "should consist in a common object and a common practice rather
than in a common belief;" that the end of its
clergy "should be good rather than truth."[1] Whatever we may think of this view of an ecclesiastical
polity, there can be no question that it is realised in
the Established Church of England. And it appears to me that a function of the British State is to
uphold that Church as a great factor in the ethical
life of the country, an effective agent of moral police.

3. THE STATE AND MORALITY

But I am here anticipating what I have to say
upon the next point; the function of the State
regarding morality. No one, I suppose, doubts
that the State is vitally interested in the ethical
life of the country. National greatness—nay, even

[1] Page 50.

national existence—depends on national character infinitely more than on any external causes. And national character is the outcome of the individual character; of the characters of the men and the women composing the nation. Assuredly the State should do all that it properly can to maintain and heighten the morality of its subjects. " All that it properly can." It is not the office of the State directly to make men moral. That is impossible. Morality is of the will. It is not a matter of compulsion. "The quality of mercy is not strained." And the same is true of every ethical quality. A power of choice is a condition of virtue. I do not doubt that Milton's masterly argument on this topic in the *Areopagitica* is familiar to most of my readers. But I may be permitted to cite a pregnant passage of it.

> Impunity and remissness for certain are the bane of a commonwealth : and here the great art lies—to discern in what the law is to bid restraint and punishment, and in what things persuasion only is to work. If every action which is good or evil in man at ripe years were to be under pittance, prescription, and compulsion, what were virtue but a name, what praise could be then due to well-doing, what gramercy to be sober, just, or continent ? . . . Were I the chooser, a dram of well-doing should be preferred before many times as much the forcible hindrance of evil-doing. For God sure esteems the growth and completing of one virtuous person, more than the restraint of ten vicious.

We may say, then, that the function of the State as to morality, is, first to maintain the conditions

necessary for freedom of individual choice, and
secondly to encourage the helps and restrain the
hindrances to right choice, so far as it can without
infringement of that freedom. This is the general
principle, although there are cases—they are most
rare—in which the State may go beyond it, for
the protection of its own supreme rights.

Let me illustrate this principle by three concrete
examples. The first two are suggested by the
words of Milton : sobriety and continence. There
can be no question that the prevalence of the habit
of drunkenness in any country is a great national
scandal and a great national mischief. I suppose it
will be universally admitted to be the right and
duty of the State to limit the places and hours at
which, and the person to whom, intoxicating liquors
may be sold by retail. And the reason, as Mill has
well pointed out, is, that the interest of the sellers
of such liquors " in promoting intemperance is a real
evil, and justifies the State in imposing restrictions
and requiring guarantees, which, but for that justification, would be infringements of legitimate liberty." [1]
But that justification cannot be urged for the legislation demanded by the advocates of what is called
"Local Option." Its essence is this : that if the
greater number of the inhabitants of a district so
choose, they should be able to forbid the sale of
intoxicating liquors therein, and to enforce teetotal-

[1] *On Liberty*, p. 180.

ism upon all who are not rich enough to keep a
supply of alcoholic drinks in their own houses.   It
is difficult to imagine any more flagrant violation of
the most elementary liberties of the subject.   If
such tyranny were attempted by an autocratic ruler
—the Sultan of Turkey or the Czar of Russia, for
example—all the world would recognise this.   But
how does tyranny lose its tyrannousness because it
is perpetrated, not by one man, but by a number of
men ?   The arguments in defence of it put forward
by its most zealous advocates, as accurately set forth
by Mill, are, that the traffic in strong drink inter-
feres with a man's social rights; that it destroys his
primary right of security, by constantly creating and
stimulating social disorder ; that it invades his right
of equality by deriving a profit from the creation of
a misery which he is taxed to support [1]; that it im-
pedes his right to free moral and intellectual development by surrounding his path with dangers, and
by weakening and demoralising society, from which
he has a right to claim mutual aid and intercourse.
Upon which Mill admirably observes, " A theory of
social rights, the like of which, probably, never before found its way into distinct language—being
nothing short of this—that it is the absolute social
right of every individual that every other individual
shall act in every respect exactly as he ought ; that

---

[1] I give this as I find it, but I confess I do not know what it means.
The right of equality before the law is the only right of equality that
I understand.

whosoever fails thereof, in the smallest particular, violates my social right, and entitles me to demand from the Legislature the removal of the grievance. There is no violation of liberty which so monstrous a principle would not justify."[1] I add that re-formed public-houses, such as under the Gothen-burg system, or under the high-licence system of certain American States, or under a government monopoly, as by the recent great reform in Russia, are by no means in this condemnation. They are legitimate and laudable attempts to fulfil, according to national circumstances, an important function of the State.

Next as to continence. But the question is part of a larger subject—the sexual relations of men and women. It is a subject in which the State is most deeply interested. Civil society springs from the family. And the family rests upon the chastity of women. It is a true saying that the ethical man is formed at the knees of his mother. The kind of men the country turns out—and that is what the greatness of a country depends upon—will ever be determined by the kind of women a country breeds. The moral tone of a country is decided by women. And their goodness or badness —as our very language witnesses—depends chiefly upon their purity. All feminine virtues are rooted in this one virtue of chastity. Renan's saying is

[1] *On Liberty*, p. 161.

true to the letter: *La force d'une nation, c'est la pudeur de ses femmes.*

What, then, is the function of the State in respect of sexual morality? Let us consider its function first with regard to the licit union of the sexes in marriage, and next with regard to their illicit union out of marriage.

There are those—Advanced Thinkers they call themselves—who hold that any interference of the State with marriage, except in certain cases for the enforcement of abortion, or for the punishment of the non-fulfilment of that new duty, is altogether unwarrantable, as an invasion of what they consider individual rights. We are assured by one of the ablest of them that " our present marriage customs and our present marriage law are destined to suffer great changes"; that "it seems not improbable that, when woman is truly educated and equally developed with man, she will hold that the highest relation of man and woman is akin to that of Lewes and George Eliot," " not a union for the birth of children, but the closest form of friendship between man and woman "; that " in the society of the future a birth will have [that is, will require] social sanction "; and that " in times of over-population, it might even be needful to punish positively, as well as negatively, both father and mother " guilty of allowing " a birth beyond the sanctioned number": but that for "a non-childbearing woman " " the sex

relationship, both as to form and substance, ought
to be a pure question of taste, a simple matter of
agreement between the man and her, in which
neither society nor the State would have any need
or right to interfere ": " a free sexual union," " a relation solely of mutual sympathy and affection, its
form and duration varying according to the feelings
and wants of individuals." So Mr. Karl Pearson,
in his work entitled *The Ethic of Free Thought;*
a misleading title, as it seems to me, for I find in
the book no trace of the ethical idea, no freedom
save that of " the beast that takes his licence in the
field of time," which I hold to be the deepest slavery.
But it may be said that these are only the private
opinions of the accomplished writer. Turn we,
then to the *Manifesto of the Socialistic League,*
published, with annotations, by its general secre-
taries, Mr. Belfort Bax and the late Mr. William
Morris—surely an authoritative exposition of the
principles of the school. We read in that document that " our modern bourgeois property marriage " is to " give place to kindly and human
relations between the sexes." And if we inquire
what these kindly and human relations are, the
annotators tell us, " Under a Socialistic system
contracts would be free and unenforced by the
community: this would apply to the marriage contract as well as others, and it would become a
matter of simple inclination; . . . nor would a

truly enlightened public opinion, freed from mere
theological views as to chastity, insist upon its permanently binding nature."

It would appear, then, that these sages regard
marriage as a mere contract, or rather as less than
that; as "a simple matter of agreement," "a matter
of simple inclination"; a nude pact, as the jurists
say, from which no "action" can arise; from which
no rights spring, in the philosophical sense, any
more than in the legal sense.   Well, marriage is not
something less than a contract.   It is a contract
and something more.   Green has correctly pointed
this out, though, perhaps, with a superfluity of
words, which I shall take the liberty to abridge:
"A right arising from contract . . . is not a
right against all the world, but a right as against
a particular person or persons contracted with to
claim a certain performance or forbearance.   The
right of husband over wife, and that of parent over
children (or *vice versa*) differs from the right arising
out of contract, inasmuch as it is not merely a right
against the particular person contracted with, but
a right against all the world.   In this respect it
corresponds with the right of property; but differs again from this since it is not a right over a
thing, but over a person. . . . The distinction
is not merely a formal one.   From the fact that
these rights have persons as their objects, there
follow important results as to the true nature of

the right, to the manner in which it should be exercised."[1]

"Most important results," indeed, which it would be foreign from my purpose to set forth in detail here. Let it suffice to observe that the only adequate conception of marriage—a conception purely rational and arising from its very essence and ends—is the permanent fusion of two personalities; a conception admirably expressed by the Roman jurist: "*Nuptiæ sunt conjunctio maris et feminæ, et consortium omnis vitæ: divini et humani juris communicatio.* And the rights springing from this union—rights which do not arise from the sanction of the State, but are antecedent to it, though, of course, in implying society in some form—are, like the parental rights so closely connected with them, among the most sacred rights of human nature. It is assuredly the function of the State to protect and enforce these rights, with all other rights attaching to personality. And it is not easy to overestimate the practical importance of that function. The origin of the State, historically considered, is the family. And the corruption of the family is the dissolution of the State. Horace, lamenting that corruption in the decadent Roman people, spoke the exact truth when he wrote—

> " Hoc fonte derivata clades
> In patriam populumque fluxit."

[1] *Works*, vol. ii., p. 536.

It is, then, the office of the State to guard with the most anxious solicitude, and the deepest reverence, the sacrosanct rights arising out of marriage. In every nation under heaven this vitally important institution has received the sanction of religion, the most powerful of all sanctions with the masses of men. And a wise statesmen will strive to the utmost to maintain that sanction, while insisting upon the just claims of the State with regard to the secular contract. The religious side of marriage should ever be the more prominent, as a matter of public policy. And here again I may cite certain judicious words of Green: "Though rights, in the strict sense, undoubtedly arise out of marriage, though marriage has thus its strictly legal aspect, it is undesirable that this legal aspect should become prominent [lest the institution should] suffer in respect of its higher moral purposes." [1]

But, unfortunately, marriage is not the only form of the union of the sexes, though it is the only licit form. What is the function of the State as regards their illicit union out of marriage? The question is of much practical importance, not only from the ethical point of view, with which I am for the moment concerned, but from another, upon which I shall touch presently. One of the notes of the age is a pronounced laxity of practice—and what is worse, of theory—about sexual matters.

[1] *Works.* vol. ii., p. 546.

Nor is it confined to any single class of society. There are too many "young ladies in gilded saloons," as Lord Beaconsfield has it, who discuss, unreservedly, things which their grandmothers would have thought it a shame even to speak of, and who assuredly do not escape moral contamination in most cases, physical in many. Their humbler sisters, in workrooms, in shops, in factories, are not slow to follow their example, and to set little store upon the teaching of the Catechism concerning the duty of chastity. The press daily vomits forth a vast mass of frankly obscene and pruriently suggestive literature and art, apparently designed for the express purpose of stimulating passions usually active enough without artificial irritants. The sexual licence practised in London, and other great cities, increases every year. And I, for one, see no prospect whatever of greater strictness. The signs of the times appear to point in the opposite direction.

One of those signs, so legibly written on contemporary life that none surely can fail to read it, is the prevailing idolatry of physical comfort, of sensuous gratification, of luxurious living. Young men of narrow means, nay, of moderate means, are—not unnaturally—averse from marriage, which means for them frugality, self-restraint, self-sacrifice. They are equally averse—as is natural—from mortifying the appetite for the lawful gratification

of which marriage was ordained. "Begad, my
good ma'am, if you think our boy is a Joseph,"
says Major Pendennis to the shocked and distressed
Helen, who cuts him short, "looking very stately."
But the fact, however shocking and distressing,
is that an exceeding great multitude of our young
men are not as Joseph. Among the virtues which
adorn them, cannot be reckoned the one for which
that patriarch is specially renowned. They do not
shrink from ephemeral connections. They do not
disdain "casual fruition." "A fact," the wise
Hindu proverb warns us, "is not altered by a
hundred texts." Here, too, I suppose, the law of
supply and demand applies. And unless you can
reconstruct human nature, or revolutionise the conditions of human society, it appears to me that the
mistress will more and more take the place of the
wife; that sexual promiscuity will become more
and more firmly rooted in our civilisation.

What, then, is the function of the State in this
matter? There are those who would meet the
sexual laxity of the age by changes, more or less far-
reaching, in the institution of matrimony. Thus,
Mr. Belfort Bax and Mr. William Morris assure us,
in the document which I just now quoted, that if
what they term "our modern bourgeois property
marriage" disappeared, "its necessary complement, universal venal prostitution," would dis-
appear also. As they would abolish pauperism by

making all men paupers, so would they abolish
prostitution by making all women concubines. We
may regard these gentlemen as the red revolutionists
of our sexual moralities. There are revolutionists
of milder types : milk-and-water revolutionists, rose-
water revolutionists, we may call them. These are
they who, while shrinking from the abolition of
marriage, would loosen, in greater or less degree, the
strictness of its bond ; who would facilitate divorce,
would give a recognised status to children born out
of wedlock, would rehabilitate the concubine and the
courtesan. I suppose M. Alexandre Dumas *fils* is
the most highly gifted and the most generally
accredited of these " reformers." I own to much
admiration for the literary ability of the author of
Le Demi Monde, L'Ami des Femmes, and *M.
Alphonse ;* but I do not think it worth while seriously
to discuss his views on sexual relations. They
appear to me mere mawkish manifestations of the
ethical limpness of our times. They recall to my
mind that profound remark of Carlyle: " The
deepest difficulty which presses on us all, is the
sick sentimentalism which we suck in with our
whole nourishment, and get ingrained into the very
blood of us, in these miserable ages." For myself, I
am convinced that the true, the only antidote to the
abounding sexual licence of our age is to uphold, in
all its severity, the ideal of marriage, holy and indis-
soluble, which Christianity has impressed upon

European civilisation. This ideal is the source of
all that is highest in the modern family. In whatever degree you tamper with it and derogate from
its strictness, you demoralise woman; you degrade
the ethical tone of society, which depends upon her
as the guardian and priestess of chastity. It was
by exhibiting the perfect type of that virtue that
the Catholic Church rescued society from a depth of
foulness to which it has never since sunk. In this
type, and nowhere else, is the rule and norm of
purity throughout the ages. Shall I be told that
the type is too perfect? Perfection is not a matter
of degree. The Christian type *is* perfect, and that
is precisely why it suffices. To tend towards perfection is a law of our nature. None save a perfect
type will draw us after it—a type to which we may
more or less approximate, but which we can never
fully realise. The vast majority of mankind ever
have dwelt, and ever will dwell, upon the lower
levels of humanity. Those elect souls who "scorn
men's common lure, life's pleasant things," are
always comparatively few. But it makes all the
difference, in any age, of what kind men's ideals
are. If they are high, severe—yes, let me venture
upon the word—ascetic, common life will be marked
by dignity, magnanimity, virility, however grave
and numerous the derelictions from the standard
commonly recognised.

But—for that is our immediate point—what is

the function of the State as to concubinage and
prostitution ? As to concubinage, the function of
the State, in my judgment, is the purely negative one of in no wise countenancing it. I believe
the old Roman law was absolutely right in holding *Pater est quem nuptiæ demonstrant,* and in
declining to recognise paternity where there is no
matrimony. The provision of the *Code Napoléon,*
based upon that law, *La recherche de la paternité
est interdite,* appears to me in accordance with the
dictates of Right, and the English law of bastardy
appears to me opposed to those dictates. Is it
objected, "This is hard on the children ?" It is
hard ; but it is in accordance with the universal law
of solidarity dominating the frame of things into
which we were born, and from which we cannot
escape. And if we try to escape, we merely en-
counter worse evils, and purchase, at our own expense, a confirmation of the truth that—

> " Because right is right, to follow right
> Were wisdom, in the scorn of consequence."

As to prostitution, the case is very different. I
do not understand how any one who will look the
facts of human life in the face can doubt that Parent-
Duchâtelet was well founded when he wrote, "Under forms which vary according to climate and
national manners, prostitution remains inherent in
great populations; it exists, and always will exist :

like those congenital maladies against which experi-
ments and systems of medicine have contended in
vain, and the ravages only of which we now strive
to limit." [1] I remember reading in one of the journals,
not long ago, of a somewhat prurient prophetess—so
she seemed to me—of what she called "social purity,"
who announced it as her mission " to put down prostitution." The good lady—I forget her name, nor
does it signify—going forth on her crusade against
the most imperious and indomitable of human appetites, with tract and tea-pot, reminded me of Mrs.
Partington going forth with her broom to sweep
back the Atlantic. Put down prostitution ! Yes,
if you can first dry up the springs which feed the
swelling ocean of human lust—want and wantoness,
laziness and luxury, the enticing vanity of women,
and the ebullient virility of men. I add—can any
one, who will clear his mind of cant, doubt that, human nature being what it is, and the conditions of
human life being what they are, the putting down of
prostitution would be the heaviest blow that could
be struck at social purity? St. Augustine, in his
profoundly philosophical treatise *De Ordine*, pointed
out fourteen hundred years ago, that to abolish courtesans would be to trouble everything with lusts.
His words are as true now as they were then ; nay,
truer. " That unhappy being," writes Mr. Lecky, in
a sadly eloquent passage, " herself the supreme type

[1] *De la Prostitution dans la Ville de Paris*, p. 625.

6

of vice, is ultimately the most efficient guardian of virtue. But for her, the unchallenged purity of countless happy homes would be polluted, and not a few who, in the pride of their untempted chastity, think of her with an indignant shudder, would have known the agony of remorse and of despair. On that one degraded and ignoble form are concentrated the passions that might have filled the world with shame. She remains, while creeds and civilisations rise and fall, the eternal priestess of humanity, blasted by the sins of the people." [1]

Considerations of this sort should fill us, not only with pity, but with awe. What can be more miserable than the lot of these unhappy women, if we really see it as it is? All the dignity of womanhood gone; all interests in life, save those of a purely animal nature, extinguished; not even the power of repentance left, in many cases, for a career of animalism has degraded them to the level of the animal, and the moral sense is atrophied. No; in place of repentance, merely regrets when their physical charms have faded; when diseases incident to their calling have made a prey of them; when destitution and desolation stare them in the face. *Triste vie est celle que je quitte,* says the dying Marguerite Gautier. Sad indeed; the saddest to which any woman can condemn herself. Fearfulness and trembling may well come upon us, and a horrible dread over-

---

[1] *History of European Morals*, vol. ii., p. 283.

whelm us, when we reflect that here, too, we are confronted with that appalling fact—evil the apparently
inevitable condition of good; that here, too, we are
brought face to face with that inscrutable law of
vicarious sacrifice.   It is a profound and heart-
piercing mystery, like that of animal suffering; a
problem beyond the reaches of our souls.

But, if we pass from speculation to practice, the
function of the State seems clear.   It is to take cog-
nisance of this monstrous fact of prostitution, to reg-
ulate what must practically be regarded as a necessary
evil, and to minimise the resultant mischiefs.   I am
far from asserting that public authority should interfere to prevent women who choose this miserable
calling from following it.   The cynical excuse of
the father of a celebrated American courtesan for
his daughter's course of life, "It's a ready-money
business, and she likes it," must disgust and dismay
us.   But certainly, if a woman who has attained an
age which authorises her to decide, prefers to walk
in this broad way which leadeth to destruction, no
human power can restrain her.   She is at liberty to
choose the evil and refuse the good, here, as in other
matters.   To say this is not, however, to admit "the
right of free prostitution"—what a travesty of the
word "right"—occasionally asserted; and that, curiously enough, by some who pose as champions of
"social purity."   The regulation of this evil trade
is no wrongful interference with individual liberty,

for the criminous commerce is in itself an impediment to social good. It is, assuredly, the function of the State to prohibit the use of our thoroughfares as a mart where public women may follow their vocation ; and to enable young men, in whom passion is strongest and reason weakest, to walk abroad without temptation staring them in the face. It is, assuredly, the function of the State to maintain, by due police regulations, order and decency in the parts of music-halls and other places of general resort, where such women congregate, and where those who need them may find them without common scandal and inconvenience[1] ; not to make foolish and futile attempts at excluding them from such rendezvous. It is, assuredly, the function of the State, and that in the interests of the unhappy women themselves, to inspect and control the houses in which they are known to dwell together, and to secure their unshackled liberty of departure thence ; not, in hypocritical impotence, to make spasmodic raids upon their habitations. All the arguments in favour of the regulation of the drink traffic, apply with far greater force to this. For the sexual appetite is much more deeply rooted in man than the appetite for alcohol. It is part and parcel of human

---

[1] The lines of Horace will doubtless occur to some readers—
    " Quidam notus homo cum exiret fornice, ' Macte
    Virtute esto,' inquit sententia dia Catonis.
    Nam simul ac venas inflavit tetra libido
    Huc juvenes aequum est descendere, non alienas
    Permolere uxores."

nature—not an artificial adjunct, the product of civilisation.

A third matter affecting the moral life of a country, regarding which the State has, as it appears to me, a function, is cruelty to animals. And I wish to say a few words about it here, because the ground upon which that function rests is often misunderstood. We are told that the State should interfere to protect the rights of animals. The unfortunate phrase is likely to prejudice the object of the excellent people who ignorantly employ it. The lower animals have, in strictness, no rights. Capability of right and responsibility for wrong go together. As the Germans put it, man is *rechtsfähig* because he is *zurechnungsfähig*. Man is the only being in the world to whom rights and their correlative duties attach. Man alone is a *person* and self-determined. "The condition of making the animal contributory to human good," writes Green, "is that we do not leave him free to determine the exercise of his powers; that we determine them for him: that we use him merely as an instrument: and this means that we do not, because we cannot, endow him with rights. We do not endow him with rights because there is no conception of a good common to him with us which we can treat as a motive for him to do to us as he would have us do to him." [1] Still, the lower animals are not mere

[1] *Works*, vol. ii., p. 513.

things. They possess that realisation of selfhood
which is a characteristic of the person. And, therefore, we may properly attribute to them—to use
Trendelenburg's happy phrase—*ein Stück persön-
liches*, an element of personality. They are our
poor relations, and their very poverty gives them a
strong claim on the sympathy—one of the highest
ethical emotions—both of individual persons, and of
the State which incorporates and represents the
personalities of its subjects. Cruelty to them is certainly demoralising ; the more so as it is a singularly
cowardly abuse of power. And it is the function of
the State effectively to restrain and severely to
punish such cruelty, even when practised in the
name of science. Torture is an unethical means of
investigation, whether in criminal courts or in physiological laboratories.

4. THE STATE AND PUBLIC HYGIENE

Another matter in which the rights of the State
come into conflict with private rights is Public
Hygiene. It is a mere truism to say that the State
should care for the corporal soundness of its subjects.
No one, I suppose, will question its function of insisting upon sanitation ; of providing physical training for the young, and healthful breathing-spaces
for the masses, in our cities ; of promoting cleanli-
ness by means of public baths and wash-houses ; of
repressing the adulteration of food and drink ; of

enforcing such preventive measures as medical
science prescribes against infectious diseases. Questions of some difficulty may, no doubt, arise as to its
best mode of action in carrying out these and the
like measures for the general advantage. Unquestionably the State should be on its guard against the
tyranny of faddists, who, as is natural in the present
empirical condition of medicine, abound among the
practitioners of that profession. But there are faddists of another kind, who are equally, or, indeed,
more prejudicial to the proper discharge by the
State of its function in respect of the public health.
There is a certain class of maladies which are not
the natural product, but the accidental accompani-
ment of the promiscuous intercourse of the sexes ;
maladies which poison the very fount of generation ;
maladies more dire in their nature, more malign in
their results, than smallpox, or cholera, or typhus.
Assuredly it is the duty of the State—the duty is
discharged in well-nigh every civilized country but
England—to circumscribe within the narrowest possible limits their baneful activity ; to employ all the
resources of medical science in order to stamp them
out. But, No, we are told ; the State must not " recognise " vice ; it must allow free trade in contagious
diseases, lest it should weaken a deterrent from the
sin of illicit intercourse. It is a monstrous scandal
that in England the hands of the State are tied
by a knot of zealots who thus argue. The excel-

lence of their motives I do not question. But assuredly they are the slaves of a sour and senseless
superstition. There is much that is noble and admirable in Puritanism. But, as a matter of fact, it
has ever been deeply impregnated with savage fanaticism ; it has ever exhibited the ugliest form of the
odium theologicum. In former ages it endeavoured
to deter men from incontinence by the stock, the
whip, the gallows. It no longer wields these weap-
ons. It seeks to employ, instead of them, the more
frightful deterrent of disease. Its fanatics are wont
to express horror of the spirit of the mediæval inquisition. They seem to me animated by a far fiercer
spirit. The official inquisitors of heresy in the Middle Ages, at all events contented themselves with
swiftly destroying in the flames the body of their
victim. The amateur inquisitors of incontinence
in this nineteenth century are not content with
dooming theirs to a worse penalty, the living death
of a life-long disease. They inflict it also upon his
innocent family ; upon his wife, upon his children,
nay, upon generations yet unborn.

5. THE STATE AND CONTRACT

A fifth instance of the conflict of the rights of the
State with private rights occurs in the sphere of
contract. Freedom of contract is unquestionably a
precious part of personal liberty, and the function
of the State—a very important function— is to pre-

serve and vindicate it. The general principle, clearly
stated by the late Sir George Jessel in a well-known
case, is that "men of full age and competent understanding shall have the utmost liberty of contract-
ing, and that their contracts, when entered into
freely and voluntarily, shall be held sacred, and
shall be enforced by courts of justice." [1] But, as we
saw in the last chapter, this freedom is not absolute.
It is a freedom on conditions prescribed by the State
for the maintenance of general right. Consider for
a moment what a contract is. It is not a mere
promise ; it is a promise which the State recognises
as binding, and will enforce with all the power of
the courts. And, so viewed, it is a limitation of a
man's freedom. This has been excellently put by
Sir Frederick Pollock : "Every person not subject
to any legal incapacity may dispose freely of his
personal property within the limits allowed by the
general law. Liability on a contract consists in a
further limitation of this disposing power by a voluntary act of the party, which places some definite
portion of that power at the command of the other
party to the contract. So much of the debtor's individual freedom is taken from him and made over
to the creditor." [2] When we speak of freedom of
contract, we mean freedom to enter into a binding
agreement for the diminution of personal liberty.

[1] *Printing and Numerical Registering Co. v. Sampson* (1875), 19 Eq.
462.

[2] *Principles of Contract*, 6th ed., p. 189.

There are many things as to which the State does not permit such freedom. There are well-recognised classes of agreements which the State does not, and should not validate and enforce, however valuable the consideration by which they are supported, however freely and formally they may have been made. Such, for example, are agreements *contra bonos mores*, agreements to oust the jurisdiction of the courts, and many other agreements which are regarded as being against public policy.

Conspicuous among such agreements should be reckoned those which are tainted by usury : although in these, for the most part, there is not that free consent which is of the essence of a contract, overmastering distress having fettered the borrower's volition. Assuredly, it is the function of the State to repress such pacts, not only through its civil courts, but, in gross cases, through its criminal tribunals. The essence of usury is extortion. It is extortion under colour of law, which is, from an ethical point of view, more heinous, in itself, than extortion by threats, or by physical violence. We are sometimes told—we are often told—that the reprobation of usury as wrong, is an exploded mediaeval superstition. It appears to me that the principle which guided the philosophers and legislators of former ages in this matter is valid for all time, and that Shylock is quite as noxious in the nineteenth century as he was in the sixteenth ; nay, more noxious, for his abominable operations are conducted upon a much wider scale. True it is that the function of money in this modern world is other than it was in the Middle Ages, where other economical conditions prevailed. In those ages almost all farming, or producing, had for its object direct use, not sale; rent, in the sense of a competition price paid for the occupation of land, was unknown; the vast developments of commerce and industry now surrounding us would have appeared the wildest and most fantastic dreams. Money is not now, as it was in earlier periods of civilisation, a mere medium of *private* exchange for the purposes of housekeeping. It is a medium of *commercial* exchange and fruitful lending; it is no longer barren, a thing to be hoarded in cellars and chests. In the mercantile society of modern life commercial credit is an essential factor; and to put money out to interest, in genuine business adventures, is, in itself, not immoral because, in itself, not unfruitful. For what usury really means— this is the definition of the Fourth Lateran Council —is "the attempt to draw profit and increment, without labour, without cost, and without risk, from the use of a thing that does not fructify." And in spite of the change of circumstances, there can be no question of the vast prevalence of usury, thus understood, in our own day; and as little of its malignancy. Leo XIII., who, fully conscious of the responsibilities of his august position, scrupulously

weighs his words, speaks, in his *Encyclical on Labour*, of the common people as "devoured" by it.
The wretched cultivators in India, in Russia, in
Austria, in Italy, in Germany, knew it only too well
in its old form : while, in a new form, it appears in
the vast incomes nefariously drawn from utterly unfruitful and unprofitable "operations" with stocks,
shares, bonds, and, in recent years, even with produce like cotton and wheat, through the system of
"options" and "futures."   Nor are these the only
proceedings of contemporary capitalists which must
be reprobated as essentially usurious ; which merit
not "a pile," but the pillory.   It is a curious instance
of the "vast unconscious hypocrisy" which wraps
us round, that men who expend much virtuous in-
dignation against the public gambling tables of
Monte Carlo, and the private gambling tables of the
"hells" in great cities, habitually practice far worse
gambling on the Stock Exchange, not for one moment
doubting that they are reputable and even edifying
members of society.

Here, assuredly, it is the function of the State to
intervene, for the protection of individual rights and
of its own supreme right.   Equally justifiable and,
indeed, necessary, is its intervention, in many cases,
for the restriction and regulation of industrial contracts.   It was the belief of our fathers and grand-
fathers—I myself was brought up in that creed—
that in such contracts the action of private interest

should be relied upon as all-sufficient. This was the teaching of the Smithian school of political economists called "orthodox"; and I can well remember the time when even to question it, was to expose one's self to the risk of intellectual reprobation. The fundamental principle of that school was what was termed free, unrestricted, and pure competition, regulating the price of things by the so-called law of Supply and Demand—of human labour among other things; for human labour was regarded as mere merchandise; *die Arbeit ist eine Waare.* The mere invocation of this so-called law was held sufficient to silence all objections to one of the most immoral and pernicious doctrines ever formulated by human perversity; a doctrine which does not recognise man as an ethical being, or the State as an ethical organism; a doctrine of which the root is Atheism and its fruit abortion. I say, "the so-called law of Supply and Demand," for, in truth, it is no law at all; it is merely an account of one of the modes in which human selfishness operates. Nothing is more singular than the unchecked dominion for a century [1] of this old "orthodox" political economy. It is "one of those delusions"—to borrow the emphatic words of Carlyle concerning another of them —"which sometimes seize upon whole communities

[1] So Professor Foxwell reckons: "We have been suffering for a century from an acute outbreak of individualism, unchecked by the old restraints, and invested with almost a religious sanction by a certain soulless school of writers."—*The Claims of Labour*, p. 249.

of men : no basis in the notion they have formed,
yet everybody adopting it, everybody finding the
whole world agree with him, and accepting it as an
·axiom of Euclid ; and in the universal repetition
and reverberation, taking all contradiction of it as
an insult, and a sign of malicious insanity, hardly to
be borne with patience." [1]   " No basis in the notion
they have formed." This is literally true. Their
so-called " principles " were not " principles " at all ;
they were merely notions, or, as Professor Cairnes
euphemistically puts it, " not positive, but hypothetic
truths ": *a priori* conceptions of the intellect, satisfying its mathematical needs, its love of order, sym-
metry, sequence, but remote from reality. Man, as
he lives, moves, and has his being in this concrete
world, they disdained to contemplate. The central
figure in their speculations was a sort of abstract
economic or city man, or rather animal ; a mere
money-hunting biped, governed solely by the lust of
lucre. And the State they regarded as an arbitrary
or fortuitous concourse of such animals, bound together by the tie of self-interest. It is hardly necessary, at the present day, to point out that this
economic man is as pure, or impure, an abstraction,
as the man in a state of nature of whom Rousseau
fabled. No such man exists, or ever existed, or ever
will exist—not even in the calico millennium of
Cobden's Apocalypse. These were the *data* of their

[1] *Shooting Niagara and After.*

pseudo-science, and on these they argued well
enough, presenting their demonstrations as "laws";
never heeding the caution conveyed in Pope's verse:
"It may be reason, but it is not man"; never re-
membering that logic, even if applied to established
facts, is by no means the all-sufficient guide of life.
Their method was described by the late Mr. Pea-
cock, not less tersely than truly: " Premises assumed without any evidence, or in spite of it; and
conclusions drawn from them so logically that they
must necessarily be erroneous."

Such was the doctrine of the old "orthodox"
Political Economy. And it issued in the establishment of a tyranny of capital of the most atrocious
kind, based upon a fictitious freedom of contract. I
know of no more shameful page in human history
than that whereon is recorded the condition of the
English working classes in coal-mines, woollen factories, and cotton factories, during the first three
decades of this century. The victims of overwork,
of under-pay, of frauds and extortions of all kinds,
notably those practised through the truck system.
Their condition was worse than that of overburdened
and overdriven horses: because those *human* faculties, those *human* needs which marked them off from
the brute beasts, were utterly ignored and unpro-
vided for. Nay, this is not the worst of it. Not
only grown men and women, but little children,
were offered up in sacrifice to "Gain, the master-

idol of this realm." The story revealed in Parliamentary Reports of 1842 and 1843, of general, deliberate, and systematic cruelty practised on girls and boys of tender age—"cruelty horrible, incredible, unparalleled even in the history of pagan slavery," a high authority calls it—cannot be read without sickening horror. It is curious that the older school of Radicals—Advanced Liberals they had begun to call themselves, as claiming, I suppose, to indicate to their party the way that it should walk in—looked upon this state of things with indifference : more, would sometimes "bless it and approve it with a text" out of the Evangelists of the old "orthodox" Political Economy. The legislative measures for its palliation were passed—I believe without a single exception—in the teeth of their strenuous opposition.

The first considerable thinker in this country to initiate a revolt against this old "orthodox" Political Economy was Samuel Taylor Coleridge. His clear eyes saw through its fictions, fallacies, and futilities, and he did not hesitate to condemn its doctrines *in globo* as "solemn humbug."[1] But it is to the German historical school that we must chiefly give the credit of the reaction against what they call *Smithianismus:* the general body of doctrines taught by Adam Smith and his disciples, some of whom departed largely—and, I

[1] *Table Talk*, p. 205.

believe, in every case for the worse—from the original positions of their master. Of this school the learned Roscher may, perhaps, be considered the founder. Its aim is to take men as they really are, belonging to a particular nation, state, and period of history : and " to investigate the laws and the character of the institutions which are adapted to the satisfaction of economic wants, and the greater or less amount of success that they have achieved." [1] To a member of it, Bruno Hildebrand, we owe the well-known work *Die Nationalökonomie der Gegenwart und Zukunft*, perhaps the most trenchant criticism of the Smithian doctrines and methods ever written. It is not necessary, for our present purpose, to catalogue the writers of this school, or dwell upon the good work done by them generally, or to indicate the excesses of some, led to " mistake reverse of wrong for right." It must suffice here to point out that one issue of the movement has been to overthrow the old doctrine of *laissez-faire*, to bring out the inefficiency of personal interest of the sole rule of economic action, to insist upon the principle that the State, as an organism—and an ethical organism —has a most important function with regard to the industrial contracts of its subjects.

To the apprehension of this principle we owe the long series of Truck Acts, Mines Acts, Factory

[1] *Grundlagen der Nationalökonomie*, p. 54.

7

and Workshop Acts, and the like measures, which
have, in some degree, broken down the tyranny
of capital. But in some degree only. Let me,
on this subject, quote a writer whose words are
always accurate, however strong the *sæva indig-
natio* sometimes underlying them. "Even now,"
says Mr. Devas, "we see multitudes working in-
human hours, with unremitting toil, for wages
seldom sufficient, and often a mockery—working,
too, in horrible, insanitary conditions, dwelling
huddled together in miserable overcrowded rooms;
uncertain, under such hard conditions, of finding
employment. And all this wretchedness after thirty
years of peace, in the very centre of accumulated
wealth and commercial power, in the very seat of
world-wide dominion." [1]

For the redress of these horrors we must look to
the ever-deepening apprehension of the truth that
side by side with those rights of capital, which the
State so efficiently protected by its laws that they
became wrongs—and wrongs of the most terrible
kind—there are rights of labour which the State
is equally bound to protect. I shall touch here
upon three of them. The first is the right to real
freedom of contract. It is a right which is made
void, not only by fraud and by force, but also by
paramount and overmastering necessity fettering
volition. And in such a case the State, upon

[1] *Manual of Political Economy*, p. 440.

which lies the obligation to be "a helper of the helpless," may interfere, and ought to interfere, for the defence of those who are unable to defend themselves. Another case in which its interference is equally justifiable and necessary is where moral relations, extrinsic to the bargain, but of vital importance to the individual and to the community, are bound up therewith. I have specially in view, not only the peculiar needs of women and children, but the duties of the adult male workman, as a husband and a father. I say that in the discharge of those duties, springing from the precedent and sacred contract of marriage, he should be protected as to hours and other conditions of toil, in any mere industrial contract.

A second right of labour is to a fair wage. This is a very different thing from the alleged right of labourers *auf den vollen Arbeitsertrag*, to the full produce of their labour, which is one of the main postulates of Socialism. No such right exists, or can exist, because it practically means confiscation of private property. The produce of labour is not, as Socialists commonly assume, a simple term; it is not identical with the goods apparently produced by a set of workmen. Those goods require many other conditions and antecedents—this arises from the organic nature of society —besides the labour of that set of workmen, who may be getting a full *quid pro quo*, fair wages, a

justum pretium, although they may earn but a frugal
subsistence; although they may, apparently, be
docked of a great piece of their *Arbeitsertrag*, of
the produce in which their labour issues. This is
a truth of cardinal importance; and it supplies the
sufficient answer to a demand of Socialists which is
at once extremely specious and utterly unethical.
Nor must we be led to forget or undervalue it by
the absurd exaggerations of it sometimes made.
The conclusion reached by a brilliant but quite
unscientific writer, that manual labourers receive
over forty per cent. more than manual labour
produces, is full of fallacies. The same must be
said of his premises. The "exceptional ability"
to which he ascribes most of the product does not,
as a rule, receive anything like an adequate share
of it. An undue proportion goes to the owners
of the soil, the machinery, the railways; to otiose
capitalists—that is, to capitalists who perform no
public duty, who apparently suppose themselves
fruges consumere nati. An insufficient proportion reaches the rank and file of the industrial
army. Speaking generally, they do not get their
fair share. Nor is this to be wondered at, since
the very notion of their fair share has well-nigh
disappeared from the public mind. The world has
ceased to remember that the labourer is *worthy* of
his hire—a *just* hire. It was certainly congruous
that Leo XIII., in his *Encyclical on Labour*, should

recall to the world this truth, and explain its meaning: "It is a dictate of nature, more authoritative and more ancient than any contract between man and man, that the remuneration of the labourer must be sufficient to support him in reasonable and frugal comfort." That is the measure of the *justum pretium*. And if it is "suspect" to any of my readers as proceeding from one whom, while perhaps not denying his wisdom and knowledge, they regard as the hiero-phant of a moribund superstition, let me refer them to a very different authority, the present Professor of Political Economy at Cambridge. In his recent work this learned author, if I rightly apprehend him, recognises a necessary level, below which wages should not fall.[1]

Assuredly, Carlyle was well warranted when he wrote, "A fair day's wage for a fair day's work is as just a demand as governed men ever made of governing; it is the everlasting right of men."[2] It is a right *against the State;* and that for a reason admirably expressed by Prince Liechtenstein in a speech in the Austrian Reichsrath:

"Labour is not merely a matter of the private order; it is a kind of function delegated by society to each member of the body politic. The peasant who cultivates his field, the artisan who works in a manufactory, are, so far as society is concerned, functionaries, just as much as the Gov-

[1] See Marshall's *Principles of Economics*, book vi., c. xii. § 19 (3rd ed.).

[2] *Past and Present* p. 84.

ernment clerk in his office, or the soldier on the field of battle. Industrial labour creates, like every other function, a series of reciprocal obligations between the society which provides it and the worker who executes it."

These reciprocal obligations were universally recognised till the rise of the Smithian School, and I rejoice to see that with the discredit and decay of that school they are again winning their way into recognition by scientific economists—nay, we may say into general recognition. Striking is the confession made by the Irish and Scotch Land Acts, that there are cases in which it is the duty of the State to provide for the judicial determination of a fair rent. The principle of these enactments is equally applicable to wages. I shall have to touch upon that point again, presently, in speaking of strikes. Here let me instance a third right of the labourer, issuing from the principle that work is a social function : his right to some public provision other than modified imprisonment in a workhouse, in return for his life of toil, when its evening has come, and he can no longer go forth to his work and to his labour. It is a right recognised by the French *Maisons de Retraite,* and still more by the Austrian *Versorgungshäuser*—institutions which may well make us blush for our "Poor Law Bastiles." I remember some words which seem to me full of wisdom, in a letter of Ranke to Frederick William IV. "The thing the masses most ardently desire is the amelioration of their social condition.

We have universal military service. If I may be permitted to say so, he who offers his life to the State deserves to be helped to live; and the soundest political science demands the recognition of that right." In this country—unfortunately, as it appears to me—we have not universal military service; but we have well-nigh universal industrial service, and Ranke's argument appears entirely applicable to those who render it to the community.

There is another result of our present industrial system—a result vitally important to the State—upon which I must touch: the constant recurrence of strikes and lockouts. Let us consider a little these portentous phenomena, for so I must account them. I remark, then, in the first place, that they mean the supercession of competition by combination. And, so regarded, they are one of the most significant facts in the world just now. I invite my readers to consider this fact from the point of view of Right.

Now, in the first place, no one can deny that combination is, in itself, perfectly legitimate. Men have a right to combine. It is part of every man's natural right to personal liberty, a right which, of course, is subject to the conditions and limitations indicated in the last chapter. Men banded together for a common purpose indefinitely increase the power of each for its attainment. I need not dwell upon what is familiar to every schoolboy, or write a dissertation upon the copy-book maxim, "Union is strength." I am at present concerned with industrial combination, and especially with the combinations of workmen usually known as Trade Unions, and the combinations of capitalists, of which the commonest forms are Federations of Employers, Rings, and Trusts.

First, then, as to Trade Unionism. I am old enough to remember—and I am not an old man— when Trade Unions were looked upon as wicked conspiracies for the ruin of capitalists : and, indeed, until of late years, the law of England has so regarded them. It is only recently in that country that combinations to control wages have ceased to be punishable offences. But, looking at the matter from the point of view of Right, the asso- ciation of workmen to maintain and advance their interests against their employers cannot, in itself, be condemned ; it is a legitimate means for a legiti- mate end. The undeniable outcome of what the old "orthodox" Political Economy called "free com- petition" was to lower wages. Too often the compe- tition was not free ; and the contracts in which it issued were fraudulent and extortionate towards the workmen. In time they discovered the advantage of collective bargaining over individual bargaining with employers of labour ; of combination over com- petition. And in the extremity of their wretch- edness they resorted to Trade Unions as a measure

of self-defence. Begun clandestinely, and often
maintained by violence, these associations gradually
made their way into toleration and recognition ; and
now they are, we may say, established factors in
our industrial system. As to the benefits which
have resulted from them, I should like to quote a
passage from Mr. Devas, whom—without pledging
myself to agreement with him in all points—I regard as one of our soundest authorities on industrial
questions. He writes as follows:

The benefits which Trade Unions have conferred, or
helped to confer, on the English artisans are many : higher
wages, shorter hours of work, removal of middlemen (sub-
contractors or sweaters), removal of many oppressive fines
and penalties, check on brutality of foremen, support to
members out of work. Also they have striven, by enforcing apprenticeship and limiting the number of apprentices,
to prevent the lack of employment ; they have given mental
and moral training to their members, teaching them to
debate and reason, to act in concert, to make provision for
the future ; and though they may have caused many more
strikes than they have prevented, they certainly have been
a prerequisite for boards of conciliation and arbitration for
settling all disputes between masters and workmen without
any strikes at all.[1]

Against all this there is, indeed, a set-off. A
result of such combinations of workmen is to
engender and perpetuate a spirit of hostility toward
employers. Mr. Devas tersely puts it: " The common interests of both masters and men remain
generally out of sight, while the opposing interests

[1] *Manual of Political Economy*, p. 222.

are ever in full view." But further. These combinations of workmen induce a spirit of indifference
toward the rights and interests of the community at
large. The members of Trade Unions display a
tendency, and more than a tendency, to separate in
thought and feeling from the rest of the community
as their natural enemy, and to delight in the thought
of waging war upon it. Hence the very idea of a
common country, with its superior claims and paramount rights, has been effaced from the minds of
multitudes. This is a national danger the gravity of which can scarcely well be over-estimated.
Further. Surely no one can view without grave
regret—the word is all too weak—the strikes in
which Trade Unionism often issues. Consider for
example, that great Welsh coal strike which, even
as I write, is fresh in all our memories. It lasted
five months. It inflicted terrible hardships upon
a vast number of innocent and helpless families.
It kept over one hundred thousand strong and
skilful arms out of employ. It compelled the post-
ponement of the naval manœuvres to which so great
importance is attached by the highest authorities on
our sea forces. It gave an immense impetus to
foreign competition with our own trade. And it
ended, practically, in the *statu quo:* a vast tragi-
comedy, a gigantic *Much Ado About Nothing* played
at the expense of many millions. I am very far
from denying, I strenuously maintain, that a strike

may be quite justifiable. But, even then, it is a
rude weapon, causing lamentable suffering to the
innocent, and frequently piercing the hands of those
who wield it. Of course, the criterion of the use
and abuse of a strike is simple enough in itself,
although its application is usually by no means
simple. It is whether the demand, to enforce which
the strike is resorted to, is a *just* demand. For
here, too, justice rules. And the eventual appeal
is to the law of Right.

We must say the same concerning the other
methods of Trade Unionism. The end—the ad-
vancement of the interests, real or supposed, of the
workmen—by no means justifies all the means
which Trade Unions, as a matter of fact, employ.
For example, what Mr. Sidney Webb, an ardent
defender of them, calls "the device of the restriction of numbers," is surely in many cases—perhaps
in most—not only injurious to industrial efficiency,
but, as he himself admits, nefarious. A recent
writer has called it, not without reason, "both an
ethical error and an economical wrong to the State."
The maxim, "Sell the minimum of labour for the
maximum of wages," is open to just the same exception as the maxim, "Buy labour in the cheapest
market and sell produce in the dearest." The restriction of output by workers is liable to precisely
the same impeachment as the restriction of output
by capitalists. The arbitrary restriction of labour—

such restriction is not always arbitrary, it may be
reasonable and right—is an ugly and immoral manifestation of human selfishness. And there is a vast
amount of evidence that the crushing tyranny of
Trade Unions has exercised a most demoralising
effect upon their members. It is a foretaste of the
despotism which would be exercised by Socialism,
wherewith Trade Unions are largely tainted. I
need not pursue this subject further. I will merely
quote a striking sentence from Mr. Sidney Webb:

> If any of the methods and regulations of Trade Unionism
> result in the choice of less efficient factors of production
> than would otherwise have been used, if they compel the
> adoption of a lower type of organisation than would have
> prevailed without them, and especially if they tend to lessen
> the capacity and degrade the character of either manual
> labourers or trained workmen, that part of Trade Unionism,
> however advantageous it may seem to particular sections of
> workmen, will stand self-condemned.[1]

It would seem to be beyond question that some of
the methods and regulations of Trade Unionism are
in this condemnation.

Let us now glance at combination among capitalists. It has arisen in two ways. First, in antagon-
ism to Trade Unions. The combination of capitalists
is a weapon forged to combat the combination of
workmen. Secondly, it is due to the growing perception by capitalists of the truth that union among
themselves is a much better thing for them than
competition among themselves ; for they may thereby

[1] *Industrial Democracy*, p. 703.

monopolise production, barter, and commerce. The
founders of Trade Unionism supposed that the
natural relation of capitalists is one of competition,
not combination. They were in grave error. The
old orthodox Political Economists believed that
their " free competition " would make an end of
monopolies. They were in grave error too. Their
" free competition " has proved to be the beginning
of monopolies upon a greater scale than the world
had seen before. It has issued in Rings and Trusts.
A Ring has been described as " a solid combination
of those who hold commodities against the public
which consumes them "—and, we may add, against
the workers who produce them. It regulates, on its
own terms, production and distribution. It has for its
express purpose " to keep up prices, to augment profits, to eliminate useless labour, to diminish risk, and
to control the output." A Trust has been defined
as " a joint-stock company of corporations," and its
object is to annihilate free trade so far as the goods
are concerned with which those corporations deal ;
it means, at best, the painless extinction of the
smaller traders ; but too often their bankruptcy or
suicide. The Trust, it is said, is able to control
every avenue of transportation, to undersell rivals,
to hinder them from receiving supplies, and from
loading or unloading the goods they may have in
hand.

Now, are we to say that such combination of capitalists is, in itself, wrong? I do not see on what ground that can be maintained. Capitalists, like workmen, are certainly at liberty to pursue their own interests in the way which they judge best— provided always that way is not unethical. Assuredly there is nothing intrinsically immoral in simplifying the mode of production and distribution. Nay, the substitution of monopoly prices for market prices is not necessarily a change for the worse. Single management effects a vast saving in cost of production, and there are instances in which the development of Trusts has resulted in the reduction of prices to the advantage of the community. But Rings and Trusts possess a giant's strength, and they are constantly tempted to use it like a giant. Too often they yield to the temptation—a fact which, human nature being what it is, need excite no surprise. What is certainly wrong is that combinations of capitalists should disregard—as we frequently find them disregarding—all considerations of justice, humanity, and civilisation in order to make money. There are occasions on which lockouts are justifiable, just as there are occasions on which strikes are justifiable. But a capitalism which absorbs not only the increase of production, but the wages hitherto required for the sustenance of the workers, must unquestionably be condemned.

The federation of labour and the federation of capital—we have come to that. What is the next step? The fact is pretty clear that machinery, while increasing the product, has, upon the whole, diminished the reward of labour. But ought this to be so? That "ought," please note, is an ethical ought. Well, I do not hesitate to say that it ought not to be so. What is the reason why it is so? The reason is that the reciprocal duties which bind men together in a commonwealth are lost sight of, both in unrestricted competition and in unrestricted combination. It is absurd to suppose that individual freedom is, or ever can be, the sole force by which society is regulated. And that because of the first principles upon which I have been insisting: that labour is a social function, that property is a social trust, that the rights of property and the rights of labour involve correlative duties. Only in an organised polity is profitable labour possible, is property valid. And this organised polity—the State—may rightly determine, in the interests of the community, on what conditions labour shall be done and property possessed. It is the duty of the State to hold in check the moneyed aristocracy—" the most brutal," Schäffle well says, " in persecuting those who in any way question its domination." It is the duty of the State to break down monopolies when they mean economic slavery, when they interfere with the right of the worker to " eat the labour of his hands." It is, to sum up, the duty of the State, as the profoundest political thinkers of the day are agreed, to cause

labour and capital to participate fairly in the profits
of increased production, and, in the discharge of this
duty, to control, to a certain extent, industrial enter-
prise. Nay, some of the ablest of living publicists
strongly urge that the State should itself direct, or
even manage, all undertakings which threaten to become monopolies, and nationalise or municipalise
so much of the land, capital, and manufactures of
a country as can efficiently be dealt with by it.
Am I told that this is Socialism? May it not, perhaps, be the antidote to Socialism? Anyhow, the
Ring and the Trust, little as their authors intend or
desire it, are most certainly playing into the hands of
Socialism. Irresponsible private despotism may well
seem to reflecting men worse than responsible public
despotism. "May well seem," I say. For, assuredly,
a much stronger case may be stated for the control
of production and distribution by public authority,
for the public benefit, than for the control of production and distribution by private associations, for
private benefit.

But to return to the point immediately before us.
The industrial war waged by means of strikes and
lockouts is a national danger of the gravest kind,
and a cause of incalculable and unmerited suffering
in numberless cases. It is a grievous violation both
of the rights of the State and of individual rights.
And the function of the modern State is to repress
it, just as the function of the mediæval State was to

put down private war. If I am asked, How? I
reply in words which I wrote some years ago:

By requiring that such disputes between capital and labour
be submitted to a public tribunal, consisting of not less than
three commissioners, equal in standing and authority to the
Judges of the High Court, who shall have power to determine, in every case brought before them, what is, *hic et
nunc*, the *justum pretium* of labour, the minimum hire which
it shall be lawful for employers to tender to their workpeople. And, if it be said that the award of such a tribunal
could not be made binding upon the workpeople, but only
upon the employer, I answer that this is sufficient. It would
be enough that a court commanding general confidence
should declare, "This is, at present, a just wage; less shall
not be given until we order otherwise." Public opinion,
the force of which in such matters is rightly great, would
strongly condemn the operatives who, by refusing to accept
the rate of wages so awarded, should approve themselves
unjust, and would leave them without pity to the sentence,
"If any man will not work, neither shall he eat."[1]

But the direct intervention of the State is not
the only way of dealing with this grave matter.
There is also the way of industrial association, which
in itself must be accounted a more excellent way.
And here the nineteenth century—and the twentieth—might well learn a lesson from the Middle
Ages. The Trade Guilds, by means of which, as
Mr. Toulmin Smith well puts it, "the principle of
association" was then in use as "a living practice

[1] *On Shibboleths*, p. 233. I add that where, as in New Zealand,
Trade Unions are incorporated, and able, alike in regard to members
and outsiders, to sue and be sued, the enforcement against them of
any legal award is comparatively easy.

8

of the common folk,"[1] are deserving of much more attentive study than they have generally received. Of course, religion had the first place in their statutes and ordinances. They held, with Plato, that faith in unseen and superseusuous realities was the true foundation of any human community. This age prefers to agree with Macaulay, that for a joint-stock company to attempt to sanctify its personality by devotional exercises is too absurd. Well, that is a question which we need not here discuss. The secular object of those guilds was to protect the craftsmen from oppression in general, and from unregulated competition in particular. And whatever may be said against them, it is unquestionable that for centuries they, on the whole, successfully accomplished their object. The effect of the French Revolution was to sweep them away with the rest of the outworn world to which they belonged. And we have nothing to take their place. But certain is it, in the well-weighed words of Professor Ingram, that "the mere conflict of private interests will never produce a well-ordered commonwealth of labour."[2] Hitze, in his suggestive book, *Die Quintessenz der Socialen Fragen*, describes the economic problem of the day as follows: "To find a social organisation corresponding to the modern conditions of production, as the social organisation of the

---

[1] *The Original Ordinances of more than One Hundred English Gilds*, Introd., p. 13.

[2] *History of Political Economy*, p. 214.

Middle Ages corresponded with the simple conditions of production then existing both in town
and country." Yes, that is unquestionably the
problem. Labour and Capital are now dissociated,
nay, are independent, distrustful, hostile: and the
longer I live the more deeply I am convinced how
entirely right Mill was in holding that for any
radical improvement in social and economical relations between them, we have chiefly to look to
a regular participation of the labourers in the profits
derived from their labour.[1] Such, I believe, is the
best remedy for the healing of the nations, sick
well-nigh unto death of this grievous wound in the
very heart of the body politic. To promote its
application by all prudent means—such means will
probably be rather indirect than direct—seems to me
not the least important of the functions of the State.

6. THE STATE AND THE LAND

I go on to a sixth instance of the conflict of public
and private rights. What is the function of the
State with regard to the land? In considering that
question, we must first remember that there is this
great difference between the soil and other subjects
of property—its quantity cannot be multiplied.
Hence it is that a man's ownership of property in
land must be regarded as being of a more limited
and restricted kind than his ownership of property

[1] See his *Principles of Political Economy*, book iv., c. vii., § 4.

in chattels. The distinction between realty and personalty which the law of England so emphatically recognises, is founded in the nature of things; and it is but lost labour that sophists endeavour to rub out that distinction. In an extremely interesting minute, Sir Henry Maine writes: "The suggestion has often been made that real property should be assimilated to personalty, more especially in respect of conveyance. There ought to be no more difficulty, it is said, in transferring a piece of land than in selling a horse. I believe the analogy to be unsound, and the route indicated a false one. There is far more promise in reversing than in extending the principle; in treating land as essentially unlike movables."[1] The doctrine of the English law that a man can hold only an estate in land, is a perfectly sound doctrine. The principle underlying the feudal system, whence that doctrine has descended to us, that the soil of the country is the common heritage of the country, is a true principle. "The conception of land as an exchangeable commodity, differing only from others in the limitation of supply,"[2] which came in upon the collapse of the feudal system, is a faulty conception; as faulty as the very different conception popularised by Mr. Henry George. The true justification of private property in land, that it is, as a matter of fact, for the general

---

[1] *Minutes and Speeches*, p. 54.
[2] See Sir Henry Maine's *Early History of Institutions*, p. 86.

benefit, has been formulated with admirable clearness and succinctness by Aquinas. "If this field be considered absolutely," he says, "there is no reason why it should belong to one man rather than to another. But if it be considered relatively to the opportunity of cultivating it, that presents a certain fitness why it should belong to one man rather than to another." [1] Private property in land he considers to be just, according to the *jus naturale*, not *in se* and absolutely considered, but relatively to the effects which flow from it. If it could be shown—which, speaking generally, it cannot—that private ownership of land is incompatible with the general good, no effectual defence of it would be possible. And the test whereby the advantage of one land system over another, of the ryotwarry, say, over the zemindary, should be judged, is the advantage of the community.

Such is the first principle governing this matter.

---

[1] The whole passage is worth quoting : "Jus, sive justum naturale est quod ex sui natura est adaequatum vel commensuratum alteri. Hoc autem potest contingere dupliciter ; uno modo secundum absolutam sui considerationem, sicut masculus ex sui ratione habet commensurationem ad feminam ut ex ea generet, et parens ad filium ut eum nutriat. Alio modo aliquid est naturaliter alteri commensuratum, non secundum absolutam sui rationem, sed secundum aliquid quod ex ipso sequitur, puta proprietas possessionum : si enim consideretur iste ager absolute, non habet unde magis sit hujus quam illius ; sed si consideretur per respectum ad opportunitatem colendi et ad pacificum usum agri, secundum hoc habet quamdam commensurationem ad hoc quod sit unius et non alterius. Considerare autem aliquid comparando ad id quod ex ipso sequitur est proprium rationis, et ideo hoc idem est naturale homini secundum rationem naturalem quae hoc dictat."—*Summa Theologica*, 2, 2, q. 57, a. 3.

And now, to illustrate its practical application, let us consider the land system of England. I wonder whether any intelligent person, who has not closed the eyes of his intelligence, can maintain that this system ought not, in the public interests, to be largely modified. Built up chiefly by landlords, it sacrifices to their interests in many ways the just claims of tenants and of the community at large. It enables a man to charge heavily for what is comparatively worthless—land unreclaimed and unimproved; to limit, arbitrarily, the use even of such land; to transfer the chief burden of taxation, which should fall upon the owner of property, to another whose interest therein is his own labour; and to confiscate enhanced values and improvements of all kinds, even expensive buildings, for which the tenant has worked and paid, and in which the landlord has had no part. The English land laws are, in these respects, unique in the world, and contrast most unfavourably with the corresponding provisions of the Civil Law and the *Code Napoléon*.

Let me not be misunderstood. I am far from denying—I strenuously contend—that the existence of large landed properties in this country is more for the common good than would be the universal prevalence of small real estates. The land is the only basis possible among us of that "directing class"—I do not use the word "aristocracy"; it is

misleading; in England, happily, we have no aristocracy—which represents, in a special way, our
national traditions; which brings to the service of
the commonwealth, leisure, independence, cultivation, hereditary aptitude, qualities of the first importance in public life; of how great importance the
present condition of France may serve to show. I
go further; I find in the fact that such properties
cannot be kept together without primogeniture, a
sufficient defence of that custom.[1]   But, side by side
with these large properties, I should like to see, as
in ancient times, the smaller estates of yeomen and
peasants. The modern mania for uniformity of tenure is one of the worst fruits of that French doctrin-
airism which has made such lamentable progress
among us. Variety of tenure is, in itself, a positive
good, for this, among other weighty reasons, that it
is a factor of individuality. I should like to see an

[1] I say the *custom* of primogeniture. And here, perhaps, a few
words of explanation may be of use to some of my readers. Primogeniture properly means the right of the eldest among males to succeed to real property. That right is of much less consequence now
than in ancient times, before alienation of such property by will was
permitted. But it is a right which our law still recognises and en-
forces where a landowner dies intestate. In such cases, provided that
he has not overwhelmed his land by an avalanche of creditors, the
law appoints his nearest male relative to succeed him. That is the
right of primogeniture. The *custom* of primogeniture is a distinct
thing, though, no doubt, it arose from the ancient right. The modern custom of primogeniture is a device for keeping a landed property
together, or, as the phrase is, tying it up, by means of settlements,
during the lives of certain existing persons, and for a period of
twenty-one years after their decease. The right of primogeniture
seldom arises save in the case of very small properties, for the large
ones are almost always settled, and is usually, in practice, a wrong

immense increase of small landowners, and I conceive
that it is a function of the State by wise legislation
to promote this.   The most effective safeguard of
the rights of landed property is to give every culti-
vator a chance of becoming a landed proprietor.   A
bold peasantry—bold because no mere *adscripti
glebæ*, but free as existing for themselves and not for
another—is not only their country's pride, but a
bulwark of their country's security and prosperity.

7. THE STATE AND THE SOCIAL ORDER

This chapter is already longer than I could have
wished.   But before I close it there is yet another
—a seventh—example of the conflict of the rights
of the State with private rights upon which I must
touch.   It is afforded by what Carlyle used to call
"the Condition of England Question."   I think it
is Mr. Ruskin who has somewhere observed—and

resulting in great hardship and injustice. My own view is that the
argument for abolishing it generally is overwhelming. I think that
when a landowner dies intestate, his land should devolve as personal
property devolves, except in the case of estates belonging to lunatics
or to minors, in whose families the custom of primogeniture has been
followed for at least three generations immediately preceding. In
these special cases alone the *right* of primogeniture should subsist.
In all other cases it should be abolished. That this reform would be
for the common good, that it would render the defence of the *custom*
of primogeniture easier, that it would be in the truest sense conservative, seems to me as clear as daylight. And it fills me with unspeakable reflections to see so-called Conservatives resisting it. But *mit
der Dummheit!* I may mention that the whole subject has been
treated with much learning and ability by Mr. Evelyn Cecil in his
work, *Primogeniture : a Short History of its Development in Various
Countries, and its Practical Effects.*

with too much truth—that "our present type of
society is, in many respects, one of the most horrible
that has ever existed in the world's history: boundless luxury and self-indulgence at one end of the
scale, and at the other a condition of life as cruel as
that of a Roman slave, and more degraded than that
of a South Sea Islander." I came, not long ago,
upon a statement by Mr. Joseph Burgess, the late
editor of the *Workmen's Times*, that there are usually
in England one million of unemployed and three
millions in want—paupers or semi-paupers. I have
not been able to verify the figures. Indeed, they
are incapable of exact verification. But even if
they are approximately accurate, which I see no
reason to doubt, they may well make us pause.
With regard to the unemployed, we must, indeed,
distinguish. There are those who are unemployed
because they are physically or mentally unfit for
work. There are those who are partly unemployed,
whose occupation is occasional, precarious, insufficient. There are those who are unemployed because
although they desire work, and are able to do it,
they cannot find it. There are those who are unemployed because they are unwilling, though able, to
work; who, unlike the Unjust Steward, *can* dig and
are not ashamed to beg. And perhaps this last
class is the largest. Mr. Spencer is well warranted
in maintaining: "There exists in our midst an enormous amount of misery which is the normal result

of misconduct, and ought not to be disassociated from it." Unquestionably he is absolutely right when he adds: "The notion that all social suffering is removable, and that it is the duty of some one or other to remove it, is simply false." But, as unquestionably, there is much social suffering which *is* removable. And we are bound to do all that in us lies to remove it. That pauperism and semi-pauperism, which is one of the ugliest features in our civilisation, seems to me, as a matter of historical fact, largely due to injustice. I shall touch on this point presently. Here let me remark that few, perhaps, really realise the gravity of the mischief which pauperism works. We may say, with strict accuracy, that it is fatal to those rights of personality the defence and enhancement of which is the end of the State: those rights of the individual which we sum up in the one word "liberty." For liberty, we must remember, is a moral good. It is the outcome of psychical endowments, not, as a widely prevalent superstition supposes, the product of ballot-boxes, or the result of a sum in addition. Truly does Wordsworth teach

> " by the soul
> Only, the nations shall be great and free."

But pauperism crushes the soul out of a man. Pauperism, I say, not poverty, which is a very different thing, and which the Roman poet rightly celebrates

as the mother of heroes.[1]   You will not convert a
nation enervated by luxury and debased by pauperism into freemen, through the most elaborate of
paper constitutions conferring the privilege of voting
ever so often.   This by the way.   My present point
is that the vast disparity of condition which exists
in the social order, the appalling chasm between the
extreme wealth of few and the extreme penury of
many, is a huge social danger.   On the one hand,
we have thousands of whom it may be said, in the
words of Mill—he is speaking of a certain class of
landlords, but his remarks may properly have a
wider application—"they grow richer, as it were,
in their sleep, without working, risking, or econo-
mising"; on the other, millions too truly described
by episcopal lips as "not so much born into the
world as damned into it."   This is, in itself, a gigantic evil.   It is not merely that so many vast fortunes
are the outcome of fraud and extortion, of wrong
and robbery, whereby speculative financiers, company promoters, "smart" traders, sweaters of all
sorts—the varieties are many—Panamists, and *ex-*

---

[1] I need hardly refer to the familiar and noble lines :

> " Regulum, et Scauros, animæque magnæ
> Prodigum, Pæno superante, Paulum,
> Gratus insigni referam Camæna,
>   Fabriciumque.

> " Hunc et incomtis Curium capillis
> Utilem bello tulit, et Camillum,
> Sæva paupertas, et avitus apto
>   Cum lare fundus."

ploiteurs of various kinds, have " made their pile."
It is also that too great inequalities, too violent con-
trasts in the distribution of wealth, are contrary to
the true law of the social organism, signifying abnormal development in one part, anæmic shrinking
in another.   Who can doubt that a remedy must be
found for " the shame of mixed luxury and misery
which is spread over our native land " ?

As we all know, Socialism proposes a remedy.
Mr. Burgess, whom I quoted just now—one of
the most moderate of its prophets—advises the
masses to " go up and possess the Promised Land,
where there will be no unemployed, no rich, and no
poor." The advice is specious.   Let us consider it
a little.   A few words on Socialism will be here
very much in place.   But we are confronted at the
outset by a difficulty.   Socialism is a very Proteus,
possessing almost as many aspects as exponents.
Professor Luigi Cossa truly observes that it " in-
cludes a rather heterogeneous number of groups,
which are named according to the aims they have
in view, the means they propose to use, the manner
in which they hold together."[1]   The professor is also
well warranted in his complaint that " classification has a hard road to travel when it enters the
tangle of jarring Socialistic sects."   It will not be
necessary, for our present purpose, to enter upon

---

[1] *Introduction to the Study of Political Economy*, translated by
Louis Dyer, p. 514.

that tangle. For, after all, these jarring sects are
agreed upon one first principle which has from the
beginning been the distinctive note of Socialism,
as a glance at its history will be sufficient to show.

I suppose for the germ of it we must go back
to a well-known passage in Rousseau's *Discourse
on the Origin of Inequality.* But its first set exponent appears to have been the Abbé Fauchet,
who in the early days of the Revolution delivered
orations at a club called the *Cercle Social* and
edited a journal entitled *La Bouche de Fer.* He
insisted "that all the world ought to live; that
everybody should have something and nobody too
much": and denounced "the wretch who desires
the continuance of the present infernal *régime,*
where you may count outcasts by millions, and
by dozens the upstarts [*les insolents*] who possess
everything without having done anything for it."
The eloquence of the Abbé, who had become a constitutional Bishop, was cut short by the guillotine
in 1793. Another of these primitive Socialists was
Marat, who pleaded in the *Ami du Peuple:* "Either
stifle the workpeople or feed them. But how
find work for them? Find it in any way you like.
How pay them? With the salary of M. Bailly."
Bailly, it will be remembered, was the patriot
mayor who floridly harangued poor Louis XVI. at
the barrier of Passy, congratulating the wretched
monarch upon being "conquered by his people,"

and was himself put to death three years afterwards by the same "people," with circumstances
of revolting cruelty. Chaumette, too, praised by
Mr. John Morley as showing "the natural effect
of abandoning belief in another life by his ener-
getic interest in arrangements for improving the
lot of man in this life,"[1] urged that, though "we
have destroyed the nobles and the Capets, there is
another aristocracy to be overthrown—the aristocracy of the rich." The poor had the same
gospel preached unto them by Tallien, who demanded "full and entire equality," and insisted
that "the owners of property should be sent to the
dungeons as public thieves"; by Fouché, afterwards Duke of Otranto and Police Minister to the
First Napoleon, who maintained that "equality
ought not to be a deceitful illusion"; that "all
citizens ought to have a like right to the advan-
tages of society"; and by Joseph Babeuf, who
exchanged his Christian name for Caius Gracchus:
"*Pourquoi vouloir me forcer à conserver St. Joseph
pour mon patron?*" he explained; "*je ne veux pas
les vertus de ce brave homme-là.*" He sought to
realise his doctrines by a conspiracy, and was
executed for his pains by the Directory. But
perhaps the most memorable of these pioneers of
Socialism was Brissot de Warville, for it is to him
that we owe the famous formula about property and

---

[1] *Miscellanies*, vol. i., p. 78.

theft: *la propriété exclusive c'est le vol*, was the original text of it. For sixty years the dictum lay buried and forgotten in Brissot's not very meritorious work, *Recherches Philosophiques sur la Propriété et sur le Vol*. There Proudhon discovered it, and made it current coin in the shortened form, *La propriété c'est le vol* appropriating it, however, without acknowledgment; perhaps, M. Janet conjectures,[1] in virtue of the right, alleged by Brissot, of everybody to everything.

This is the corner-stone, elect, precious, upon which all Socialism rests. The literature of the subject is immense, and is rapidly growing every day. Herr Stammhammer, in his *Bibiliographie des Socialismus*, enumerates some five thousand works more or less immediately dealing with it; and the catalogue is by no means complete. But whatever diversities of operation the prophets of Socialism exhibit, in all worketh one and the self-same spirit. All bring, in effect, the charge against such of us as have property—that we are thieves. That is the head and front of our offending. The substance of their indictment against us is, "Property is theft." Is this true?

Perhaps there is much more truth in it than is pleasant for us to think about. Certainly, it is not true of property in the abstract. That, I trust, has been sufficiently shown in previous pages of

[1] *Les Origines du Socialisme Contemporain*, p. 95.

this work. But what if we consider property in the concrete ! All but Socialists will, I suppose, agree that private property, in its original idea, is the guaranty by the State to the individual of the fruits of his own labour and abstinence. But can anyone deny that a great deal of it, as it exists, in fact, is largely the result of theft and worse offences, whereby its owners and their progenitors have appropriated the fruits of the labour and abstinence of others ? To take England only, how many noble houses derive their abundant possessions from the ruthless spoliation of the religious foundations under Henry VIII. : foundations which, whatever else they may or may not have been, were so many centres, throughout the land, of Christian charity—a very different thing from Poor Law relief ; which were, in a true sense, the patrimony of the poor. "To the rapacity of that aristocratic *camarilla* of adventurers," as Professor Rogers writes,[1] surrounding the nonage of Edward VI., we owe the destruction of the thirty thousand religious guilds which had been the great institutions of thrift and self-help—"the benefit societies of the Middle Ages," the Professor calls them—and the foundation of English pauperism. Or, to come down to our own time, certain it is, in the well-weighed words of Mr. Chamberlain, that "the vast wealth which modern progress has created has run into pockets";

[1] *A History of Agriculture and Prices in England*, vol. iv. Pref.

that " the great majority of toilers and spinners have derived no proportionate advantage from the prosperity which they have helped to create." But to withhold that "proportionate," advantage or share which is justly theirs, is to wrong them, or, in plain English, to rob them. And, unquestionably, by such wrong and robbery, a vast amount of existing property has been heaped together, and is kept together.

It would seem, then, that there is an unpleasant amount of truth in the indictment brought by Lazarus against Dives. The answer commonly made is, that however unethically the wealth may have been gained, of which his purple and fine linen, his sumptuous fare and gorgeous palaces, are the emblems, he has kept "the windy side of the law," and therefore must not be meddled with. Let us hear Herr Lasson expound the argument: " Existing property is lawful : otherwise it might be assailed in the courts of law. It has all been gained under the authority of legislation. Who could presume to separate the just from the unjust in what is all conformable to law? It is the very business of law to cut short this untenable thinking and deeming about right. . . . The principal and most important thing is that we should recognise the sacredness of existing property, for with it all law-abiding, all civilised life would fall." [1] We may doubt whether Lazarus will find that a

[1] *System der Rechtsphilosophie*, p. 609.

very conclusive argument. A rejoinder to it is
suggested by the Duke of Argyll in an interesting
page of one of his most interesting works. "Any
law which gives to one set of men a right to live on
the industry and property of others, starts, of necessity, a spirit of idleness and imposture on the one
side, and not less certainly evokes a spirit of suspicion
and resistance on the other." [1] This judicious observation is directed against the old English Poor
Law. But probably Lazarus will consider it no less
applicable to dukes than to paupers. He may even
find in it a justification for viewing with sinister
eyes the class described by Burke as "those who
hold large portions of wealth without any apparent
merit of their own." And thanks to the remarkable
political arrangements now existing in the greater
part of the civilised world, Lazarus, in his millions,
is our master. Nor is it surprising if he turns a
willing ear to those who promise him, in exchange
for his vote, the transformation of his material condition by drastic legislation on proprietary rights.
When I was last in Paris a song which declared,
with a significant disregard of grammatical nicety—

> "Ce n'est pas toujours les mêmes
> Qu'aura l' assiette au beurre"

was very popular among "the masses." It set me
thinking. As a matter of historical fact, property
has always followed political power. But this is

[1] *The Unseen Foundations of Society*, p. 562.

the first time in the world's annals that power has been lodged in the hands which now hold it. And the quantity of butter is limited.

I shall have to return to this subject in a subsequent chapter. Here I should remark that however well founded Socialism may be in its criticism of the evils of the existing social order, the remedy which it proposes for them necessarily involves infinitely worse evils. For Socialism, like Pauperism, is fatal to those rights of personality which are summed up in the world "liberty." The very essence of despotism, whether it be the despotism of the one or of the many, is, as Aristotle has pointed out, that it is "tyrannously repressive of the better sort." But no system which the brain of man has ever devised carries that tyrannous repression so far as Socialism. Liberty—let me repeat what I have said in an earlier chapter—means the power of a man to make the most and the best of himself; to develop fully his personality. And, however private property may have been abused, it is, in itself, realised liberty. It is essential to the development and maintenance of personality in this workaday world. It is requisite for the very existence of the family. But Socialism, if true to its principles, means the confiscation of private property, the destruction of the family, and the annihilation of individual freedom. It proposed to remedy what it calls—not altogether without reason—the slavery

of labour, not by vindicating the liberty of the
labourer, but by establishing a system of universal
servitude. This monstrous proposal we are bound
to resist, even, if necessary, to the shedding of blood.
And to the shedding of blood the matter is not
unlikely to come in the long run. For Socialism is
rather a sect than a party. Its votaries are animated
by a spirit akin to that of religious enthusiasm.
They are largely of the stuff of which martyrs are
made. Assuredly the privilege of sealing their
testimony with their blood should be withheld from
them as long as possible. But it may not be always
possible. And, as assuredly, the preservation of
civilisation is of far more account than are the lives
of fools and fanatics, few or many.

The real value of Socialism lies not in its pre-
posterous proposals and unrealisable Utopias, but
in this : that it is, what Professor Ingram has well
called it, " the inevitable and indispensable protest
of the working classes, and their aspiration after
a better order of things." And, assuredly, it is a
function of the State to " extract from the intermin-
able popular and philanthropic utterances constitut-
ing Socialistic literature the underlying ideas, and to
translate them into scientific conceptions of Right." [1]

---

[1] *Das Recht auf den vollen Arbeitsertrag in geschichtlicher Darstellung.* von Anton Menger, p. 3. I may refer my readers who desire
practical illustrations, to an excellent chapter in Mr. Devas's
Manual of Political Economy (p. 458), wherein nine important
economic reforms needed by Great Britain and Ireland are clearly
and cogently stated.

CHAPTER V

THE truth that civil society is an organism—a truth specially needful to be insisted upon at the present day—must not make us forget the truth that it is also a mechanism. "The tendency to political life," writes Bluntschli, " is found in human nature; and so far the State has a natural basis : but the realisation of this tendency has been left to human labour and human arrangement." [1] The question to be considered in this chapter is, What are the true principles on which that tendency should be realised ? What is the right arrangement of the State ?

The mechanism of the State is, of course, a very large subject, including, as it does, every provision for the right discharge of their public duties by rulers and ruled. One great first principle, re-cognised by all publicists from Aristotle down-wards, is that there should be a well-marked separation between its several powers. The Aris-totelian division need not detain us here, for it

---

[1] *Allgemeine Staatslehre*, p. 18.

applied to a very different stage of political evolution.   In the existing state of society the classification
so widely popularised by Montesquieu, is well-nigh
universally recognised as indicating the true method.
No one will deny that the legislative, the administrative, and the judicial provinces ought to be kept
well apart.   No one will deny the necessity for the
independence and dignity of the judiciary, for the
responsibility of public officials in respect of their
public acts, for the equality of all before the law,
for the provision of such securities for the liberty
of the subject as the writ of *habeas corpus* and
trial by jury afford.   I add that although all this
is admitted in theory, it is not easily realised in
practice.   The history of the century which has
passed away since Washington's death amply war-
rants the caution conveyed in his Farewell Address :
" The spirit of encroachment tends to consolidate
the powers of all the departments in one, and thus
to create, whatever the form of government, a real
despotism." [1]

" Whatever the form of government "—which,
indeed, is, in itself, a matter of less importance than
the spirit in which the institutions of a country are
worked.   Without adopting Pope's opinion, " What-
e'er is best administered, is best," it may be safely
asserted that there is no immutably best form of
government; that what is best for one age and one

[1] *The Writings of George Washington*, vol. xii., p. 226.

condition of civilisation may be worst for another.
The best form of government for a people is that
best fitted to the elements of which it is composed,
to the period of its development, to its local habit-
ation and historic traditions.   The rights of the
subject may be amply secured under a monarchy or
an aristocracy ; they may be trampled under foot in
a democracy.   That is certain, if any lesson of history
is certain.   Of course, it does not in the least follow
that the form of government is a matter of indifference.   The accommodation of the mechanism of
the State to the exigencies of any given condition of
society, is one of the gravest problems of practical
statecraft.   We live in an age when representative
government, or self-government, is generally recognised—to quote the words of Mill—as "the
ideal type of the most perfect polity, for which, in
consequence, any portion of mankind are better
adapted in proportion to their degree of general
improvement."[1]   The most highly civilised nations
are, as a matter of fact, supposed to be now adapted
for it.   The topic to which we will confine ourselves
in this chapter is, What are the first principles on
which such government should be framed ?

And first, let me notice, very briefly, a conception
of representative or self-government which is most
common and most erroneous—a conception which
reduces it to a sum in addition.   We are told that

[1] *Considerations on Representative Government*, p. 70.

it consists in assuring the preponderance of the
greater number of the votes of men—that is, of the
opinions expressed by their votes. "Opinions!"
Pray, what is the worth of the individual opinion
of the average voter upon any political subject?
And how can it gain in value if multiplied by
millions? Mr. Lorimer, in his interesting book,
The Constitutionalism of the Future, relates that "a
very learned and ingenious friend" of his "believes
the political capacities of all men who can read a
penny newspaper to be equal." It appears to me
that if a man can believe that, he can believe
anything. It is the very fanaticism of doctrinarian-
ism. And of what avail is it to argue with fanatics?
Let us leave them their liberty of foolishness, merely
stipulating that, in return, they leave us our liberty
of common sense. The individual opinion of the
average voter upon the efficacy of the coarser kinds,
whether of the spirituous stimulants supplied at the
public-houses, or of the spiritual stimulants supplied
by the Salvation Army, may be entitled to respect.
But who that is not given over to a strong delusion
to believe a lie, can really value his individual
opinion upon any problem affecting the interests,
especially the larger and remoter interests, of the
commonwealth? Nay, he is seldom the best judge
even of his private interests in matters to which the
one or two rules ordinarily governing his understanding do not extend. If the preponderance of the

greater number of opinions were the true account of self-government, then self-government would stand condemned by its intrinsic absurdity.

But it is not the true account. Let me proceed to indicate what the true account is. The principle upon which self or representative government rests, appears directly deducible from the nature of civil society as an ethical organism. As I observed in the First Chapter, the ideals of Right which con-stitute the absolute jural order, whence positive law derives moral and rational validity, are binding upon the conscience of the State, as such, just as they are binding upon the conscience of the individual, as such: they are the fundamental principles determinative of the proper construction of a polity ; and of them the ideal of justice is the first, and embraces, in some sort, all the others; whence the dictum with which we started, and which must ever be borne in mind, that justice is the foundation of the State: *Justitia fundamentum regni* And what is justice but, as the old Roman jurisprudent defined it, " the constant and perpetual will to render to every man his right ? " (*jus suum*). Now, in the organisation of the State the problem is to assure to each subject that political right which is really his. It has been shown in the Third Chapter[1] that a man, as an ethical being in an ethical organism, is entitled to some share, direct or indirect, of political power—

[1] See pp. 46, 47.

a share correspondent with his personality. And personality varies vastly from little more than zero upwards. There is a true sense in the Carlylese doctrine that the mights of men are the rights of men. Character, race, fortune—yes, and all the forces which constitute the individual—ought to have free play. Human freedom, as Aristotle defines it, means belonging to one's self and not to another. And this implies the right of every man to be valued in the community for what he is really worth. Political inequality springs necessarily from men's inequality as persons. To sum up in words which I have elsewhere used : "In so far as men are in truth equal, they are entitled to equal shares of political power. In so far as they are in truth unequal, they are entitled to unequal shares of political power. Justice is in a mean—it lies in the combination of equal and unequal rights." [1]

In a civilised community, then, we find vastly varying individualities ; and the more civilised it is, the greater is the variation. We find also, as a result of those varying individualities, a number of classes and interests, diverse but dependent upon one another, and all necessary to the perfection of the body politic. Hence the necessity for what Schäffle calls, in a sufficiently uncouth phrase, indeed, "*eine gliederungsmässige Territorial- und Berufs-Vertretung*"; the due representation of the local and

[1] *On Shibboleths*, p. 104.

professional interests and capacities of the commonwealth is, I take it, what he means.   This is a matter
of great importance, and is discerned to be such by
the chief political philosophers of our age.   Krause
and Ahrens, Mohl and Bluntschli, among the Germans, have expounded it more or less fully; and M.
Prins, one of the most eminent of Belgian publicists,
has discussed it with much force in his remarkable
work on *Democracy and Representative Government*.
Even Proudhon, who excelled in appropriating the
ideas of others and in clearly enunciating them,
qualifies the merely mechanical system of representation by equal and universal suffrage as " mystifica-
tion " and " tyranny," and demands for every social
and political element in the nation its proper influence.   *La représentation nationale*, he writes, *là où
elle exist comme condition politique, doit être une
fonction qui embrasse la totalité de la nation dans
toutes ses catégories de personnes, de territoire, de
fortunes, de facultés, de capacités et même de misère.*[1]
I take these to be the words of truth and soberness,
although they proceed from the pen of Proudhon.

A representative government, then, as its very
name implies, should represent all the elements of
national life, all the living forces of society, in due
proportion.   All should be subsumed in the reason

[1] *Théorie du Mouvement Constitutionel au dix-neuvième Siècle*,
p. 101.

of the organic whole. Schiller well insists that just because the State is essentially an organisation formed by itself, and for itself, it can be actually realised only in proportion as its constituent parts have brought themselves in harmony with its true idea.[1] And its true idea is that it should be a city at unity with itself; the unity of diverse activities working, each in its own mode, for the common good, under the law of Right. Mirabeau happily said, *Les assemblées représentatives peuvent être comparées à des cartes géographiques qui doivent reproduire tous les élémens du pays avec leur proportions, sans que les élémens les plus considérables fassent disparaître les moindres.*[2]

This is the true ideal of representative or self-government. And if we are asked, How is it to be realised? the answer, as I intimated just now, is, That is a problem not so much of political science, or of political philosophy, as of practical statecraft, which must be differently worked out in different countries and at different periods. We should remember that it is not a new problem. Many popu-

---

[1] Aber eben deswegen, weil der Staat eine Organisation sein soll die sich durch sich selbst und für sich selbst bildet, so kann er auch nur insoferne wirklich werden, als sich die Theile zur Idee des Ganzen hinaufgestimmt haben.—*Ueber die ästhetische Erziehung des Menschen.* Vierter Brief.

[2] Compare Trendelenburg. "Bleibt es die Aufgabe einer gerechten Verfassung die Bestimmungen des Grundgesetzes immer in ein proportionelles Verhältniss zu den gegebenen und aufstrebenden Machtstellungen zu bringen."—*Naturrecht auf dem Grunde der Ethik,* § 205.

lar speakers and writers, who might, perhaps, be
fairly expected to know better—Members of Parliament, newspaper puplicists, *et hoc genus omne*,—
are in the habit of talking and writing as if representative government were a distinctly modern institution. In fact, it is by no means a modern
institution. It prevailed in one form or another—
we need not go back farther for our present purpose
—throughout mediæval Europe. It disappeared, almost everywhere except here, in the Cæsarism which
was the political expression of the Renaissance, although its vestiges, its ruins, were to be found in
most continental countries until the last decade of
the last century. Then the torrent of the French
Revolution swept them away, and, for good and
evil, renewed the face of the earth. The essential
characteristic of that mediæval regimen was that it
represented groups, classes, institutions; as in England, the Lords Spiritual and Temporal, the counties, cinque ports, boroughs, and universities. It
was based upon local interests and divisions. It was,
Bishop Stubbs tells us, "an organised collection of
the several orders, states, or conditions of men . . .
recognised as possessing political power"[1]; in other
words, of all the political factors of a people.

In England, this species of representative government prevailed down to the passing of the first
Reform Act. That the old unreformed House of

[1] *The Constitutional History of England*, vol. ii., p. 163.

Commons—to speak merely of that chamber—was truly representative, is not, I suppose, now denied by any competent authority. The Duke of Wellington—who, although no political philosopher, was "rich in saving common sense," beyond, perhaps, any other man who has made a name in English history—declared that unreformed House to be not only "the most efficient legislative body that has ever existed," but also "as *complete* a legislative body as can be required." This was in a speech in the House of Lords in 1831. And in addressing the House in 1832, he further expressed himself in the same sense:

We have, under the existing system, the county representation, and the representation in cities and boroughs. The county representation consists, principally, of freeholders, and the members for counties represent not only the lower classes, but the middle and higher orders. The representatives for the great maritime towns, and for the larger description of towns in the interior of the country, represent, likewise, the lower and middle classes. The representatives for the pot-walloping boroughs, for the scot-and-lot boroughs, and for the single borough of Preston where the franchise is vested in the inhabitants at large, represent the lowest orders of the people; and in this manner this borough representation represents all classes and descriptions of persons who have anything to do with the business transacted in the House of Commons.

A very different authority, Mr. Bagehot, in his extremely interesting essay on the Unreformed Parliament, has put forward the same view, "It gave," he tells us, "a means of expression to all classes whose minds required an expression."[1] And again, "The English Constitution of the last century, in its best time, gave an excellent expression to the public opinion of England"[2]; the reason why this was so being indicated in a dictum of Sir James Mackintosh—its date is 1818—which he quotes: "A variety of rights of suffrage is the principle of the English representation." The Reform Act of 1832 changed all that, and introduced a new era in English political life. On this I shall have to dwell in the next chapter.

Of contemporary attempts on the Continent of Europe to solve the problem of representative or self-government, three may fitly be noticed here. One of the most interesting is that made in the Kingdom of Prussia. The members of the Prussian House of Representatives (Abgeordnetenhaus) are chosen by universal suffrage. But the suffrage is indirect and unequal. Property, and the bearing of public burdens, as well as mere numbers, are taken into account. The House of Lords consists of a number of nobles who sit there by hereditary right, of certain great officers of State, and of life peers appointed by the King, some *proprio motu*, others upon the nomination of the universities and the thirty-eight principal cities. In the election of that very important body, the Kreistag—the chief

[1] *Works*, vol. iv., p. 397. He adds, "The representation of the working classes then really existed" (p. 398.)
[2] *Ibid.*, p. 383.

organ of local administration—the suffrage is not universal; and plural voting prevails, in recognition of the principle of a balance of the various provincial interests, so that no one of them shall preponderate over the others.[1] The provinces of Prussia, it should be remembered, are not, like the French departments, arbitrary and artificial districts, but historical territories. In Austria, the Lower Chamber of the Reichsrath is elected by four classes of voters, organised in a sort of system of estates, in which the franchise varies from what is practically manhood suffrage[2] to a somewhat high property qualification in the class of great landowners. In the Upper, some of the members sit by hereditary right, others by Imperial nomination, and with them are joined all the Archbishops and Bishops possessing princely status in the kingdoms and countries represented by the Reichsrath. But, as the powers of the Austrian Reichsrath are largely limited by the privileges vested in the Provincial Diets, it is a less important body than at first sight appears.[3] In

---

[1] Not the least important of Prince von Bismarck's achievements was the remodelling of the local government of Prussia, by a series of laws enacted between 1872 and 1883, and having for their main object the separation of local from general administration.

[2] Men in domestic service are excluded from it.

[3] The same must be said of the German Reichstag, elected by direct universal suffrage, which, fortunately for Germany (see p. 204), has practically no control over the administration, and not a great deal over legislation; the parliamentary system not existing in the German Empire.

Belgium, according to the constitutional revision of 1890–93, persons possessing "general capacity, civil rights, and full age (twenty-five)," are entitled to one vote in elections for the Chamber of Deputies. A second vote is accorded to men of thirty-five who are householders and who pay a small specified tax on their house, and to men of twenty-five of greater wealth; and those who possess certain educational diplomas, or who have occupied positions implying a higher education, have a third vote. This system was introduced to provide an antidote to the mischiefs found to result from the equal and quasi-universal suffrage previously existing. It applies to elections, not only for the Lower Chamber, but for the Senate. A certain proportion of the members of that body are directly chosen by the general electors in the several provinces, according to population. From these Senators a pecuniary qualification is required. It is not required from another class of Senators, who are chosen by the provincial councils. Princes of the Royal House are Senators in their own right. To criticise the Belgian plan of multiple voting is, of course, an easy task. Why graduate the suffrage from one to three? Why the ages of twenty-five and thirty-five? Why fix the property and educational qualification for extra votes as they have been fixed, and not otherwise? Why, indeed! I suppose the

only answer is, that age, headship of a family,
property, and education ought to count; and that
it is better for them to count according to the rough-
and-ready process of the Belgian constitutional
revisionists, than not to count at all.   No doubt
the system proposed by Professor Lorimer in his
Constitutionalism of the Future, under which one
voter might be endowed with twenty-five votes, is
theoretically far more perfect.   Still, in proceeding
tentatively—haltingly, if you will—in this grave
matter, the Belgians have proved themselves worthy
descendants of their wise ancestors whose liberties
they inherit.   Their practical sagacity in politics
presents a remarkable contrast with the speculative
folly of their French neighbours.

For in France, and in the countries which have
framed their political institutions upon the French
model, representative government cannot properly
be said to exist.   The French system—which I
shall have to consider further in the next chapter
—is not an organic, but an atomistic system.
The only element in the national life of which
it takes account is mere numbers.   For the
representation of other elements far more important in the body politic, it makes no provision,
not even in its Senate.   As little can the French
system be said to secure self-government.   In the
individual man, self-government means the supremacy of the intellectual nature over the sensitive;

the predominance of the moral over the animal self.
The lower powers and faculties of a self-governed
man are brought into subjection, and kept in
subordination, to the higher. And so he realises
his proper end as a rational being. I may add that
in such self-government resides the highest part of
liberty, which is ethical; according to that admirable dictum of St. Basil: "Who is free? He that
is his own master." This is the true account of
self-government by the individual man. It is also
the true account of self-government by a nation of
men. For the State, in the words of Schiller, "is the
objective, and, so to speak, normal form in which the
manifoldness of the subjects seeks to combine itself
into a unity [1];" or, as Browning puts it—

> "A people is but the attempt of many
> To rise to the completer life of one."

The rule of that completer life, for a people as
for one, is reason; not the individual reason, but
the abstract reason. The man "who to himself is
a law rational," alone realises the true idea of self-
government. We must say the same of a nation.
Manifestly the man who is carried about by every
storm of passion, by every wind of impulse, by
every gust of emotion, is not self-governed. Nor
is the State that is so swayed. But in every
commonwealth numbers—the masses, as the phrase
is—represent passion, impulse, emotion. And the

[1] *Ueber die ästhetische Erziehung des Menschen.* Vierter Brief.

country which is dominated *arbitrio popularis auræ*
is no more self-governed than is a ship without
rudder or steersman.   The politics of the people is
very like the justice of the people.   Blinded by
terror or maddened by hate, they seize a suspected
person and hang him on the nearest telegraph post.
Their lynch law dispenses with inquiry, evidence,
proof.   So in their politics, passion, impulse, emotion,
take the place of ratiocination, knowledge, justice.
Passion, impulse, emotion, no doubt have their
proper office in the State, as in the individual man.
But whether in the individual man or in the State;
they must be subjected to the only rightful law-
giver and governor—Reason.   It is one function of
political parties to be the organs of passions, impulses, emotions; and I need not observe how important a part such parties play in the modern State.
Of course, they are no new phenomena in history.
They are, in one form or another, as old as human
society.   There is in man—we may see it exemplified in every schoolboy—an innate tendency to
take sides.   " Party feeling," Sir Henry Maine well
says, " is one of the strongest feelings acting on
human nature."   It is, he thinks, " probably far
more a survival of the primitive combativeness of
mankind, than a consequence of conscious intellectual differences between man and man." [1]   However that may be, there can be no doubt that, as

[1] *Popular Government*, p. 31.

Bluntschli argues at length in a thoughtful work,[1] not, I believe, much known in England, political parties are indispensable to the working of representative institutions, as instruments of that mobility in persistence which is the condition of life for the political as for the physical organism.

It will be well, therefore, to say here a few words regarding political parties as they exist in this age, and of the party government in which they issue. The original home of party government is England, whence other countries have adopted it, with more or fewer changes. It is the product of a very peculiar set of circumstances in English history. North, in his *Examen*,[2] gives a very amusing account of the origin of the terms " Whig " and "Tory." It seems that "Tory " was a nickname first applied to those who opposed the Bill for the exclusion of the Duke of York in the Parliament of 1679. According to North, the word originally denoted "the most despicable savages among the wild Irish," and was applied to the Duke's partisans "because the Duke favoured Irishmen." " Being," North adds, " a vocal clever-sounding word, readily pronounced, it kept its hold," and "the anti-exclusionists were stigmatised, with execration and contempt, as a

[1] *Character und Geist der politischen Partcien.*
[2] Page 371. A pungent, but partisan account of the difference between Whigs and Tories is given by Swift in No. 35 of the *Examiner.*

parcel of damned Tories, for divers months together." Then, "according to the common laws of scolding, the Loyalists considered which way to make payment for so much of Tory as they had been treated with, and to clear scores." After essaying various repartees, they at last hit upon "Whig," "which was very significative, as well as ready, being vernacular in Scotland for corrupt and sour whey. And so the account of Tory was balanced, and soon began to run up a sharp score on the other side." "This," North affirms, "fell within my own personal knowledge and experience."

The names thus originally used as invectives, were gradually adopted by those to whom they were applied. And from the close of the seventeenth century, the two great parties designated by them have been prominent factors in English public life. It was not, however, until the accession of the House of Hanover, that party government, in the proper sense of the word, was established. William III. and Anne both set themselves persistently against it. William naturally relied chiefly upon the political leaders who had been most active in raising him to the throne. Yet he never renounced his preference for a mixed ministry, composed of moderate Whigs and moderate Tories, between whom, probably, he saw no great difference [1];

[1] So Pope :
"In moderation placing all my glory ;
While Tories call me Whig, and Whigs a Tory."

and during almost the whole of his reign he succeeded, in some degree, in attaining it.   Indeed, as
Hallam quaintly puts it, he "was truly his own
minister, and much better fitted for the office than
most of those who served him." [1]   Anne, though her
own personal leanings were to the Tories, by no
means desired, as she expressed it, "to be their
slave"; she wished them to predominate in her
counsels, but not to monopolise power, and to reduce
her authority to a shadow.   "Her plan was, not to
suffer the Tory interest to grow too strong, but to
keep such a number of Whigs still in office as should
be a constant check upon her ministers." [2]   After
her death the conditions of government were greatly
changed.   It was inevitable, Hallam thinks, that the
Whigs should come exclusively into office under the
line of Hanover; and George I.'s ignorance of
England and English disqualified him from presiding over the deliberations of his ministers, after the
manner of his predecessors, and reduced the monarchy
to the shadow of a great name.   The Sovereign
"was no longer the moderating power, holding the
balance in a heterogeneous and divided Cabinet,
able to dismiss a statesman of one policy and to
employ a statesman of another, and thus in a great
measure to determine the tendency of the Government.   He could govern only through a political

---

[1] *Constitutional History of England*, vol. iii., p. 292 (8th ed.).
[2] Sheridan's *Life of Swift*, p. 124.

body, which, in its complete union and in its command of the majority in Parliament, was usually able, by the threat of joint resignation, which would make government impossible, to dictate its own terms."[1]

Such was the beginning of the system of party government which has existed to this day, and which has been so largely imitated throughout the civilised world. It is not necessary, for the present purpose, to trace in detail its vicissitudes during the well-nigh two centuries that it has existed in England. The broad fact is, that through all that tract of years, England has been really ruled by successive juntos of politicians, whose title to office has been that they could command a majority in the House of Commons. The influence of the Crown has, of course, been more at one time and less at another. Had George III.'s ability been on a level with his character, he might, not improbably, have recovered much of his lost prerogative, and have vindicated for himself an authority similar to that now exercised by the Prussian monarch. He failed in the attempt; and succeeding British sovereigns have been content to reign without governing. "The reputation of public measures," wrote Junius, in 1770, "depends upon the minister who is responsible; not upon the king, whose private opinions are not supposed to have any weight against the advice of his

---

[1] Lecky's *History of England in the Eighteenth Century*, vol. i., p. 227.

council, and whose personal authority should therefore never be interposed in public affairs. This,
I believe, is true constitutional doctrine." For a
century that doctrine has been universally accepted,
and the real governing power in England has
been an informal committee, not of the Legislature,
as is sometimes said, but of the party able to command a majority in the Lower House of the Legislature.

This is party government as a fact in English
history, where, as Bluntschli observes, it has been
more clearly exhibited than elsewhere. Let us now
briefly consider the theory upon which it rests. Perhaps the first apologist—certainly the first considerable apologist—is Burke. "Party" he defines as
"a body of men united for promoting, by their joint
endeavours, the national interest upon some particular principle in which they are all agreed." He
argues that such "connexions in politics" are "essentially necessary for the full performance of our public duty"; because "where men are not acquainted
with each other's principles, nor experienced in each
other's talents, nor at all practised in their mutual
habitudes and dispositions by joint efforts in business, no personal confidence, no friendship, no common interest subsisting among them, it is evidently
impossible that they can act a public part with
uniformity, perseverance, or efficacy."

He continues:

Therefore every honourable connexion will avow it is their
first purpose, to pursue every just method to put the men who
hold their opinions into such a condition as may enable them
to carry their common plans into execution, with all the
power and authority of the State. As this power is attached
to certain situations, it is their duty to contend for these
situations. Without a proscription of others, they are bound
to give to their own party the preference in all things; and
by no means, for private considerations, to accept any offers
of power in which the whole body is not included ; nor to
suffer themselves to be led, or to be controlled, or to be over-
balanced, in office or in council, by those who contradict the
very fundamental principles on which their party is formed,
and even those upon which every fair connexion must stand.
Such a generous contention for power, on such manly and
honourable maxims, will easily be distinguished from the
mean and interested struggle for place and emolument. The
very style of such persons will serve to discriminate them
from those numberless impostors who have deluded the ignorant with professions incompatible with human practices,
and have afterward incensed them by practices below the
level of vulgar rectitude.[1]

Let us turn from this fine rhetoric of the most accomplished thinker that ever adorned English political life, to a publicist of a different school and age
and nation, Herr Bluntschli : a thinker of a far
lower order, but careful, candid, and conscientious,
although, no doubt, theological prejudices sometimes
cloud his judgment. His little work, *The Character
and Spirit of Political Parties*, of which I spoke
just now, is not, indeed, a masterpiece of political
science ; but it is the best-reasoned exposition of the
subject with which I am acquainted, and may, in

[1] *Works*, vol. ii., p. 335.

some sort, serve, according to his design, as "the physiological key" to it.

Herr Bluntschli begins by laying down the proposition that, wherever there is free movement of political life in a State, political parties appear; and that the richer and freer such life is, the more sharply and clearly defined are the lines of party. Political parties, he insists, are not, as so many narrow and timid spirits suppose, a perilous evil, a disease of the body politic, but are, on the contrary, a condition and a token of sound public health: the necessary and natural manifestation and outcome of the mighty inward springs (*Triebe*) of national existence. He next goes on to consider the true nature of a political party. In the first place, he reminds us that it is, as its name (*pars*) implies, only a portion of a greater whole. It contains the consciousness of merely a part of the nation, and must not be identified with the totality, with the people, with the State. Again, parties are not limbs (*Glieder*) in the political organism; they are free and voluntary associations of individuals who, by reason of a common feeling and judgment, associate themselves for common public action. Of political parties, properly so considered—"natural political parties," he sometimes terms them—Herr Bluntschli allows four: Radicals, Liberals, Conservatives, and Absolutists, or Ultra-Conservatives; and he considers, at some length, the characteristics and functions of each of them. We

need not follow him in detail through this interesting discussion, but I may observe that, founding
himself upon an ingenious speculation of Friedrich
Rohmer, he finds in the psychological law, ruling
the stages of human life, the key to the spirit and
character of political connexions.[1]   In Radicalism,
we see the love of ideals, often unreal and unprac-
ticable, the delight in abstractions, the thirst for
novelty, the disdain of experience, which characterise
youth.   Liberalism corresponds with the period of
early manhood which has put away childish things
and the illusions of fancy, when the more developed
understanding (*Verstand*) discerns facts as they are,
and traces their connexion ; and which, desiring and
striving for their amelioration, avoids " raw haste,
half-sister to delay."   " The love of freedom is most
eminently seen in the young man, who, having out-
grown the authority of tutors and governors, now,
for the first time, thinks and acts independently,
proving things for himself, and doing freely what
is suited and fitted to him.   That is also the most
forcible characteristic of all true Liberalism.   But,"
adds Herr Bluntschli, " the Liberal knows well that
freedom is not a coin which circulates from hand to
hand ; that it is the revelation and development of
a personal faculty."   Conservatism he describes as
less sparkling (*weniger glänzend*) than Liberalism
but as making a firmer, more durable, and more

[1] P. 84.

solid impression; as like the fully developed man of from thirty to forty, not so intent upon the acquisition of new possessions as upon the preservation and improvement of things already gained. The specially characteristic ideas of Conservatism, our author tells us, are Piety (*pietas*), Loyalty, and Law (*das Recht*). But its starting-point is the real; it goes on from the reality to the idea. "The true Conservative does not shut his eyes to the claims, the advance, of all innovating time; he merely insists that the movement towards the future shall respect the conditions of the past."[1] Absolutism, or Ultra-Conservatism, is the political counterpart of unproductive and unreceptive old age. The ideas proper to it have neither the splendour of youth, nor the fulness of wisdom, the depth of feeling, characteristic of perfect manhood. They are lacking in virility. They are of a somewhat feminine type. Peace and stability are wont to appear to it the highest good.

Such, in briefest abstract, is Herr Bluntschli's account of the four "natural political parties." He points out that in practice they tend to coalesce into two, Radicals and Liberals forming one, and the dual Conservatism the other. They all express tendencies and faculties of the body politic; they all have their proper function in the State and in the Parliament which, I suppose, he would agree with M.

[1] P. 138.

Fouillée in considering (although he does not use
the expression) a sort of national brain (*une sorte
de cerveau national*). Constitutional government he
regards as depending upon their proper working and
due balancing according to the exigencies of the age.

No doubt one of the most valuable offices per-
formed by political parties is to watch and criticise
the conduct of the Government.[1] It is a truth so
trite as long ago to have become a truism, that there
is always in human nature a tendency to abuse power.
The fact that every act of an administration is liable
to discussion and censure in Parliament, is a valuable
check upon that tendency. Obviously, such discussion and criticism may be, and often are, carried too
far. It is easy for a party to sink down into a faction, and it is often extremely difficult to distinguish
the one from the other. Herr Bluntschli imputes
this difficulty to the looseness and uncertainty of
ordinary language.[2] He tells us, however, in effect,
that a faction is a degenerate party, and is as salt
which has lost its savour. A political party, he insists, should be animated by a political principle,
and follow a political object; combinations repre-

[1] Mr. Chamberlain, in a very suggestive speech, delivered at Oxford
on the 7th of May, 1890, claimed for the party system the merit of
"securing an exhaustive criticism, an examination into all new
measures; of affording a stimulus, and even a healthy stimulus, to
individual ambition and to the ingenuity of rival politicians." But
he went on to admit—and the admission is most significant—that
"when great national interests are at stake, when the safety of the
commonwealth is involved, the party system breaks down."
[2] P. 9.

senting nationalities, or religious convictions, or class
interests, he terms "spurious" parties. The word
"political" he takes to mean, resting on the State,
in unison with, not opposed to, the State, and serv-
ing the common welfare. Political parties may display unwisdom, both as to the ends they follow and
the means they employ, without ceasing to be properly parties. But when they place themselves above
the State, and subordinate public interests to their
own interests, then they cease to be parties, in the
true significance of the word, and become factions.
And that brings him to what he considers the distinctive mark of a faction, which is this: that instead of seeking to serve the State, it seeks to make
the State serve it; that it follows not political—
that is, commonly beneficial *(gemeinnützliche)*—but
selfish ends. "If," he further insists, in an emphatic
passage, which concludes his discussion of this point,
"if party zeal and party passion become so overmastering that parties would rather tear the country
to pieces than join hands for its delivery and welfare,
if a party abuses the public authority of which it
has gained possession, unjustly to oppress and per-
secute those who do not hold with it, if parties combine with a foreign enemy against their own country
and the nation to which they belong,—then so un-
patriotic a course expels the essential idea of a political party, and the party becomes a faction." [1]

[1] *Ibid.*, p. 12.

We must allow that the political history of England during the present century exhibits more than one instance of the degeneracy of party into faction. It also illustrates forcibly another evil incident to the system of self- or representative government, as worked by political parties. The true function of a Parliament is not to administer, but to watch and supervise the administration. There is, as Mill points out, "a radical distinction between controlling the business of government and actually doing it."[1] It is the tendency of representative bodies, driven by the forces of party interests—which, if analysed, often prove to be private interests in disguise—to ignore that distinction. Indeed, such bodies afford, at the present day, the most signal manifestation of the "spirit of encroachment," spoken of by Washington in the warning words cited a few pages back. The House of Commons, Lord Beaconsfield wrote in *Sybil*, presents, on "studious inspection, somewhat of the character of a select vestry, fulfilling municipal rather than imperial offices, and beleaguered by critical and clamorous millions." It is time, high time, that the House of Commons should lose that character. The true principle has been enunciated with equal terseness and force by Mill. "The Parliament of a nation ought to have as little as possible to do with local affairs."

It is but a small quantity of the public business of a

[1] *Considerations on Representative Government*, p. 89.

country [he further observes] which can be well done, or
safely attempted, by the central authorities ; and even in
our own government, the least centralised in Europe, the
legislative portion at least of the governing body busies itself
far too much with local affairs, employing the supreme power
of the State in cutting small knots which there ought to be
other and better means of untying. The enormous amount of
private business which takes up the time of Parliament, and
the thoughts of its individual members, distracting them
from the proper occupations of the great council of the nation, is felt by all thinkers and observers as a serious evil,
and, what is worse, an increasing one.[1]

But this is not the only evil springing from the management of local affairs by the Imperial Legislature.
Another, and perhaps a greater evil, is that it im-
pairs those habits of independence of thought, of
self-reliance, of self-control in a people, which are
alike the chief factors and the chief guaranties of
civil and religious liberty.

So much concerning the office of political parties
in the mechanism of representative or self-government, as existing at the present day. It remains to
speak of the function of the chief of the State in
such a regimen. A chief of some sort there must
be, whether he hold the supreme magistracy for life
or for a term of years. In him is personified that
sovereignty which is the fundamental idea of the
State, however great the limitations of his prerogative in the exercise of it. Limitations, again, there
must be, for the very idea of self- or representative

[1] *Considerations on Representative Government*, p. 266.

11

government, is incompatible with the idea of an autocratic ruler. A first function of constitutions, written or unwritten, is to prescribe those limitations.

It may not be amiss to observe here, that limited or constitutional monarchy is no more the creation of modern times than is representative or self-government. For example, we find such monarchy at the very beginning of English history, in the year 493, when, according to the Chronicle, "the two ealdormen, Cerdic and Cymric his son, came to Britain and became Kings of the West Saxons." Descendants of Woden though they claimed to be, they were by no means absolute rulers. The type of kingship which they introduced into this country, differed, in most important particulars, from Roman Cæsarism. The selection of the Sovereign from among the members of the Royal House belonged, both in form and substance, to the Witan. To the Witan belonged also the power, in grave cases, of deposing him. The advice and consent of the Witan was necessary to the validity of his laws. Great as were his privileges and prerogatives, he was hedged in, on all sides, by constitutional restrictions. "Cerdic of Wessex, the fierce Teutonic chief, out of whose dignity English kingship grew," was as truly a limited monarch as is his far-off descendant, our present gracious Sovereign.[1]

---

[1] No doubt the Norman Conquest brought a considerable accession of royal authority. But William the Conqueror professed to stand in the same position as Edward the Confessor, whose chosen heir he

Perhaps it is among the chief achievements of
England in practical politics—that field where she
has won so many magnificent triumphs—to have
worked out the true idea of modern constitutional
monarchy; to have assigned to the Throne its proper
place in the representative or self-government of the
age.   And although this is, of course, the realisation
of first principles, it has not been effected by any
conscious employment of them.   It is the natural
outcome of constitutional development, "the long
result of time."   British monarchy has grown into
its present form *occulto velut arbor œvo*, ever manifesting that adaptation to environment which is a
chief law of life.   And I think it exhibits one of
the most striking examples in all history of the successful fitting of old institutions to new needs.   I
suppose the maxim, "The King reigns, but does not
govern," expresses accurately the function of a
limited monarch.   It is easy enough to burlesque
that type of kingship.   "Supreme Majesty, with
hypothetical decorations, dignities, solemn appliances,
high as the stars, tied up with constitutional straps
so that he cannot stir hand or foot for fear of

claimed to be.   Nor was it an empty profession.   He set himself to
rule as an English king, binding himself at his election and coronation by the accustomed oaths; and, upon the whole, he observed
them fairly well.   The feudalism which he brought with him, no
doubt, introduced a disturbing element into our constitutional history ; and under his immediate successors the distinctively English
idea of kingship was largely obscured.   But it was never lost.   It is
the cornerstone upon which the existing edifice of our political liberties rests.

accident "[1]—such is Carlyle's mocking account. But
the fact that this kind of monarchy commended
itself as the fittest to Lord Chatham, who stands so
high among his heroes—"a clear, sharp, human
head, altogether incapable of falsity "—might have
led him to doubt whether it is altogether disposed
of by his flouts and gibes. In practical politics Lord
Chatham is certainly a better authority than Carlyle ;
and Chatham doubtless discerned that this theory of
kingship, while it left the Sovereign indefinite freedom for good, effectively minimised his power for
evil.

"The English," wrote Montalembert in his book,
The Political Future of England, " have left to royalty the pageantry (*la décoration*), the prestige of
power ; they have kept for themselves the substance
of it." The pageantry and prestige surrounding the
British Throne are manifest. As manifest is their
utility in the mechanism of the State. It is a saying
of the first Napoleon, " You can govern man only
through the imagination ; without imagination he is
no better than the brute." This is true generally.
It is especially true of Frenchmen. And perhaps
the absence from the Third Republic of all that appeals to the imagination, in some degree explains the
anarchical animalism now prevailing in France. Imagination is a faculty absolutely necessary to *human*
life. It is at the basis of civil society. Emotions

_____

[1] *History of Frederick the Great,* vol. vii., p. 146.

are called forth by objects, not by our intellectual
separation and combination of them.   Mere abstractions and generalisations do not evoke feeling.   Loyalty, by which I mean devotion to persons, springs
eternal in the human breast.   And nowhere is it
more eminently seen, more beautifully displayed,
than in the Teutonic races.   In Englishmen, there
is innate a veneration for the men and women in
whom the institutions of the country seem—so
to speak—embodied in visible form.   But that is
not all.   The moderating, controlling, restraining,
guiding influence exercised by the British Sovereign
is assuredly most real and most important—more real
and important than, I think, Montalembert realised
—although, from the nature of things, it is usually
most hidden.   And here I am reminded of a story
of St. Thomas Aquinas being consulted concerning
the election of an abbot.   The choice lay between
three.   "Describe them to me," said Aquinas.
"What manner of man is the first on the list?"
"Most learned," was the answer.   "Well, let him
teach."   "And the second?"   "Most saintly."
"Good; let him pray."   "And the third?"   "Most
prudent."   "Ah, that is your abbot; let him rule."
Now, the virtue of prudence, the first and most essential qualification for a ruler, as this great thinker
discerned, is unquestionably more necessary to a constitutional Sovereign than to any other.   The duties
of limited monarchy are among the most difficult

and delicate that can devolve upon any human
being. They are also of singular complexity when
the monarch is, so to speak, the central principle—
anima in corpore is Aquinas's phrase—of a vast and
widely spread political mechanism, such as that
united under the British Crown. Of this unity the
Crown, let us remember, is not merely the type and
symbol, but also the efficient instrument. It is the
binding tie

> " That keeps our Britain whole within herself,
> A nation yet : the ruler and the ruled."

And here we may note a cogent argument for the
descent of the Crown in a princely family. Bishop
Stubbs, discussing the reasons which led the Saxons
to vest the sovereignty in the House of Cerdic, observes: "A hereditary king, however limited his
authority may be by constitutional usage, is a
stronger power than an elective magistrate : his personal interests are the interests of his people, which
is, in a certain sense, his family : he toils for his
children, but in toiling for them he works also for
the people whom they will have to govern : he has
no temptation to make for himself or them a stand-
ing-ground apart from his people." [1] The Bishop is
writing of the sixth century. His words are just as
applicable to the nineteenth, and will be just as applicable to the twentieth. And the reason is that
they express fundamental truths of human nature—

[1] *Constitutional History of England*, vol. i., p. 67.

first principles which are not of an age, but for all time. They are not only a justification for the institution of hereditary monarchy, but for its continuance in those lands "of old and settled government" which are fortunate enough to possess it.

But further. The British Crown is something more than the centre and instrument of national unity: it is the effective pledge of moderation and longanimity, of uprightness and honour in public life. We have only to turn our eyes to other nations to realise that this is so. Two examples may suffice: one from the Old World, the other from the New. Look at France. Thrice during the last century she has been a republic, and always with the same result; immeasurable corruption, undisguised intolerance, the ostracism of men of light and leading, the sway of political adventurers of the lowest type; a republic twice—well-nigh thrice— ended by a Saviour of Society and a military despotism. It is only under the monarchy, whether of the elder or younger branch of the restored Bourbons, that tranquillity, decency, and the enjoyment of rational liberty were obtained by her. Or think of Brazil, as she flourished under the mild sway of her accomplished Emperor, the one country in South America where the true end of the State was kept in view. And then consider her as she now is, sunk to the infamous level of the neighbouring republics, the happy hunting-ground of bankrupt desperadoes

who have reduced the art of government to the art
of pillage. I remember an occasion when a radical
member of the House of Commons was volubly
contrasting, much to our disadvantage, our political
institutions with those of the United States, regarding the practical working of which, however, he
seemed to know singularly little. When his eloquence had ceased to flow, I turned to a distinguished
American scholar and statesman whose face I had
been watching with some amusement, and said,
" Well, what do *you* think of benighted Britishers ? "
He replied, " *O fortunatos nimium, sua si bona
nôrint.*" I could extract nothing more than that
from the diplomatic lips. And perhaps it was
enough.

CHAPTER VI

IT is the constant peril of the State that its authority should be misused for the exclusive or undue promotion either of individual or of class interests. Evidently, if this happens, whatever be its form—whether, to follow the Aristotelian classification, preponderating power be vested in one, in a few, or in the many—its true end, the maintenance and amplification of public and private rights, in general, is, more or less, defeated. When, in the place of that end, the advantage of the ruler, or ruling class, is solely, or unduly pursued, it becomes what the philosopher calls a perversion (παρέκβασις). The Monarch is converted into a Tyrant, the Aristocracy into an Oligarchy, the Democracy into an Ochlocracy. But of these three varieties of the corruption of the State, the last is incomparably the worst. It is the most corrupt, the most cruel, and the most costly, while, as Schiller warns us, it is suicidal by reason of a law arising from the nature of things—

"Der Staat *muss* untergehn, früh oder spät,
Wo Mehrheit siegt und Unverstand entscheidet."

And here the philosophic poet does but sum up the teaching of the world's wisest thinkers. Not only "Aristotle and Polybius," but all the great masters of political science, have regarded "the democracy of numbers as the final form of the degeneracy of all governments." [1] This degeneracy, or corruption, as it exists in the present day, is our topic in the present chapter. It is the prevailing disease of the body politic in the most civilised nations; the *morbus democraticus* of which they are sick, some of them well-nigh unto death. Let us first inquire into the genesis of this kind of Democracy; next, let us judge it in its principles and in its working; and, lastly, let us consider the various remedies proposed for its evils.

Now, Modern Democracy is the direct issue of the French Revolution. So much will be admitted on all hands. But what is the essence, the inner meaning of the French Revolution? A chain of moral causation runs through the ages. No great event in the life of nations, in the history of the world, is isolated. Every present is necessarily the outcome of all the past. Yes; there is a sovereign necessity issuing from the nature of things—*inexorabilis Fatorum necessitas*—which shapes the course of history irresistibly, irrevocably, not to be changed by any human power. This is not Determinism.

---

[1] See Mill's *Dissertations and Discussions*, vol. iii., p. 65.

It is the truth which Determinism veils. And it is a truth quite compatible with that other primary verity that the human will is free, not absolutely, but relatively, and largely guides the destined succession of events. The French Revolution, then, not to ascend further the stream of time, was the inevitable reaction in the political order against the movement vaguely called the Renaissance, which we may take to have culminated between the years 1453 and 1527—the dates respectively of the fall of Constantinople and the sack of Rome. Whatever else the Renaissance was or was not— and it was much else—it most assuredly was a return to Pagan absolutism. This I have shown elsewhere[1] at length, and I may be permitted to refer my readers thither, for a justification of what I here advance. The Renaissance cannot be summed up in the formula, "a new birth unto liberty." It might with as much truth be called a new birth unto servitude. This it was assuredly, both in the political and the economic order. The notion of irresponsible and unlimited lordship *(dominium)*, whether in government or in wealth, was alien to the mediæval mind. Let it not be supposed that I have any sympathy with the religious romanticism which paints the Middle Ages as a period of seraphic sweetness. I know too well the dark side of their history for that. But certain it is that

---

[1] See my *Chapters in European History*, vol. i., pp. 254-297.

civil authority and private property were regarded
then as essentially limited and fiduciary; as subject
to the moral law and the rights of the community.
In politics, as in economics, the influence of the
Renaissance was simply de-ethicising. It laid loose
the reins upon the neck of monarchical despotism,
and upon the neck of private cupidity. Kings
throughout Europe, as military organisation advanced, cast away the cords of provincial and
municipal franchises, which, throughout the mediæval
period, had more or less effectively restrained them;
the rights and liberty of the subject were no longer
heard of; the maxim of Pagan Cæsarism—*Quod
principi placuit legis habet vigorem*—once more
became the first principle of rule. And as the
world grew rich, and capital assumed a form and
an importance quite unknown in the earlier order-
ing of society, the old belief that wealth was
weighted with duties, that it was a trust rather
than a possession, grew dim; and the wealthy
asserted, ever more and more confidently, their
right to do what they would with their own. The
French Revolution, as I have observed in the
third chapter, was a protest for the natural and
imprescriptible rights of man, political and economical, in an era when the very conception of
such rights seemed to have almost disappeared from
the public mind. It meant the death of Renaissance
Absolutism, and the birth of Modern Democracy.

There is a pregnant remark of Mills that the *philo-sophes* usually saw " what was not true, not what was." And this saying is as applicable to the men who led and shaped the French Revolution, and whom the *philosophes* had trained. The immediate problem before them was the redistribution of polit-ical power. The great bulk of the people had been nothing in the *ancien régime.* That the revolution-ary legislators justly discerned to be wrong. Pro-ceeding to " mistake reverse of wrong for right," they decided that the masses should be everything in the brand-new polity. Those long debates which occupied the mind of France for so many months before the meeting of the States-General, as to how the voting should take place in them, raised a ques-tion the real gravity of which none of the disput-ants, probably, perceived. How should they have perceived it, utterly unversed, as they were, in true political science, and crammed full of the sophisms of Rousseau and the Social Contract ? The real issue was this : whether the legislature and the gov-ernment should represent all the constituent ele-ments of a nation, or merely one class—the numerical majority. The world's great thinkers who had pre-ceded the revolutionary era, from Aristotle to Aqui-nas, from Aquinas to Spinoza, had taught the theory of the public order insisted on in the last chapter —that due weight and influence should be given, according to their importance, to all the jarring

elements of human society, the undue preponderance
of any being obviated. As we saw, this was done
in the Middle Ages—roughly indeed, but as effectively as that stage of civilisation allowed—by the
representation in the National Councils of the Estates of the Realm. It is perfectly true that in 1789
the nominal estates of the French monarchy were
little more than titular. The division of spirituality,
nobility, and commonalty by no means sufficed as a
classification of the elements which then made up the
combination and subordination of civil life in France.
Hence, no doubt, the comparative ease with which, as
Burke expresses it, "the three orders were melted down
into one." The practical effect was to throw all political power into the hands of the *Tiers*, with its double
representation. It was the victory of a merely mechanical, or arithmetical, principle in the political organism, the principle of counting heads; the principle
which has found most recent expression among ourselves in the shibboleths; "One man, one vote";
"Equal electoral districts"; "Every man to count
for one; no man for more than one"; the principle
which M. Arthur Desjardins has summed up in a
pregnant sentence, "that the will of the greater
number shall prevail, even if in error, over the will
of the most intelligent of minorities."[1]

[1] See his very able article, "Le Droit des Gens et la Loi de Lynch
aux États Unis," in the *Revue des Deux Mondes*, May 15, 1871. It
must not be supposed that M. Desjardins is an admirer of this kind
of democracy.

And this principle is the very primary note of
Modern Democracy.   It is the characteristic which
chiefly differentiates it from all that the world has
hitherto known by that name, and which led Mill to
designate it " False Democracy." [1] The fundamental
position of contemporary radicalism is that all adult
men—and perhaps women—in a country should be
politically equivalent; and that supreme political
power should be exercised by a majority of them—
that is, by delegates chosen by the majority and
paid to do its bidding.   It is a doctrine which by
no means commended itself to British Liberals of
the older school—to speak, for the moment, of them
only—and which is almost passionately disavowed
by Mill, unquestionably the greatest of them.   For
myself—it is always best to be frank—I cannot pre-
tend to be satisfied with the political philosophy of
that eminent man as a whole, although I find much
in it of unspeakable value.   Like all his philosophy,
it is vitiated by the Benthamism which dulled his
fine intellect and darkened his generous heart.   I
search his pages in vain for any real apprehension
of the primary verity that the State is an ethical
organism, rooted and grounded in those eternal principles of Right which constitute the moral law—a
verity confessed by the world's greatest political
teachers, from Plato and Aristotle to Kant and Hegel.   How should he have really apprehended it,

[1] *Considerations on Representative Government*, p. 146.

when his ethical doctrine is purely empirical, based
on calculations of profit and loss, on "the conviction," from which, as he tells us, he "never wavered,"
"that happiness is the test of all rules of conduct
and the end of life," [1] and devoid of the fundamental,
aboriginal, indecomposable idea of justice as a divine
order ruling through the universe?

But, however inadequate Mill's mechanical conception of the social organism, he saw clearly that
the Jacobin conception, in which, as he expresses it,
"exclusive government by a class usurps the name of
democracy," [2] is more inadequate still. He warns
us that "if the constituency were made co-extensive
with the whole population, the majority, in every
locality, would consist of manual labourers; and
when there was any question pending on which
these classes were at issue with the rest of the community, no other class would succeed in getting
represented anywhere." [3] He insists, "though everyone ought to have a voice, that everyone should
have an equal voice is a totally different proposition:
[that] if, with equal virtue, one is superior to the
other in knowledge and intelligence—or if, with
equal intelligence, one excels the other in virtue—
the opinion, the judgment of the higher moral and

[1] *Autobiography*, p. 142.

[2] *Considerations on Representative Government*, p. 155. In the
same page he speaks of "the falsely called democracies which now
prevail, and from which the current idea of democracy is exclusively
derived."

[3] *Ibid.*, p. 135.

intellectual being is worth more than that of the
inferior; and [that] if the institutions of the country
virtually assert that they are of the same value, they
assert that which is not."[1]   He pronounces the
belief, "whether express or tacit," "that any one
man is as good as any other . . . almost as detri-
mental to moral and intellectual excellence as any
effect which most forms of government can produce."[2]   He urges, "Until there shall have been
devised, and until opinion is willing to accept, some
mode of plural voting which may assign to education,
as such, the degree of superior influence due to
it, and sufficient as a counterpoise to the numerical
weight of the least educated class; for so long the
benefits of completely universal suffrage cannot be
obtained without bringing with them, as it appears
to me, more than equivalent evils."[3]   Of Mill's argument on behalf of "universal but graduated suffrage" I shall speak later on.   I have already noted
how strongly he opposed the introduction of secret
voting in the election of members of Parliament.[4]
Not less strongly did he oppose the payment of
members of Parliament, on the ground that "the

---

[1] *Ibid.*, p. 165.   So at p. 159 he contends that every man "should
be legally entitled to have his opinion counted at its worth, though
not at more than its worth."   I do not remember that he ever discussed the question.   What *is* the real worth of the average voter's
opinion on political subjects?
[2] *Ibid.*, p. 174.
[3] *Ibid.*, p. 171.
[4] See p. 47.

calling of a demagogue would be formally inaugurated " thereby.   He adds :

> The occupation of a member of Parliament would thereupon become an occupation in itself, carried on, like other professions, with a view chiefly to its pecuniary returns, and under the demoralising influences of an occupation essentially precarious.   It would become an object of desire to adventurers of a low class, and six hundred and fifty-eight persons in possession, with ten or twenty times as many in expectancy, would be incessantly bidding to attract or retain the suffrages of the electors, by promising all things, honest or dishonest, possible or impossible, and rivalling each other in pandering to the meanest feelings and most ignorant prejudices of the vulgarest part of the crowd.   The auction between Cleon and the sausage-seller in Aristophanes is a fair caricature of what would be always going on. [1]

But Mill is " the voice of one crying in the wilderness."   He has no disciples left.   The more cultivated of the new school of Radicals may, indeed, honour him with their lips, but their heart is far from him.   The years which have passed away since the publication of his book *On Representative Government* have witnessed a complete transformation in the ethos of the party with which he was closely associated.   Gradually it has become indoctrinated with the Rousseauan political philosophy.   Consciously or unconsciously, its exponents think the thoughts and vent the verbiage of Jacobinism.   I know of no clearer, franker, or more succinct statement of their doctrines than that which is given in a little book, published not long ago, and very largely

---

[1] *Considerations on Representative Government*, p. 209.

circulated—*The Radical Programme.* The authors speak—and with reason—of the Franchise and Redistribution Acts of 1884 as having wrought "nothing less than a revolution, though a silent and peaceful one." They rejoice that "three-fifths of the electors of the House of Commons belong to the working classes." They pronounce that "manhood suffrage, equal electoral districts, and the payment of members are each, in their turn, indispensable." They add: "An equitable system of Parliamentary representation is absolutely inconsistent with the minority vote, and no sound Radical can acquiesce in such a device for minimising, and it may be nullifying altogether, the power of the majority." "*The power of the majority.*" That is the keynote of the whole book. The postulate upon which it proceeds is the sophism against which Mr. Mill so earnestly contended—that a country should be governed "by a mere majority of the people, exclusively represented," that is, by their hired mandatories; that the foundation of the public order is a sum in addition.

I suppose that no one has done so much as Mr. John Morley to indoctrinate the Liberal party with these principles. And certainly nothing could more forcibly illustrate the low state of political science in England than that the Liberal party should have gone to school for it to Mr. Morley. A clear, cultivated, and conscientious writer he unquestionably is.

That is evident upon every page of his works. Not
less evident is the scantiness of his studies in statecraft, the poverty of his political philosophy. For
him the French Revolution is "a new gospel"[1];
Robespierre is "the great preacher of the Declaration
of the Rights of Man"[2]; and the sophisms and
sentimentalities of Rousseau are the Alpha and
Omega of politics. The "shallowness" and "the
practical mischievousness of the Social Contract,"
Mr. Morley of course admits, as, at this time of day,
every man out of Bedlam surely must. But underlying it he finds what he calls "the great truth"
that a nation "consists" (the word is his) of "the
great body of its members, the army of toilers," that
"all institutions"—*all*, note, without exception—
"ought to have for their aim the physical, intellectual, and moral amelioration of the poorest and most
numerous class. This [he adds] is the People,"[3]
with a capital P. And by way of corollary to that
proposition he lays down that, unless we have paid
members of Parliament, "we cannot be sure of hearing the voice of the People."[4]

So much may suffice as to the history and the
substance of that new political movement specially
characteristic of this age, which we may properly
call with Mill, "False Democracy." It is false

[1] *Rousseau*, vol. i., p. 1.
[2] *Diderot*, vol. i., p. 48.
[3] *Rousseau*, vol. ii., p. 194.
[4] Speech at Newcastle, Oct. 1, 1891.

because it does not really mean the rule of the Demos,
or People. " The poorest and most numerous class "
is not the People.   It is not even the most considerable element of the People.   There are other elements—we cannot insist too often and too strongly
upon this truth—far more important in a nation
than poverty and numbers.   It is false, again, because it rests upon the manifest sophism of the
equivalence of all men in the body politic : "any
man equal to any other : Quashee Niger to Socrates
or Shakespeare ; Judas Iscariot to Jesus Christ."
A manifest sophism, surely, which, nevertheless, has
become an accepted article of belief, or first principle,
not only among ignorant and foolish voters, and the
demagogues whose natural prey they are, but among
persons of culture and education, accredited teachers
of men, who might reasonably be expected to clear
their minds from cant.   Thus, for example, in a
book by no means destitute of merit—Professor
Macy's work on *The English Constitution*—I came,
the other day, upon the following astounding sentence : " The advent of Democracy "—by which he
means the False Democracy which we are now considering, the rule of the adult male population told
by the head—" and the advent of the age of scientific research are not two things ; they are different
manifestations of the same thing." [1]   This is indeed
a dark saying.   A primary lesson of physical science

_____

[1] *The English Constitution*, p. 477.

is the fact of the natural inequality of men, of races, of nations. A primary principle of political science is the inequality of right resulting from this fact. If men are unequal physically, morally, intellectually, most clearly they should not be equal in the body politic. Mill was assuredly well founded when he wrote, " Equal voting is in principle wrong "[1]—well founded, indeed, in a deeper sense than the words bore for him. By "wrong " he meant merely inexpedient. Sovereignly inexpedient equal voting certainly is. But that is not the only or the chief reason why it is wrong. It is wrong because it is contrary to the nature of things, which is ethical; because it is *unjust.* It is unjust to the classes, for it infringes their right as to persons to count in the community for what they are really worth ; it is " tyrannously repressive of the better sort." It is unjust to the masses, for it infringes their right to the guidance of men of light and leading, and subjects them to a base oligarchy of vile political adventurers. It is unjust to the State which it derationalises, making it—to borrow certain pregnant words of Green—" not the passionless expression of general right, but the engine of individual caprice, under alternate fits of appetite and fear." [2] Professor von Sybel is absolutely well warranted when he tells us, in his *History of the Revolutionary*

[1] *Considerations on Representative Government,* p. 173.
[2] *Works,* vol. iii., p. 282.

4

Period, that the Rousseauan theory, which is, so to speak, incarnate in False Democracy, "raises to the throne, not the reason which is common to all men, but the aggregate of universal passions."

Before we pass on to survey the actual working in the world of this False Democracy, and the corruption of the State in which it issues, let us glance briefly at the various apologies put forward for it. They may be reduced to three, which may be termed, respectively, the Abstract or *a priori*, the Utilitarian, and the Sentimental. For the Abstract or *a priori* defence of False Democracy it will be best to go to its inventor, Jean Jacques Rousseau. His central political doctrine is what is often called "the sovereignty of peoples," and what might be more correctly called the sovereignty of the individual. Rousseau postulates unrestricted liberty and boundless autonomy as the normal condition of the abstract man who is the unit of his system. He holds that all the adult male inhabitants of any country are entitled to absolute political equality, that each of them may claim, by natural right, an equal share in the government of the territory where he happens to be born. And the great political problem, according to him, is " to find a form of association which defends and protects, with all the public force, the person and property of each partner, and by which each, while uniting himself to all, obeys only himself." The Jacobin disciples of Rousseau, who

endeavoured to translate his speculations into fact,
supposed themselves to have solved this problem by
the assignment to each adult male of an equal mor-
sel of sovereignty, or—for that is what it practically
comes to—of an equal infinitesimal share in the election of one of the depositaries of sovereignty.   It is
true that by this arrangement the sovereign individual will often find himself compelled to obey laws of
which he disapproves.   How can he then be said to
retain his sovereignty and to obey only himself?
Rousseau answers that every sovereign individual,
by entering into an imaginary Social Contract, makes
over all his rights to the community, his consolation
being that if the State is above him, no one else is,
and that he is a member of the sovereign despotic
authority, whose sovereignty—although constraining
him to do or suffer what he dislikes—is, in effect,
his sovereignty.

Mr. John Morley tells us, " Of this doctrine Rousseau assuredly was not the inventor," and refers it
apparently to " the great Aquinas," whom he represents as teaching that " only the reason of the multitude, or of a prince representing the multitude, can
make a law."   I may be pardoned for doubting
whether Mr. Morley's acquaintance with "the great
Aquinas " is very intimate.   I have elsewhere written :

If, as would seem, Mr. Morley imputes to Aquinas the
doctrine that, "the reason of the multitude" is the ultimate
source of human authority, he greatly errs.   Nothing could
be further removed from the teaching of the Angelic Doctor.

The original and pattern of all earthly law, ever to be kept in mind by the human legislator, is, as Aquinas holds, that *lex eterna* which is the necessary rule of ethics, and of which, the reason of the multitude, is no more the accredited organ than is the will of the prince. To this it may not be superfluous to add that "the multitude" meant for Aquinas, not what it meant for Rousseau and means for Mr. Morley, a fortuitous *congeries* of sovereign human units, but an organic whole, implying all that may be gathered from Darwinism and elsewhere as natural and necessary in the organism.[1]

But whether Mr. Morley's studies in "the great Aquinas" have been profound or superficial, we may be quite certain that Rousseau had never read a line of him. We may be equally certain that Rousseau derived his fundamental political conception from Hobbes, assigning to the collective sovereignty of all, the unlimited dominion which that thinker had attributed to the single sovereignty of the prince; but, like him, postulating as the source of it, a contract into which all members of the community are supposed to have entered. It is hardly necessary to repeat that this contract is wholly fictitious. The divine right of majorities taught by Rousseau, like the divine right of kings inculcated by Hobbes, rests upon "the thing that is not." To expose Rousseau's political sophisms is, as the old Greeks would have said, to kill the dead over again. And yet those sophisms constitute the stock in trade of the Continental Radicalism, as a glance at the speeches of the late M. Gambetta may serve to show.

[1] *A Century of Revolution*, p. 11.

It has been the habit of Englishmen, Heine noted, to neglect general principles in politics; and he thought—with reason, as it seems to me—that we have carried that neglect much too far. However that may be, certain it is that in this respect the New Radicalism—of which, I suppose, Mr. John Morley is the accredited philosopher—has departed widely from the old British traditions. It is essentially *doctrinaire*—a mere transplantation of French Jacobinism. Let us go on to consider the Utilitarian apology for False Democracy presented by the Old Radicalism, of which Bentham was the evangelist, of which Bright, Milner, Gibson, and Cobden were the chief apostles. That Old Radicalism spoke no word of man's natural rights. It did not believe in them. It grounded its worship of majorities upon the principle of utility. Its catchword was "the greatest happiness of the greatest number." This was, in its judgment, the end of the State. And the way to realise this end, it held, was to vest political power in the greatest number. Identity of interest between the holders of political power and the community, was its panacea; and it sought to effect that identity by making the majority supreme. The argument of Bentham is, in effect, this: all people that on earth do dwell, seek what it is to their interest to have: it is to the interest of the majority to have good government: therefore the majority should bear rule.

Such is the Utilitarian apology for False Democracy.   It is, in truth, if tested by facts, as untenable
as the old *a priori*. Bentham, indeed, in spite of
his professed devotion to facts, was really as great
a *doctrinaire* as Rousseau himself. The common
sense on which he prided himself too frequently
proved, in practice, uncommon nonsense. The conception of man as an animal dominated by self-
interest is quite unreal. Man is habitually swayed
by a number of impulses, emotions, passions, hallu-
cinations, altogether unaffected by Utilitarian calculations. Again, to desire one's own advantage is
one thing ; to know how to attain it is quite another.
Everyone will admit that this is so in the case of
children.   And surely Napoleon was well warranted
when he pronounced the vast majority of adult men
mere grown-up children, physically mature, but
intellectually quite undeveloped. To which it must
be added, that even if it should chance that an
individual voter perceives and pursues his immediate advantage, in bringing his vote to bear
on a particular question, it does not in the least
follow that what is for his advantage is for the
general benefit. Moreover, with universal or quasi-
universal suffrage, the number of voters who
are capable of even grasping the idea of the
general benefit, must, of necessity, be infinitesimal.
Consider, with a mind cleared of cant, the average
British elector as actual life discloses him, a skilled

or an unskilled artisan. How is it possible for
him, I will not say to form an intelligent judgment on the graver questions of domestic or
foreign politics, but to discern, even in the dimmest
outline, their real bearing, their true significance?
"Put before him the simplest train of argument,
invite him to exactness, ask him to define, beg
him to consider differences, and you strike him
dumb, unless, perchance, by way of answer, he
damns your eyes. He views things disconnectedly,
unable to make use of that 'large discourse, looking before and after,' which would interpret their
connection. The very notion of causation is strange
to him. Condemned by a law which shall not
be broken—for it issues from the nature of things
—to a life of manual toil, 'his phenomenal existence, his extensionless present, his momentary
satisfaction'—this alone has any reality for him,
and his energies are concentrated on its maintenance." [1]   He is the natural prey of demagogues
who buy his vote by fawning flattery, by loath-
some lying, by abominable appeals to his meanest
motives, by profligate promises made in inexhaust-
ible profusion, and incapable of performance.
Goethe has defined a majority as "a few strong
men who lead, some knaves who temporise, and
the weak multitude who follow, without the faint-
est idea of what they want."   True, the weak

---

[1] *A Century of Revolution*, p. 187.

multitude do not know what they want. How
should they?   But the strong professional politician
—strong with all the strength of his emancipation
from ethical scruples—who leads the multitude,
knows very well what he wants.   "*Qu'est ce que le
peuple veut après tout?*" asks Chaffion in M. Sardou's
comedy: "*il ne veut que de garanties, ce pauvre
peuple. Quelles garanties?*" demands Rabagas.
"*Quelque chose pour nous,*" his colleague replies. Can
any man honestly say that this is not true? And
if it is true, does it not supply a sufficient answer
to the Utilitarian apology for False Democracy?
Burke has excellently observed, "I see as little of
policy or utility, as there is of right, in laying down
a principle that a majority of men, told by the head,
are to be considered as the people, and that as
such their will is to be law."[1]   It is a spurious
Utilitarianism which, in the long run, is not useful
to the State, but ruinous.

The Sentimental apology for False Democracy
rests upon the belief—or profession—that the
instinct of the masses, like that of creatures lower
in the scale of existence, never, or hardly ever,
goes astray ; that it is really a form—an unconscious
form—of right reason, and the most trustworthy.
I know not who has more copiously, or passionately,
urged this apology in our own day than the late
Mr. Gladstone.   And, no doubt, here is the secret

---

[1] *Works*, vol. vi., p. 216.

of the popularity which he enjoyed during the latter
years of his erratic career. The idol of the populace
is the "man full of words," "the excellent stump
orator," who, "in any occurrent set of circumstances
can mount upon his stump, his rostrum, tribune,
place in Parliament, or other ready elevation, and
pour forth thence his appropriate 'excellent' speech,
his interpretation of the said circumstances, in such
manner as poor windy mortals around him shall
cry 'Bravo!' to." Mr. Gladstone has been surpassed by few in this gift, and his rhetoric was
of a kind peculiarly fitted to take captive the
imagination of the masses: grandiose, turgid, de-
nunciatory, unctuous—and vague. Moreover, there
was in it a special brand of religiosity, potent to
charm the ears of a certain variety of the British
Dissenter.[1]   It is a matter of history how adroitly

[1] I have often thought that Mr. Gladstone must have modelled himself on Robespierre, whose discourses will be found to present a most
curious resemblance to his. The deputy Meillan, who listened to
much of the Incorruptible's eloquence, describes it as "a tissue of
declamation." M. Taine's judgement of it is *pas un détail indi-
viduel, vrai, caractéristique, rien qui parle aux yeux et qui évoque
une figure vivante ; aucune impression nette et franche ; dans le mot
vide il introduit le sens contraire;* which surely might serve as a
faithful description of Mr. Gladstone's speeches. Meillan goes on to
tell us concerning Robespierre, *nous étions obligés, chaque fois qu'il
parlait, de lui demander où il voulait en venir.* That is precisely
the question which Mr. Gladstone's hearers ever had to ask. Once
more, there was about Mr. Gladstone, as about Robespierre, what
Mr. Morley calls "a kind of theocratic distinction." *Robespierre
prêche, Robespierre censure: il a tous les caractères d'un chef de
secte,* writes Condorcet. This is just as true of Mr. Gladstone, whose
early wishes, it is understood, inclined him to the ecclesiastical state,
and who always took the keenest interest in religious controversy—
of a kind.

he used this endowment to flatter King Mob. In
that respect he was not surpassed by the most
extravagant orators of the First French Revolution.
Like them, he appears to have believed that the
populace can do no wrong. On the terrible 20th of
June, when thirty thousand ruffians, the *élite* of
Parisian blackguardism, marched upon the Tuileries
to the cry of *Ça ira,* and poor bewildered Louis the
Sixteenth naïvely asked help of the National Assembly, Vergniaud answered, with the greatest serious-
ness, *Que ce serait faire injure aux citoyens que de
leur supposer de mauvaises intentions.* Mr. Gladstone's apology for the Plan of Campaign was conceived in a precisely similar spirit. He declined to
see in that abominable conspiracy to break the law,
anything more than "a substitute without authority
for the law." "How can you say," he demanded,
"that those men were wrong who, by the Plan of
Campaign, saved people from eviction and starva-
tion?"[1] Like Mr. Morley, from whom he probably
learnt the lesson, he came to regard the poorest and
most ignorant of Her Majesty's subjects as forming
"the nation." To these he opposed "the classes,"
inquiring "are the classes ever right when they
differ from the nation?"[2] It was an odd fate that
converted him in his senescence into the chief
preacher of "those general principles of democracy,"

[1] Speech at Hampstead, July 1, 1888.
[2] Speech at Liverpool, June 29, 1886.

as he termed them, to which, in his early manhood, he hoped "this country would oppose a more organised, tenacious, and determined resistance than any other country which is prominent upon the great stage of the civilised world."[1]

But although Mr. Gladstone, in his long career, changed in that respect, as in much else, there were some things in which he did not change. From first to last he manifested a curious adroitness—indeed, in one of his pamphlets he piques himself upon this endowment—of discerning the "ripeness" of questions, and of thereby avoiding "inconvenience in the race of life."[2] From first to last he displayed a quite unique capacity for obtaining and retaining office, by dexterously setting his sails to the quarter whither—the metaphor is his—the wind was veering.[3] To resist the devil was not in him, if the foul fiend appeared in the shape of popular plaudits, or a probable Parliamentary majority. On the contrary, he agreed quickly with the adversary, who was at once transformed for him into an angel of light, and gave copious, if not cogent, reasons for his conversion. To say the truth, his reasons were seldom cogent, and were, not unfrequently, conundrums. And this brings us to another psychological peculiarity

[1] *The State in its Relations with the Church*, vol. ii., p. 389 (4th edit.).
[2] *The Irish Question*, p. 22.
[3] *A Chapter of Autobiography*, p. 45. I am far from suggesting that he was a conscious impostor.

of his which Lord Macaulay noted at the outset
of his political life, and which was as notable at
the end of it—his habit of seeking refuge from the
consequences of false philosophy in equally false
history.   Do the annals of the world show, as he
alleged, that the unreasoning instinct of the masses
has been invariably, or even frequently, right?
Why, from the beginning, their choice has fallen
on Barabbas.   If Mr. Gladstone had not been, as
Carlyle rightly judged, "incapable of seeing verita-
bly any fact whatever," he would have discerned
that, even now, under the system of False Democracy, it is Barabbas who bears rule in a large part
of the civilised world.   I shall have to speak of that
presently: Here let me put it to the common sense
of my readers—Would any sane man go to the
masses, in any country, in quest of right reason?
Who can deny the truth of the description of them
which Milton puts into the mouth of Incarnate
Deity?

> A herd confused,
> A miscellaneous rabble, who extol
> Things vulgar, and, well weighed, scarce worth the praise.
> They praise and they admire they know not what,
> And know not whom, but as one leads the other.
> And what delight to be by such extolled,
> To live upon their tongues, and be their talk?
> Of whom to be dispraised were no small praise ;
> His lot who dares be singularly good.

But if the Puritan poet of the seventeenth century
is held to be out of date, let us turn to the Utili-

13

tarian philosopher of the nineteenth. In his *Principles of Political Economy* Mill points out "the extreme unfitness of mankind in general, and of the labouring classes in particular, for any order of things that would make any considerable demand upon their intellect and virtue." And in his *Subjection of Women* he invites us to "consider how vast is the number of men in any great country, who are little better than brutes." Right reason the endowment of the numerical majority? No; Schiller spoke the exact truth when he said that the majority is not merely irrational, but senseless. *Mehrheit ist der Unsinn.* The Sentimental apology for False Democracy is as futile as is the *a priori* apology, or the Utilitarian apology.

As for us, let us do what Mr. Gladstone, and the *doctrinaires* confederate with him, would by no means do: let us look out upon the world around us with open eyes, and see what the working of False Democracy actually is. And first consider it in its birthplace—France. There, thanks to the clean sweep which the Revolution of 1789 made of ancient institutions and traditions, it has not encountered the obstacles which have more or less retarded it in other countries. There you have what its admirers call *le suffrage universel, direct, égalisé, rasé, et nivelé* in all its perfection, as the expression of that sovereignty of the man

and the citizen which is the corner-stone of the
Rousseauan political edifice. How does it work?
A striking book, by one of the ablest of French
publicists, which lies before me as I write, M.
Benoist's *La Crise de l'État Moderne*, may assist
us to answer that question.

"The sovereignty of the man and the citizen."
But it may be objected that the Rousseauan theory
rather regards sovereignty as residing in the entire
nation, one and indivisible. No doubt that is so.
"I am the State," said Louis XIV. "The people
is the State," is the doctrine now received in
France. I have no objection to the doctrine in
itself. I think that, if the word "people" be
properly understood, it is perfectly true. But let
us see what it really means in contemporary France.
It is well observed by M. Benoist, "The only
expression of sovereignty is the suffrage. If there
are ten millions of electors, there are ten millions of atoms of sovereignty. Indivisible in theory,
sovereignty is realised only in division."[1] The
French Revolutionary theory does not really mean
that the nation, in its corporate capacity, is sovereign. It really means—as every schoolboy can
see—the complete subservience of the numerical
minority, or rather of what is accounted as such,
to what passes for the numerical majority. I use
these qualifying words advisedly. For, as a matter

[1] *La Crise de l' État Moderne*, p. 9.

of fact, the titular majority in France is no more
a real majority than the titular sovereignty of
the man and the citizen is a real sovereignty.
Some very curious statistics on this subject will
be found in an appendix to M. Benoist's volume.
I content myself here with giving the net result
of them. Let us take the general election of
1893—a fairly representative year. The number
of registered electors in France in 1893 was 10,-
443,378. Of these, 7,147,903 are stated to have
voted. The total number of votes obtained by
the successful candidates was 4,512,550. The result, therefore, was that the majority of the electors,
viz., 5,930,828, were not represented at all in the
Chamber elected in 1893[1]; that number being
made up of 3,018,024 who did not vote, and 2,912,-
804 who voted for unsuccessful candidates. Such
is one result of universal and equal suffrage in the
country which originated it, and which has carried it to its greatest perfection. The majority of
sovereign men and citizens is absolutely disfran-
chised. The country is ruled by the so-called representatives of a minority.

"The so-called representatives." For, as the

---

[1] I find that the result of the three preceding French general
elections was similar, as will be seen from the following table :

	Votes obtained by the Deputies elected.	Voters not represented.
1881	4,567,052	5,600,000
1885	4,042,064	6,000,000
1889	4,526,036	5,800,000

majority is a sham majority, so is the representation
a sham representation. The deputies in no sense
represent the principles, opinions, desires—whatever they may be worth—of the Sovereign and
equal men and citizens whose votes are cast for
them. They represent, as a rule, merely the cun-
ning and cupidity of a gang of professional politicians to whom they owe their nomination and
election. M. Benoist's account of the matter is so
piquant, that I will give it:

One fine morning someone bethinks himself that there
will be a general election in six months' time. The Deputy of the Division is used up ; he has ceased to be popular ;
perhaps he belongs to the opposition, and then it is a duty
to oppose him; or he has shown that he has not as much
influence as he ought to have in those high quarters whence
are rained down places and favours; and then it is a crying
need to replace him. Anyhow, this somebody, who is not a
somebody but a nobody—the first man in the street possessing a good deal of vanity and a little knowledge of the
world—finds a second somebody, equally a nobody, who
goes off and finds a third. As soon as there are three of
them, X, Y, and Z, a committee is formed: president, vice-
president, and secretary and treasurer. The committee
calls a general meeting, where each of its members takes
care to bring the friends he can most surely rely upon. He
unfolds to them what he has done; and consults them as
to what he is to do. What he has done is ratified by ac-
clamation. As to what he is to do, *carte blanche* is given
him. Before this general meeting the committee was mod-
est, and called itself provisional. Afterwards it is established, installed, patented. . . . And now the candidate ?
It is the business of the committee to find one. X, Y, and Z
confer every evening. There are mysterious comings and
goings to and from their homes. They are looking out for

a man. The constituency is in expectation. At last they decide. There is another general meeting. The name of the candidate is put to vote. There is a show of hands. X, Y, and Z's man receives the solemn approval of two hundred lesser Z's, Y's, and X's. He is from that time a candidate—*their* candidate, *the* candidate. Who has conferred this character upon him? The general meeting. Who proposed him to the general meeting? The committee. Who has empowered the committee to do that? The first general meeting. Who had convoked the first general meeting? The committee. Who had empowered the committee to do that? No one. But no one calls in question the credentials, either of the general meeting, or of the committee, or of the candidate. He is the champion, declared, privileged, warranted, by the guaranty of the progressive Republicans of the District. And who are these progressive Republicans? Oh, you know very well; they are What's-his-Name, and then X, Y, Z ! [1]

The chosen candidate represents then, as M. Benoist puts it, "a committee which represents nothing," "a small, self-constituted clique of local politicians." But is there no means whereby a candidate may render himself independent of the committee? Let M. Benoist answer the question: "There is for the candidate one and only one way of freeing himself from the committee, and that is to put his trust in hard cash; there is one and only one means to avoid doing homage to the committee, and that is not to hold his seat like a feudal fief from the committee, but to buy it outright. Universal inorganic suffrage is organised and is worked by two forces only: the committees

[1] *La Crise de l' État Moderne*, p. 20.

and money. But the committees are fatal to its universality, and money deprives it of the character of a suffrage."[1]

But how do candidates, once nominated, win their election? M. Benoist declares bluntly, that "the corruption of the candidate by the elector, and of the elector by the candidate," is the normal state of things in France. And again: "Corruption is at once the corollary and the corrective of inorganic universal suffrage which, rejecting all distinctions and even classifications, falls into the hands of the most impudent, and which ceases to be anarchical only when it ceases to be universal."[2] Anyhow, the Deputy, in one way or another, buys his power—there are many ways of buying. And when he gets into the Chamber, he proceeds to sell it. He attaches himself to one of the twenty odd groups existing in the Chamber—political parties, in the proper sense of the word, there are none there—and awaits a purchaser. "Ministers," an acute American observer, Mr. A. Lawrence Lowell, remarks, "must seek support as best they may; and as they cannot rule the majority, they are constrained to flatter and follow it; or, rather, they are forced to conciliate the various groups, and, as the members of the various groups are very loosely held together, they must grant favours to the individual

[1] *La Crise de l' État Moderne*, p. 22.   [2] *Ibid.*, p. 18.

deputies in order to secure their votes." "This satisfaction of local and personal interests," as Mr. Lowell euphemistically calls it, is, he tell us, "a necessity." He adds, "The favours which the deputies demand and exact, as the price of their votes, extend over a large field; nor do they show any false modesty about making their desires known."[1] They are seldom, indeed, the sort of men to show false modesty—or true. They are, as a rule, political adventurers of a very low type—lawyers without clients, doctors without patients, pedagogues without pupils; the most mediocre of mediocrities. How should they be other? Is it to be expected that men of light and leading should be eager to soil their hands with political life as it exists in France? "The wire-pullers," Mr. Lowell asserts, in his guarded way, "are not over-anxious for really strong characters, because they prefer men whom they can control and use for their own purposes. If they want anything, they exert a pressure on the Deputy, who, in his turn, brings a pressure to bear on the ministers; and hence it has become a common saying that the electoral committees rule the deputies, and the deputies rule the Government."[2] "Thus," writes M. Benoist, "is forged and riveted a whole chain of dependencies: the Minister is dependent

---

[1] *Governments and Parties in Continental Europe*, pp. 130, 131.
[2] *Ibid.*, p. 135.

upon the chiefs of groups, who are dependent upon the deputies, who are dependent upon the committees; and thus at the end of the chain, at the very last rung, Power, everywhere and always, drags about the clog of Number. Hence the humiliating mediocrity, the lamentable sterility of our actual politics—nor can they be other than mediocre and sterile under the present regimen "[1]; that regimen of inorganic universal suffrage which recognises numbers as the sole power in the State, which subordinates the highest interests of the nation to the "stupid and dumb brutality of figures," which means "the omnipotence of the masses" with their "foolish credulity, puerile inconstancy, envious cowardice, savage brutality." To the like effect is the testimony of the late M. Scherer, in his well-known pamphlet on Democracy. He describes the existing political order in France as "a vast ascending scale of corruption, the local committee governing the Deputy, the Deputy the Government, and the Government the country; a great evil and a great shame."

And what is a greater evil and a greater shame, is the hopeless acquiescence of the French people in this colossal infamy. It is a very notable circumstance that the few deputies who have striven for the purification of the French Republic by their

---

[1] *La Crise de l'État Moderne*, p. 25.

too well-founded denunciations and exposures of parliamentary corruption, were nearly all among the unsuccessful candidates at the last general election. The wire-pullers had their revenge. The great mass of the electors, so far as they are capable of forming any opinion on the subject, regard corruption as a natural characteristic of their representatives. *Le peuple ignorant croit aujourd'hui que "patriote" et "brigand" c'est égal,*[1] it was officially reported in the year IV. of the Republic. The same belief still prevails very widely. I remember a distinguished French publicist describing to me the ministries which succeeded one another so rapidly in France as *les premiers venus, jetés au pouvoir par je ne sais quelle petite intrigue, et n'y restant qu'en servant les intérêts personnels des ingénieurs parlementaires.* These "parliamentary engineers" are the Bosses of France, who set up one phantasmal ministry after another, filling meanwhile their own pockets. *Quidquid delirant reges, plectuntur Achivi.* Such is the corruption of the State which is the issue of False Democracy in France.

And here France may stand for the type of the Latin races generally. The corruption of the State by False Democracy is as great in Spain, in Portugal, in Italy; nay, in the last-mentioned country it is, perhaps, greater. In Germany, False Democracy has been kept under by the iron hand of the Hohenzollerns.

[1] Taine, *Le Régime Moderne*, p. 226.

When Frederick William IV. consented to give
a constitution to his subjects, he invented the
formula, " A free people under a free king." It
was reserved for his successor to translate the formula into practice. King William, from first to last,
showed plainly that he meant to remain at liberty to
fulfil his monarchical office; to guard and strengthen
the State founded by his ancestors; to extend it as
they had done; and, for these ends, to organise his
army in accordance with the exigencies of the times.
Of the constitutional conflict which resulted from
his carrying out this determination, it is not necessary to speak here. But I may observe that, practically, the German Emperor is to Germany what
the Prussian King is to Prussia. The representatives of Germany have two political rights: they
fix each year the amount of the contingent; and no
new tax may be levied without their consent. The
Emperor chooses his ministers with small regard to
the parties in the Reichstag, and prescribes their
policy. Most English publicists who treat of the
politics of Germany—their treatment is not often
marked by profound knowledge of the subject—
regard this condition of things as deplorable, and
would gladly see False Democracy prevailing there.
The wisest German thinkers are of a different opinion. We may take Herr Schäffle as a specimen
of them. His personal sympathies, as might be
expected from so strong a Liberal, are with the

Parliamentary system. But he owns, that in the exclusive predominance of universal and equal suffrage, democratic government would probably be fatal to his country. The following passage from this weighty writer may be worth pondering :

> No nation has gone so far in the unlimited adoption of universal suffrage as the German people, in elections for the Reichstag. Is it due to this that precisely in Germany the despisers and accusers of universal suffrage are apparently most numerous ? In all directions, throughout the German Empire, we hear it said that the effect of universal suffrage has been to render the German Reichstag poorer in capacities, in characters and leaders, with each successive election ; that only those social powers (*nur jene sociale Mächte*) which specially and strongly influence the masses— labor leaders, parsons, peasant kings, anti-Semitic screamers and croakers—attain to ever-increasing authority and an ever extremer position ; that social democracy, ultramontanism, agrarianism, anti-Semitism become, and must become, ever stronger under universal suffrage ; that the formation of fresh coalitions of Parliamentary parties, incapable of ruling, strong only in negation, ever more and more embarrasses the Government ; that the most weighty interests of the nation find no representation, or, if any, only an accidental and altogether disproportionate representation.[1]

Let us now glance at the United States of America where False Democracy has had free course, and is glorified. And we will take as our guide Mr. Bryce's well-known work, which, certainly, is written in no spirit of hostility to American institutions. It is abundantly clear that in the New World, as in the Old, the corruption of the State is the practical

---

[1] *Deutsche Kern- und Zeitfragen*, p. 134.

issue of False Democracy. Corruption! It is the
great fact "writ large" on well-nigh every page of
Mr. Bryce's volumes. "Neither party," we read,
"has any principles or any distinctive tenets. Both
have traditions. Both claim to have tendencies.
Both have, certainly, war-cries, organisations, interests enlisted in their support. But those interests
are, in the main, the interests of getting or keeping
the patronage of Government. Tenets and policies,
points of political doctrine and points of political
practice, have all but vanished. . . . All has
been lost except office or the hope of it."[1] "What,"
said an ingenuous delegate to the National Convention held at Chicago in 1880, "what are we here
for, except the offices?"[2] "In the Federal Civil
Service there are about 120,000 places. Here is
a vast field . . . for the gratification of personal and party interest."[3] "The civil service in
America is not a career. Place-hunting is the
career; and an office is not a public trust, but a
means of requiting party services, and also a source
where party funds may be raised for election purposes."[4] "Patronage is usually dispensed· with a
view to party considerations or to win personal support."[5] "Politics have been turned into the art of
distributing salaries, so as to secure the maximum
of support from friends with the minimum of offence

[1] *The American Commonwealth*, vol. ii., p. 344.
[2] *Ibid.*, vol. ii., p. 455.   [4] *Ibid.*, vol. ii., p. 489.
[3] *Ibid.*, vol. ii., p. 518.   [5] *Ibid.*, vol. ii., p. 524.

to opponents. To this art able men have been forced
to bend their minds; on this Presidents and ministers have spent those hours which were demanded
by the real problems of the country." [1] "Elections
are entirely in the hands of party managers, and the
people have little to say in the matter." [2] Politics
in America are, in fact, "a squabble over offices and
jobs."

That is the real meaning of the processions,
the speech-making, the shouting, the torches, the
badges, and the flags, which are such well-known
instruments of American political campaigns. On
the 29th of October, 1884, Mr. Bryce tells us, the
business men of New York, who supported Mr.
James Gillespie Blaine in his candidature for the
Presidency, held what is called a parade. They
numbered twenty-five thousand, it seems: nearly
one-third of them lawyers, and another third "dry-
goods men" who represented £30,000,000 worth of
business. "They started from the Bowling Green,
near the south end of Manhattan Island, and marched
straight up the city along Broadway, where Mr.
Blaine reviewed and addressed them. Rain fell
incessantly, and the streets were deep with mud;
but neither rain above nor mud below damped the
spirits of this great army, which tramped steadily
along, chanting:

[1] *The American Commonwealth*, vol. ii., p. 488.
[2] *Ibid.*, vol. ii., p. 199.

"Blaine, Blaine, James G. Blaine,
    We don't care a bit for the rain.
    O—O—O—O—III—O." [1]

The spectacle of twenty-five thousand business
men engaged in such psalmody to honour a gentleman of the calibre of Mr. James G. Blaine, is probably one of the most singular which this planet has
ever exhibited.   It is not necessary for me to give a
detailed account of that popular hero.   On one occasion people were whiling away a wet afternoon in
a country house, where Voltaire was staying, by tell-
ing stories of thieves.   It came to his turn, and he
began, "There was once a farmer-general," and, then,
pausing for a few moments, added, " I forget the rest;
but that is the essence of the tale."   So it is sufficient
to say of Mr. James G. Blaine that he was a politician.   "The American politician," writes Mr. J. R.
Lowell, "is a member of an army of office-seekers,
whose warfare is . . .   waged chiefly with a rival
army of office-seekers, and the spoils of victory, in
the form of public offices, . . .   are allotted
strictly to the officers who have organised and disciplined these voters—to persons more vulgarly called
the workers or wire-pullers of the party." [2]   "Politician," Mr. Bryce tells us, "is a term of reproach . . .
among the better sort of citizens over the whole

---

[1] *The American Commonwealth*, vol. ii., p. 580.   In the State
elections held in Ohio shortly before, Mr. Bryce explains, "the Republicans had been victorious, and the omen was gladly caught
up."
[2] *Essays on Government*, p. 107.

Union. 'How did such a job come to be perpetrated?' I remember once asking a casual acquaintance, who had been pointing out some scandalous
waste of public money. 'Why, what can you expect
from the politicians?' was the surprised answer."[1]
"Politicians," he elsewhere observes, "belong to, or
emerge from, a needy class."[2]   They constitute "an
army," "the desire for office, and for office as a means
of gain," being "the force of cohesion [which] keeps
leaders and followers together," and "the source of
the power the committees wield."[3]   They have "the
spirit of self-interest to rouse them," and "the bridle
of fear to check any stirrings of independence."[4]
They are organised into rings, which are dominated
by Bosses.   "What the client was to his patron at
Rome, what the vassal was to his lord in the Middle
Ages, that the leaders and workers are to their Boss
in the great translantic cities,"[5] where "Ring-and-Boss-
dom has attained its amplest growth, overshadowing
the whole field of politics."[6]

This is the source of the immeasurable corruption
of public life in the United States, for the Boss is, as
a rule, utterly venal: he regards and uses power
merely as a way to wealth.   In Mr. Henry George's
terse phrase, he "makes a business of gaining power
and selling it."[7]   And, as Canon Barnett has truly

[1] *The American Commonwealth,* vol. ii., p. 400.
[2] *Ibid.,* vol. ii., p. 463.   [5] *Ibid.,* vol. ii., p. 450.
[3] *Ibid.,* vol. ii., p. 458.   [6] *Ibid.,* vol. ii., p. 468.
[4] *Ibid.,* vol. ii., p. 450.   [7] *Social Problems,* p. 17.

pointed out, "the penalty"—one penalty—of that corruption "is written in the broken lives and bitter passions of the poor."[1] The Great Republic is really ruled by an aristocracy, or kakistocracy, of Bosses, of whom it is not too much to say that they directly appoint the President, and the Members of the House of Representatives, and, indirectly, the Senate.[2] The vast majority of the House of Representatives are "politicians,"[3] in the American sense, without any visible means of subsistence, in many cases, but the beggarly stipend attached to their office, whence naturally enough the House "has little sense of its own dignity,"[4] "does not enjoy much consideration,"[5] and produces legislation "scanty in quantity and generally mediocre in quality."[6] Its energies, in fact, are devoted to quite other matters than legislation for the benefit of the country. "Toil for the public good is usually unfruitful in the House of Representatives. . . . But toil for the pecuniary interest of one's self and one's friends is fruitful."[7] The Senate has become, practically, an assembly of plutocrats. "Some," Mr. Bryce tells us, "are Senators because they are rich: a few are rich because they are

---

[1] See his interesting paper on "The Poor of the World," in the *Fortnightly Review*, August, 1893, p. 222.

[2] The Senators of the United States are nominated by the State Legislatures.

[3] "Politicians pure and simple," Mr. Bryce says (vol. i., p. 197). "Corrupt and astute" would be more accurately descriptive adjectives.

[4] *The American Commonwealth*, vol. i., p. 105.

[5] *Ibid.*, vol. i., p. 193.   [6] *Ibid.*   [7] *Ibid.*, vol. i., p. 268.

Senators."[1]   A very considerable American authority asserts, "The mind and moral sentiment of the
American people are not represented [in Congress].
The Government is below the mental and moral level
even of the masses."[2]

And what shall we say of the President?   Perhaps it will be best to let Emerson speak.   "The
President," writes that philosopher, "has paid dear
for his White House.   It has commonly cost him all
his peace and the best of his manly attributes.   To
preserve for a short time so conspicuous an appearance before the world, he is content to eat dust before the real masters who stand behind the throne."[3]
But, curiously enough, these real masters have themselves to reckon with a faction which, whatever else
may be said of it, does represent a principle, or, at

[1] *The American Commonwealth*, p. 158.   My own information
would lead me to believe that not a few Senators are rich because
they are Senators.   Mr. Henry George writes, " In our National Senate sovereign members of the Union are supposed to be represented,
but what are more truly represented are railway kings and great
moneyed interests, though occasionally a mine-jobber from Nevada
or Colorado, not inimical to the ruling powers, is suffered to buy himself a seat for glory."—*Social Problems*, p. 18.

[2] Fisher's *Trial of the Constitution*, p. 347.   Venality is not, indeed,
of the essence of bosshood.   Nay, Mr. Bryce affirms, "a Boss may be
a man of personal integrity."   "The atmosphere of oaths and cock-
tails" which surrounds him may blind him to the sordidness of his
occupation and the noxiousness of his methods.   "It must not be
supposed," Mr. Bryce writes, "that the members of Rings, or the
great Boss himself, are wicked men.   They are the offspring of a system.   Their morality is that of their surroundings.   They see a door
open to walk to power, and they walk in.   The obligations of patriotism or duty to the public are not disregarded by them ; for these
obligations have never been present to their minds."—*The American
Commonwealth*, vol. ii., p. 455.

[3] *Essays*, p. 80 (Macmillan's edition).

the least, a passion.   One Boss bids against another
to win the votes of a section of the electorate, described by an indignant writer in a New York journal,
as "a nation within a nation—a nation of naturalised
Irishmen, enjoying the privileges of American citizens, and feeling no responsibilities except to that
portion of the Irish people who are in revolt, more
or less open, against the Government of Great Britain."[1]   Surely then, to sum up, Mr. Henry George is
well warranted when he writes, "The experiment of
popular government in the United States is clearly
a failure.   Speaking generally of the whole country
. . . our Government has, in large degree, become,
is, in larger degree, becoming, government by the
strong and unscrupulous. . . .   In many cities
the ordinary citizen has no more influence in the government under which he lives than he would have in
China.   He is, in reality, not one of the governing
classes, but of the governed.   He occasionally, in
disgust, votes for 'the other man,' or 'the other
party,' but generally to find that he has effected only
a change of masters, or secured the same masters under different names.   And he is beginning to accept
the situation and to leave politics to politicians, as
something with which an honest, self-respecting man

[1] The New York *Puck*, April 11, 1889. The writer continues, "Perhaps it is harsh to blame the newspapers for taking their cue from
the statesmen, who, all over the country, bow down before this alien
fetish. Yet we may fairly look to the press, the censor of politics, to
be superior to the politicians."

cannot afford to meddle."[1] Mill, who weighed his
words, went so far as to say that in the United
States, "the first minds of the country are as effect-
ually shut out from the national representation, as if
they were under a formal disqualification."[2] Certain
it is, that the special note of the public life of that
country is intense sordidness. This it was that
wrung from Emerson the pathetic lament—even
truer, now, alas! than when it was uttered—"Who
that sees the meanness of our politics but inly
congratulates Washington that he is long already
wrapped in his shroud and forever safe; that he was
laid sweet in his grave, the hope of humanity not yet
subjugated in him?"[3]

Such is the working of False Democracy in the
United States. Let us now look at it in England.
Our political arrangements differ in some very important respects from the American. Instead of an
elective President, who for his four years' tenure of
office governs, and possesses the substantial powers
of royalty, we have an hereditary Sovereign, who
reigns and does not govern, and whose influence upon
public affairs, however important, is chiefly indirect
and moderative. Instead of ministers responsible to
the chief of the State, we have ministers responsible
to the House of Commons. The separation between
the executive and legislative powers, so clearly

[1] *Social Problems*, p. 16.
[2] *Considerations on Representative Government*, p. 157.
[3] *Essays*, p. 216.

marked in the United States, is much fainter in England. The Prime Minister and his colleagues are not only the heads of the departments entrusted to them, but are also the initiators of new legislation. But we have this in common with the political condition of the United States, that among us, too, the principles and practices of False Democracy prevail, They have supplanted the old British theory of constitutional government.

For, as I observed in my last chapter, the Reform Act of 1832 made a new departure in English political life. The profoundest thinker among living Englishmen, when that measure was introduced, denounced its authors as doing "the utmost in their power to rase out the sacred principle of a representation of interests, and to introduce the mad and barbarising scheme of a delegation of individuals."[1] These words of Coleridge are as accurate as they are vehement. When the Duke of Wellington told the House of Lords "the principle of this measure is not *reform*"—reform he fully acknowledged to be necessary—when he declared that the spirit animating the movement of which it was the outcome was "the consequence of the French Revolution," he was absolutely well warranted. The feature in the measure to which he most strongly objected was "a uniform system of election." It was the introduction into the country of political atomism, of a representation

[1] *Table Talk*, p. 144.

of mere numbers—a principle so utterly at variance
with our traditions as to lead him to predict,
" From the period of its adoption, we shall date
the downfall of the Constitution." I need hardly
observe that the Reform Act of 1832 by no means
possessed that form of finality which its authors
claimed for it. Lord Althorp declared in the House
of Commons, "I have every reason to hope that the
change we propose will be permanent." And on
another occasion he told the House : "I am sure
that the people of this country are not so fickle as to
give reason to apprehend that when they have no
practical evil to complain of, that they will still wish
for change for the sake of change itself. It has been
truly said that what this country requires is quiet
and a cessation from anxiety and agitation." So
Lord Grey, in the House of Lords, anticipated " permanent contentment" from his Bill. "It was desirable," he said, " that if the question was to be
entered into at all, it should be done in such a manner as to afford a hope that it might be effectively
and permanently adjusted."

Curious pronouncements are these read in the
light of subsequent history. Principles are the
strongest things in the world. They have a life of
their own. They work themselves out by logical necessity. And they often produce consequences most
alien from the minds of those who have adopted them,
for an immediate purpose, in ignorant indifference

to their real nature. The Reform Act of 1832 was
but the beginning of a series of similar statutes,
sometimes initiated by those who sat in the seats of
Lord Grey and Lord Althorp, sometimes by so-called
Conservatives desirous to "dish" them; but all un-
derlain by the Rousseauan or Jacobin principle of
the political equivalence of men and of the absolute
right of numerical majorities; and each carrying
that principle farther. The net result of them, and
of the accompanying changes in local government is,
that if the English system, as it exists at this moment, were really representative, all power would be
in the hands of the manual laborers, skilled and unskilled. That clear-sighted publicist, Mr. Bagehot,
warned his generation: "We should be very cautious how we now proceed to found a new system
without any provision [for giving] the requisite influence to the instructed classes, and with no coun-
terbalancing weight to the scanty intelligence of
very ordinary persons, and the unbridled passions
of the multitude."[1] His warning fell on deaf ears.
We have not been very cautious. We have been
absolutely reckless. In their eagerness to outbid
one another for that popular support which would
give them place and power, our two great political
parties have stuck at nothing. It is notable that
the most flagitious and most disastrous of the so-
called "reforms," the clean sweep made in 1884 of

[1] *Works*, vol. iv., p. 424.

the old historical constituencies, and the close approximation to equal electoral districts, was, in a
very large degree, due to the leader of the so-called
Conservatives.[1]   I say " so-called Conservatives."
For what is it that the Conservative party wants to
conserve ?   What *idea* is there behind the frightened,
unintelligent opposition of the average Conservative
to changes which, in his heart of hearts, he believes
to be inevitable ?   The Conservative party is no less
committed, implicitly, to the principle of False Democracy than is the other party.   And the only
means by which it can obtain or retain office is by
doing homage to that principle.   Of course, Lord
Salisbury's object in 1884 was to secure some agreement with his adversaries which would prevent his
party from being " dished."   But there is simply

[1] On this subject see an interesting page (p. 164) of Herr von
Gneist's *Die nationale Rechtsidee von den Ständen und das preussiche
Dreiklassenwahlsystem*.   It is not easy to imagine any wider departure from English constitutional principles than the destruction effected by the Third Reform Act (1884–85) of the ancient franchises of
counties and boroughs—the unavoidable consequence, Gneist remarks, of universal and equal voting—or than the gradual development of caucuses and their machinery, and the ever-increasing
degradation, as Burke had prophesied, of our " national representation into a confused and scuffling bustle of local agency " (*Works*,
vol. iii., p. 360).   Perhaps few of us really realise the magnitude of
these changes, which, as Herr von Gneist observes, are " more easily
discerned by outsiders than by the society concerned."   He continues
in a passage which contains enough truth to be worth quoting :

" To outsiders, this mighty edifice [of the British Constitution] appears almost a ruin.   The professional politician of the Continent
might be tempted to regard with a certain malicious joy the present
development of Parliamentary government in the land of hereditary
wisdom.   There, too, is the old formation of the great Parliamentary
parties torn into six or seven factions, which, again, exhibit in themselves points of difference whence will issue still further subdivisions,

no rational ground on which he can now resist the
cry for absolutely equal electoral districts, and " one
man one vote "; in other words, for a purely numerical system of representation.   The principle was
conceded in 1884 ; and principles are stronger than
the men who play fast and loose with them ; much
stronger, which perhaps is not saying a great deal.
Anyhow, the upshot is that the Duke of Wellington's prophecy has been fulfilled to the letter.   The
downfall of the old Constitution under which England achieved more than Roman greatness, is
complete.   We have experienced " a revolution in
due course of law."   What is, practically, universal
inorganic suffrage now prevails in England, as in
France.

The question then arises, Why has it not, as yet,

There, too, have the Radical parties arisen, whose programme seems
incompatible with the working of a constitutional ministry.   There,
too, extreme parties combine with their direct opposites for a fac-
tious opposition, which falls asunder as soon as there is question
of assuming the responsibilities of government.   There, too, the personal level of the representatives is declining, as is also the observance
of Parliamentary manners and decencies.   There, too, fortuitous
alternations of party ministries seem likely soon to be the rule, as in
France and Greece.   There, too, appear unintelligible changes of
opinion in the newly constituted electoral districts—more like changes
of the weather than anything else—which place the existence of
every Administration in question, and seem to make adherence to a
settled policy impossible.   In place of the old Whigs and Tories with
their programme—corresponding to what are called in Germany the
middle parties—there have arisen in the Parliament new groups,
with class interests (*neue gesellschaftliche Interessengruppen*), which
gradually swell to majorities, and which have in common with one
another only the negative characteristic that, neither singly nor in
coalition with one another, are they in a position to carry on Parliamentary government."

produced in England so much mischief as in that?
Why is it, to quote the words of Professor Macy,
that, "while democracy has run riot in France,
the English have by common consent taken on democracy in a restrained, conservative manner?"[1]
No doubt national history is rooted in national character. And national character has its own laws.
A people has its proper life, its distinctive physiog-
nomy. The British temperament is alien from "the
schoolboy heat, the blind hysterics of the Celt."
Moreover, in 1789, France, in a single night of ver-
bose intoxication, broke with all her old historical
traditions. In England old historical traditions are
a great power. Mr. Bagehot well observes: "There
has ever been a *structure* in English political society:
every man has not walked by the light of his own
eyes; the less instructed have not deemed themselves the equals of the more instructed; the many
have subordinated their judgment to that of the
few. They have not done so blindly, for there has
always been a spirit of discussion in our very air:
still they have done so—opinions have always *settled
down* from the higher classes to the lower; and in
that manner, whenever the nation has been called on
to decide, a decision that is really national has been
formed."[2] "England," he elsewhere quaintly says,
"is a deferential country": nay, "the type of deferential countries." "The nominal constituency is not

---

[1] *The English Constitution*, p. 482.   [2] *Works*, vol. iv., p. 383.

the real." We may admit that this is so, and that—
to quote Professor Macy again—" the present constitution depends for its stability upon the rational
and conservative character of the people." [1]   But
characters are modified, nay, are largely transformed,
by the influences brought to bear upon them.   And
that in nations as in the individuals of whom nations are composed.   The wide diffusion, one might
almost say the unquestioning acceptance, among us
of purely arithmetical or mechanical conceptions in
politics, and the consequent belief in the absolute
right of majorities, constitute a most grave danger.
For such conceptions necessarily tend to realise
themselves in fact.   Add to this that responsible
politicians—I employ the word in all the degradation of its American associations rather than pros-
titute the venerable name of statesman—responsible
politicians, I say, in their eagerness to pander to
and to trade upon popular passions, have used every
rhetorical artifice to split up our national solidarity
and to array the masses against the classes.   Their
inflammatory diatribes breathe the very spirit of
Rousseau's anathemas upon the culture, the wealth,
the leisure, to which they owe their own position
and influence.   They teach, almost in terms, his
doctrine that civilisation is depravation : *l'homme
civilisé est un être dépravé*"; that the instincts of
the ignorant and untutored child of nature—the

[1] *The English Constitution*, p. 480.

rough, in fact—are the best qualification for the exercise of political power. But certain it is that when the masses in any country, realising their possession of preponderating political power, use it for the purpose of swamping the better-educated and better-off minority, the decadence of that country has begun.

For—let us lay this fact to heart—the quintessence of that vast chaotic movement which I have called, with Mill, False Democracy, is not political, in the ordinary and corrupt sense of the word, but social. Its end is not a mere rearrangement of the mechanism of the State for the benefit of wire-pullers as bosses. No. What advantageth it to the mechanic, groaning under the forced toil of over-competition, to the agricultural labourer, as truly a mere animated tool—ἔμψυχον ὄργανον—as the slave in Aristotle's time, that he possesses an infinitesimal share in the election of one of the rulers of his country, unless his material condition is improved thereby? Equality of right is only a barren notion unless it be wedded with fact. The matter is summed up with admirable terseness in M. Ledru Rollin's famous declaration: "To arrive at social amelioration through the political question" (*passer par la question politique pour arriver à l'amélioration sociale*)—"such is the course of the Democratic movement." This is a truth to which Lazarus will no doubt request the attention of Dives. And Lazarus is now master of

the situation, as Dives fully recognises when solicit-
ing his vote in Parliamentary elections. Will he be
any longer content to lie at the gate in his rags,
watching through the bars the rich man within,
clothed in purple and fine linen, and faring sump-
tuously every day, in the hope, not always gratified,
that some stray crumbs may fall to him from that
luxurious table? I think not. Between the two
classes, of which these are the divinely drawn types,
there is what Mill euphemistically calls "complete
opposition of apparent interest." And well may
that thoughtful writer proceed to inquire: Even
supposing the ruling majority of poor

sufficiently intelligent to be aware that it is not for their
advantage to weaken the security of property, and that it
would be weakened by any act of arbitrary spoliation, is
there not a considerable danger lest they should throw upon
the possessors of what is called realised property, and upon
the larger incomes, an unfair share, or even the whole, of the
burden of taxation, and, having done so, add to the amount
without scruple, expending the proceeds in modes supposed to
conduce to the profit and advantage of the labouring class? [1]

This inquiry of Mill's may, with advantage, be
pondered a little. I shall observe upon it, that, as a
matter of history, no fear of weakening the security
of property has ever withheld the classes which
possessed none, from acts of arbitrary spoliation
when they have had the power of bettering their
condition thereby. Experience testifies to the truth
of Grattan's saying: "If you transfer the power in

[1] *Considerations on Representative Government*, p. 120.

the State to those who have nothing in the country, they will afterwards transfer the property." This is, of course, what Socialism proposes to do. And of Socialism, in the judgment of the late M. Scherer —one of the clearest-headed and most far-seeing of French Liberals—the Falsely Democratic Republic existing in his country "is bound, by the very law of its being, to make trial." Whether or no he was right in so thinking, I do not undertake to say. At all events, his opinion on the matter is worth far more than most people's. Certain it is, however, that the very foundation of Socialism is the doctrine of the absolute power of numerical majorities. "Its essential law," as one of its chief exponents at the Namur Congress, a certain "Citizen" Volders, declared, "is to ensure the free exercise of the force of numbers."[1]   But, short of systematic Socialism, incalculable mischief may result from the madness of the Many, intent upon levelling down, in the economic order, by legislation utterly opposed to the true principles of political science; upon achieving, at all events, an approximate equality by way of abasement. The attempt is, of course, doomed to ultimate failure, because it is contrary to the laws of human nature. I do not know who has pointed out this truth with greater force than Aristotle in the Eighth Book of the *Politics*. Absolute equality,

[1] Quoted by Desjardins, *De la liberté politique dans l'Etat moderne*, p. 238.

once attained, immediately begets a discontent with itself and a striving after inequality, and sooner or later leads thereto. Its usual issue, politically, is in Cæsarism, veiled or avowed, and, economically, in the usurpations of the usurer.

Is Socialism, then—whether systematic or unsystematic—"the consummation coming past escape" upon the civilised world? Or is there any cure for the prevailing corruption of the State which will save it from such dissolution? any antidote to the irrational egalitarianism which is the essential *virus* of False Democracy? Seven such remedies, or antidotes, have been proposed. I will briefly consider them before concluding the present chapter.

1. POPULAR EDUCATION.

And first let me speak of popular education. Is it possible to neutralise the evils of universal inorganic suffrage by educating the voters? We all remember Lord Sherbrooke's dictum on this subject. It would be interesting to know how far he had thought the matter out. "To educate our masters." Is it possible to bestow such an education upon the average voter—or, we will say, "the man and the citizen," if that cant phrase is preferred—as will qualify him for the exercise of the sovereignty which False Democracy confers upon him? I have spoken of him, in a previous page, as actual life really dis-

closes him to our observation, his mind's eye dim, its
range circumscribed, the images pictured upon it
blurred, inaccurate, and misleading. Can we look
to primary schools, whether voluntary or board, to
cure these defects of his political vision? Admitting,
for the sake of argument—and it is a very large admission—that his will is sincerely and honestly directed to the task, how is it possible for him to
acquire such an amount of knowledge and intellectual discipline as will qualify him for forming a sane
judgment even upon the essential elements of public
problems? I am far from denying that it is as possible for the peasant as for the prince to be educated,
in the proper sense of the word—the sense expressed
by Milton: "I call a complete and generous education that which fits a man to perform justly, skilfully,
and magnanimously all the offices, both public and
private, of peace and war." Yes, the true conception
of education is put before us in these majestic words:
to teach a man his duties, and to discipline and develop his intellect and his will for their accomplish-
ment. That every manual labourer, skilled or
unskilled, owes duties to his country, and that these
duties involve corresponding rights, I do not deny, I
strenuously maintain. But, assuredly, the sovereign
functions bestowed upon him by universal and equal
suffrage are not among those duties or those rights;
assuredly the education capable of being imparted
to him by primary or other schools cannot possibly

fit him for such functions, cannot possibly qualify him to sway the rod of empire and to determine the fate of nations. Reading, writing, and arithmetic, a little elementary history, a little elementary geography—what an equipment for such a task! Of all the manifestations of human folly, surely the glorification of the educational nostrum in politics is one of the most foolish.

You forget, it may be said, the newspaper press, that glorious instrument of popular enlightenment. Ah, no; I do not forget the newspaper press. But a stranger instrument of political education it is not easy to conceive. I suppose the newspapers really are the chief source of the jumble of notions which have drifted into the head of the average voter, and which he calls his opinions, or, it may be, his principles. These are, for the most part, if we carefully examine them, formulas void of sense, false aphorisms, claptrap phrases, disingenuous arguments, nicknames, watchwords, empty platitudes, and the most ambiguous of commonplaces. I need not dwell longer upon what must be evident to everyone who will impartially consider the matter. Some years ago, having occasion to write upon the Ethics of Journalism, I ventured to express my opinion that "the newspaper press, during the last quarter of a century, has done more than anything else to de-ethicise public life; to lay the axe to the root of duty, self-devotion, self-sacrifice, the elements of the

moral greatness of a nation which is its true greatness."[1]   I have seen no reason since to modify that
opinion.

2. COMPULSORY VOTING

Another antidote to the *virus* of inorganic universal suffrage which has been confidently recommended, is compulsory voting.   Certain it is that, as
a rule, the people who stay away from the ballot-
boxes are precisely the men for whose political opinions some real value may be claimed.   These may
well disdain to vote when their votes will be
swamped by the ignorant crowds led captive by the
wire-puller at his will.   It is proposed—in one or
two countries the proposal has been acted upon—to
compel them to vote, under penalties.   But surely
there is something ridiculous in the notion of a
sovereign thus compelled to exercise his sovereign
functions.   Such a sovereignty is curiously like a servitude.   And what penalties?   Deprivation of franchise?   That will hardly be a penalty to one who
does not care to exercise it.   Fine or imprisonment?
What a monstrous invasion of individual freedom!
Surely liberty to vote implies liberty not to vote.
Surely the voter is the proper person to determine
whether he should vote.   It is a matter for his own
conscience.   He may possess just enough of knowledge to realise his vast ignorance regarding the

[1] *On Right and Wrong* (3rd ed.), p. 173.

merits of the issues put before him; his utter incapacity for rationally deciding them.   He may—like
Catholics in Italy at the present time—consider himself bound to lend no countenance to the government under which he is enforced to live.   In these
and the like cases, his duty is clearly *not* to vote.
And to compel him to do so is, plainly, a gross violation of sacred rights of conscience.

3. DOUBLE OR INDIRECT ELECTION

Some publicists—conspicuous among them is the
late M. Taine—have recommended a system of double
election, or election by two stages, in place of the
system of direct and equal universal suffrage.   It
looks well on paper; and a distinguished Belgian
statesman attributes to it "a remarkable power of fil-
tration."   But the facts hardly warrant this view.
No doubt the theory is excellent.   The ignorant and
incompetent mass of voters refrain from exercising
themselves in great matters which are too high for
them, and select fit and proper persons, possessing
the qualifications they themselves lack for rationally
discharging the task of election.   But the actual result of this system, wherever it has been tried,—so
far as I am aware,—has been to convert the electors
chosen under it into mere delegates.   And that is
entirely to nullify it, to render it an empty form,
worthless in practice.   Thus the French Senate,
which is the outcome of a very cunningly devised

scheme of double election—the Life Senators were suppressed by the law of 1884—is not appreciably superior to the Lower Chamber. The Senators, indeed, are, for the most part, used-up deputies. "Indirect elections in Prussia," writes Mr. A. Lawrence Lowell, "have worked in the same way as our [the American] method of choosing the President by means of a college of electors; that is, the Prussian electors do not really select the representative, but are themselves almost always voted for in the name of a definite candidate whom they are pledged to support." "And more," he adds, "this must necessarily be the case whenever the electors have no other function than the election."[1] Probably, Mr. Lowell is right in that opinion. At all events, I think we may safely assert that this system of double election demands from the preparatory elector—if we may so call him—an amount of self-abnegation, or, at least, of discipline, which he seldom possesses; while it presupposes in the secondary elector—thus to designate him—the same moral qualities, together with a rare degree of courage, firmness, and independence.

4. VOTING BY PROFESSIONAL CATEGORIES

M. Benoist, who feels as strongly, and has exposed as unsparingly as any living publicist, the evils of the False Democracy at present prevailing, has his own scheme for remedying them. It is a brand-new

[1] *Governments and Parties in Continental Europe*, p. 308.

scheme,[1] and merits careful examination, both on
account of the respect due to its distinguished author, and of the ingenuity which he has displayed
in its construction. The distinctive feature of it is
that the electors shall be organised in *professional
categories*, which shall choose representatives *from
among themselves*—not from outside. M. Benoist
does not propose to interfere with direct, equal, and
universal suffrage. But he would recast it, so that
not only numbers but interests may be represented.
He would classify the electors in each electoral
district, in—say—eight groups, according to their
occupations, and to each group he would assign representatives according to their numbers. Number,
the counting of heads, still remains in M. Benoist's
scheme the point of departure. He would reallot
the five hundred seats in the French Chamber—for
he is writing with immediate reference to France—
among the eighty-seven departments according to
population. And he would distribute the number
falling to each department by this arithmetical operation, among the professional groups according to
their numerical strength. His professional groups—
it will be best, perhaps, to keep the French nomen-
clature—are: I. *Agriculture*; II. *Industrie*; III.
Transports, postes et télégraphes; IV. *Commerce*; V.
Force Publique; VI. *Administration Publique*; VII.
Professions Libérales; VIII. *Rentiers*. Of these

---

[1] See chap. vi. of his *La Crise de l'État Moderne*.

the fifth, *Force Publique,* does not count for much, as, under the existing law, the army does not vote. Let us now see how M. Benoist's scheme would work out in one of the most considerable of the departments of France: *le Nord.* Nineteen seats would fall to it; and they would be thus distributed: I. *Agriculture, 5 Deputies;* II. *Industrie, 9 Deputies;* III. *Transports, postes et télégraphes, 1 Deputy;* IV. *Commerce, 3 Deputies;* V. *Force Publique,* VI. *Administration Publique,* VII. *Professions Libérales, and* VIII. *Rentiers*—all taken together—1 Deputy. No one of these last four categories is numerous enough by itself in *le Nord* to claim a representative; and M. Benoist urges that we may therefore lump them together without doing too much violence to logic or reality. This important department, then, if M. Benoist's scheme were adopted, would contribute to the Chamber five farmers, probably peasants—for remember, the election is by counting heads, and jealousy of those above him is a dominant passion with the average French elector; nine *industriels,* probably mechanics; four traders, probably small shopkeepers; one representative of transports, etc., probably a postman or a telegraph clerk; and one representative of the army and navy, the liberal professions, the civil service generally, and persons of independent fortune; the only one of the lot, we may be pretty sure, who would belong to the classes as distinguished from the masses.

Now, what are we to say of M. Benoist's scheme? Does he really imagine that his system of electing deputies by, and from, professional categories, would result in a Chamber truly representative of the French nation—its wealth, its industries, its energy, its intelligence, its culture, its traditions, as well as its numerical strength or, to express it otherwise, would render available, for the common weal, all the constituent elements which make it a great people? Unquestionably, he is well warranted in regarding the professional politicians, who constitute the majority of the French deputies, as a curse to their country. They represent nothing but corruption and the basest interests and passions. But can he suppose that his system would make an end of them? No doubt they are chiefly recruited, at present, from among indigent lawyers and doctors. But the place of deputy, with its salary and its opportunities of trading upon the power which it confers, is a prize which would attract equally a sharp-witted peasant, or mechanic, or small trader or postman or telegraph clerk. The *personnel* of the Chamber would be changed by M. Benoist's scheme. But the professional politician would still dominate it, although he would come chiefly from the operative classes. Three-fourths of the Chamber, as M. Benoist conceives of it, would be elected by peasants and mechanics who would form an overwhelming majority in the categories of *Agriculture* and

Industrie, and who would certainly, as a rule, choose men of their own position in life to represent them; for, as I have already observed, hatred and distrust of those socially above them is, usually, one of the strongest passions of the French peasant and me-chanic. As certainly the greater number of those representatives would adopt politics as a trade. What would be gained by M. Benoist's scheme? Like the present system, that scheme would place preponderating political power in the unfittest hands. And this is its sufficient condemnation.

The truth is that M. Benoist does not go to the root of the matter, and that simply because he dares not. Indeed, he himself owns as much with a can-dour which is somewhat winning. The reason of the political woes of France is this: that the polity existing in that country is founded upon a lie—the baseless and baneful fiction of human equality. The first and fundamental proposition of the *Declaration of the Rights of the Man and the Citizen,* in which Rousseau's disciples embodied his gospel, is abso-lutely false. Men are not born and do not continue equal in rights. They are born and they continue unequal in rights, just as they are born and con-tinue unequal in mights, and therefore they are not entitled to equal shares of political power. M. Benoist fully recognises this. "Inequality of value among men," he writes, "is a natural fact. And the practical consequence which spontaneously flows

from it is this: Since inequality is a fact, equality
ought not to be a right; since all men are not identical, all should not have the same power as electors.
No! Men are not equal to one another physically,
morally, intellectually, or from any point of view of
natural fact; and therefore they ought not to be so
politically." [1]   These are the words of truth and
soberness.   And yet, as we have seen, M. Benoist's
scheme is based upon this very equality, the falsity
of which he thus exposes.   Why?   His answer is
very simple.   "For fifty years in France we have
had universal, equal suffrage.   We can't touch it.
Argumentum ex necessitate."   To this the rejoinder is
plain, and has, indeed, been supplied by an observation of Rousseau himself—one of the luminous truths
which light up from time to time the black darkness
of his sophisms.   "If the legislator establish a principle at variance with that which results from the
nature of things, the State will never cease to be agi-
tated until the principle has been expelled, and in-
vincible Nature has resumed her sway."   Which
seems to me a still more cogent *argumentum ex-
necessitate* than the one adduced by M. Benoist.

5. THE REFERENDUM

The Referendum is a popular vote on laws and
public questions, which have already been discussed

<hr>

[1] Page 101.

by the legislative body. Its home is the Swiss Republic, a confederation of twenty-two sovereign
States, the larger of which possess elected legislatures, while the smaller legislate by mass meetings.
In the larger the population does not exceed half a
million; in the smaller it is about twelve or thirteen
thousand. Under the Swiss Constitution of 1874
alterations of the Constitution are subject to the Referendum, and any legislation of the Federal Parliament may be so subject. "The appeal," writes
Professor Dicey,[1] "is to the people's judgment of a
distinct, definite, clearly stated law. . . . It does
not facilitate any legislation which Parliamentary
wisdom or caution disapproves. It merely adds an
additional safeguard against the hastiness or violence
of party. It is not a spur to democratic innovation;
it is a check placed on popular impatience." There
are two reasons, the Professor notes, why its introduction into this country—to speak merely of England—is advocated : that it supplies, under the
present state of things, the best, if not the only possible check upon ill-considered alterations in the
fundamental institutions of the country, and that it
tends to sever legislation from politics. I must refer my readers to his extremely interesting and able

---

[1] *Contemporary Review*, April, 1890, p. 496. The professor adds in
a note, "Of course, in making this statement, I do not refer to the
right given under the *Constitution Fédérale*, Art. 120, to 50,000 Swiss
citizens of demanding the preparation of a scheme for revising the
Constitution. This right is what Swiss authors call the Initiative,
and is certainly not an essential part of the Referendum."

paper for his discussion of those reasons, merely
noting here the conclusion at which he arrives : that
"there is more to be said for, no less than against,
the popular veto than English thinkers are generally
ready to admit." It appears to me that the success
of the Referendum in Switzerland—which seems to
be pretty generally allowed—is due to the extremely
peculiar political conditions of that country. It is a
country in which there are no classes and no masses ;
no glaring inequalities of wealth, education, or social
standing; it is an agricultural country, possessing
neither mines nor manufactures, and undisturbed by
industrial struggles ; it is a country in which direct
legislation in the little peasant republics has been a
regular constitutional feature from the very beginning of its history. We may say that in Switzerland
something very like equality of fact prevails among
the electors. The Democracy resting there on equal
and universal suffrage is not a wholly false, but
an approximately true Democracy. In England it
is far otherwise. Society there, as in most European nations, is highly complex and artificial,
and implies vastly varying individualities, very numerous and extremely diverse classes and interests.
An appeal to the majority of the population told by
the head, in such a country as this would be a direct
appeal to " the yes and no of general ignorance." It
would be a fresh step in the wrong direction ; or, to
change the metaphor, and to borrow a French phrase,

it would be the crowning of the pseudo-democratic edifice.

6. THE MULTIPLE VOTE

A far more promising device for mitigating the evils of False Democracy is the Multiple Vote. Mill, as we have seen in a previous page of this chapter, urged its adoption with much earnestness. And I am not aware that his main argument has ever been answered. Indeed, it seems to me unanswerable. The justice of conferring upon those of greater capacity a more potential voice than upon those of less, in the management of joint interests, is, indeed, in itself so manifest, that only a fool or a fanatic could gainsay it. And the experience of Belgium, touched upon in the last chapter, shows—what hardly required demonstration—that there is no practical difficulty in making such concession with regard to the electoral suffrage. "If it be asked," writes Mill, "to what length the principle admits of being carried, or how many votes might be accorded to one individual upon the ground of superior qualification, I answer that this is not, in itself, very material, provided the distinctions and gradations are not made arbitrarily, but are such as can be understood and accepted by the general conscience and understanding. But it is an absolute condition . . . [that] the plurality of votes must on no account be carried so far that those who are privileged by it, or the class, if any, to which they mainly belong, shall outweigh by means of it all the rest of the community."[1]   This is so clearly reasonable as to require no comment.   Mill adds, "Plural voting, though practised in vestry elections and in those of poor law guardians,[2] is so unfamiliar in elections to Parliament, that it is not likely to be soon or willingly adopted ; but as the time will cer-tainly arrive when the only choice will be between this and equal suffrage, whoever does not desire the last, cannot too soon begin to reconcile himself to the former."

7. A STRONG UPPER CHAMBER

But multiple voting, however carefully and justly organised, would be, at the best, but a

---

[1] *Considerations on Representative Government*, p. 169.

[2] And we may note that, in elections to School Boards—which have come in since Mill wrote—England has the cumulative vote.   I must here say a word on the chaotic state of the English law as to the elec-toral franchise.   In the first place, the kinds of electorate are diverse. There are the Parliamentary, the Parochial, the County Council, and Municipal—to say nothing of the School Board.   And these electorates comprise many varieties of electors : for example, Freeholders, who have the Parliamentary and Parochial votes, but not the County Council unless they occupy their freeholds ; £10 Occupiers and Householders who, if of the male sex, are richly endowed with well-nigh every kind of vote ; Service Voters and Lodgers, of the same sex, who have the Parliamentary vote only : Peers, single women, and widows, who, being Occupiers, have the County Council and Parochial vote, but not the Parliamentary ; and Married Women Oc-cupiers, who have only the Parochial vote.   The distinction between an Occupier and a Lodger is, in the highest degree, artificial : nor does it entirely depend, as is generally supposed, upon the residence or non-residence of the landlord.   And it is not easy to imagine more arbitrary and absurd anomalies than those which attach to residen-tial qualification.   These vagaries of the law are due to a piece-meal system of legislation, and to the great number of judicial decisions, some of them contradictory, by which it is supplemented.

palliative for the mischiefs of False Democracy. The
true conception of representative government, as
we saw in the fifth Chapter, is that all independent elements, all powers which exercise any considerable influence on the life of a nation, should
be duly represented. And a popularly elected
chamber, even if the electoral machinery received
all the improvements so cogently advocated by
Mill, would still represent, principally, numbers,
the element of least importance in the national
life. This, indeed, he candidly confessed. "Those
whose opinions go by the name of public opinion," he remarks, "are always a mass, that is
to say, collective mediocrity. . . . Their thinking is done for them by men much like themselves, addressing them, or speaking in their name,
on the spur of the moment, or through the newspapers. I do not assert that anything better is
compatible, as a general rule, with the present
low state of the human mind. But that does
not hinder the government of mediocrity from
being mediocre government. No government by
a democracy or a numerous aristocracy, either
in its political acts or in the opinions, qualities,
and tone of mind which it fosters, ever did or
could rise above mediocrity, except in so far as
the sovereign many have let themselves be guided
(which, in their best times, they always have
done) by the counsels and influences of a more

highly gifted one or few." So Mill, in his essay *On Liberty*. And in his *Representative Government*, he insists that a Second Chamber should be "composed of elements" which "would incline it to oppose itself to the class interests of the majority, and qualify it to raise its voice with authority against their errors and weaknesses." In order to possess that authority, it should specially represent those factors in the national life which will never be adequately represented in an assembly due to the accident of popular election.

This truth has been recognised in the constitution of the Upper Houses in most European countries. And M. Benoist would accompany his reform of the French Chamber by a reform of the French Senate, which he wishes to see elected in equal proportions by the Councils General, the Municipal Councils, and the various corporate bodies of each department. In this way, he urges, the individual would be represented in the Chamber through the professional group to which he belongs; and local unions, administrative and civil —social organisms, we may call them—would be represented in the Senate. The example of the United States is here much in point. Mr. J. R. Lowell is well warranted when he claims, "The Americans are the only people who have set themselves to work to solve the problem of restraining the power of the majority."[1] And it is notable that of all the institutions devised by the founders of the United States, the Senate alone has, in any marked degree, fulfilled their expectations. The Presidency, notwithstanding the elaborate machinery intended to place it above party, is now the chief prize of contending factions. "The venality of the [State] legislatures has become a byword and a reproach."[2] The House of Representatives is a House of corrupt adventurers, the salaried servants of Bossdom and Ringdom, where "single thought is civil crime and individual freedom mute." But the Senate, "although doubtless the State legislatures are often guilty of shameful corruption,"[3] in the choice of Senators, preserves a much higher level of integrity and wisdom than the lower chamber. "Once in the Senate, a man may serve his country with fearlessness and honour."[4] And it is, at this moment, "one of the most powerful political bodies in the world."[5] Now "the Senate of the United States," as Sir Henry Maine has pointed out, "is in strictness no more a democratic assembly than the House of Lords. It is founded on inequality of representation, not on equality."[6]

[1] *Essays on Government*, p. 83.
[2] Jennings's *Eighty Years of Republican Government in the United States*, p. 122.   [3] *Ibid.*, p. 121.   [4] *Ibid.*, p. 161.
[5] Maine's *Popular Government*, p. 226.
[6] *Ibid.*, p. 186. Each of the forty-four States comprising the Union, whatever its size, is represented by two Senators.

But let us come to our own England. It is
often said that a reform of the House of Lords
is the necessary complement of the reform of the
House of Commons. And that is true, though
for a reason not usually in the minds of those who
make the assertion. One immediate effect of the
Reform Act of 1832 was to purge out of the House
of Commons some of its most valuable elements
and greatly to debase it. In 1833, Coleridge said:
"You see how this House of Commons has begun
to verify all the ill prophecies that were made
of it—low, vulgar, meddling with everything,
assuming universal competency, flattering every
base passion, and sneering at everything noble,
refined, and truly national." [1] And from that
time until now, the character and tone of the
House have sunk lower and lower, until it has
offered us the spectacle of honourable members
belabouring one another on the floor, while
spectators in the gallery, not unnaturally, hissed
and cried "Shame." It is the true function of
the House of Lords to supply the deficiencies
of this degraded and decadent assembly, and to
remedy its blunders. In a speech of Mr. Gladstone's, at Edinburgh, on the 27th of Septem-
ber, 1893, I find the following proposition:
The Lords "are not the representatives of the
people." The answer is simply this: "It all

[1] *Table Talk*, p. 215.

16

depends upon what you mean by 'the people.'
If you mean the populace, the proposition is true.
The House of Lords does not represent the populace, and that is precisely its great merit, nay,
its very *raison d'être*.   If you mean what the
Romans meant by *populus*, and the Greeks by
δῆμος, if you mean the nation, the proposition is
not true.   The House of Lords, even as at present constituted, is far more truly representative
of that which makes the nation what it is, of
its wisdom, its experience, its culture, its independence, its great historical traditions, its imperial instincts, than the House of Commons."
So much must be clear to any dispassionate observer.   Equally clear must it be to him that to
enable the House of Lords to maintain its proper
position in the national counsels two reforms are
necessary.   The first is the suspension or extin-
guishment, at the instance of the Lords themselves,
of the peerages of those who are a public scandal
and an open disgrace to their order.   Let me not
be misunderstood.   It is no part of the duty of
the House of Lords to make inquisition into the
details of any peer's private life, after the manner
which approves itself to the prurient apostles of
social purity.   But it is fitting that peers notorious
for conduct which, if they were in the army, would
entail the loss of their commissions, as unworthy
of an officer and a gentleman, should be deprived of

honours which they dishonour. And I can conceive of nothing better fitted to justify Mill's sneer
against the Conservatives as "the stupidest party,"
than their persistent indifference, nay, their dogged
opposition to this reform.

But there is another reform much more necessary
and important, and much more far-reaching, which
should be applied to the Upper House. It is
at present constituted by heredity and selection.
The importance of the principle of heredity, no
one even superficially acquainted with contemporary science will doubt. But certain it is that
in the House of Lords, as actually existing, selection does not adequately operate.[1] No doubt, members of that House, especially those who feel that
their assembly is the Ark of the Constitution,
are the most proper persons to propose such a
remodelling of it as may enable it to breast the
surging waves of the democratic deluge. Unfortunately, they, for the most part, too much
resemble those antediluvian Conservatives of whom
it is written, "They did eat, they drank, they married wives, they were given in marriage—until
the flood came." So does it threaten to be with
this generation. It may, therefore, be permitted
to a student of political science to sketch briefly,

[1] I believe Mr. Bryce entirely well warranted when he writes:
"In England, during many years, thinking men of both parties
have been convinced that something ought to be done to reconstruct
the Upper Chamber."—*The American Commonwealth*, vol. i., p. 489.

and in the barest outline, a scheme which may,
perhaps, be not unworthy of their Lordships' consideration, for the reconstruction of their Chamber
in accordance with the needs of the times, by the
wider application to it of the principle of selection.

Now, to deal in the first place, then, with the
existing body of peers sitting in the House of
Lords by hereditary right, I would submit that
direct selection might well be employed in respect
of them, as it has been employed for well-nigh
two centuries in respect of the Scotch peers, and
for the better part of a century in respect of the
Irish. The peers of England, of the United Kingdom of Great Britain, and of the United Kingdom
of Great Britain and Ireland, numbering close
upon five hundred, are now entitled to sit and
vote in the Upper House. Certainly not more
than one-tenth of them take part habitually in
the business of the House; nay, are ever seen
in it, save upon the rarest occasions. I do not
know that the public interests lose by their absence. It would certainly be no loss to them,
but rather a gain, if they were present by representation. I would suggest that the five hundred
peers now sitting by hereditary right should be
represented by one-tenth of their number. Perhaps no better process could be devised for that
purpose than the one set forth by Mill.[1]   The

[1] See his *Considerations on Representative Government*, p. 246.

sixteen representative Scotch peers are elected for each Parliament. The twenty-eight representative peers of Ireland are elected for life. I would not disturb these arrangements; but the fifty representatives of the peerages of England, of Great Britain, and of Great Britain and Ireland, might be elected for a term of seven years. Variety of tenure is, in itself, a positive advantage.

The principle of representation might, however, be also indirectly applied to the hereditary peers in whatever peerage, by allowing the holding of certain great positions to entitle them to sit and vote in their House. This category should certainly include the Prince of Wales (Duke of Cornwall); the hereditary Earl-Marshal and the hereditary Great Chamberlain; all peers holding the Lord Lieutenancy of a County, or the rank of Field-Marshal, or Admiral of the Fleet, or filling or having filled the office of Cabinet Minister, Lord Chamberlain, Lord Chief Justice of England, Master of the Rolls, Ambassador, Viceroy of Ireland, India, or Canada, or Governor of any Indian presidency or British colony.

The space obtained in the House of Lords by the elimination of so many of the hereditary peers now entitled to seats there, might be filled, to some extent, by life peers.[1] The Crown should have the

---

[1] These peers should be nominated originally in the Act for the Reform of the House of Lords, vacancies being subsequently filled up as they occur by the Crown. Among them might be a certain number

power of bestowing a life barony, carrying with it a seat in the House of Lords, upon, say, one hundred commoners, of unusual distinction for public services, or in literature, art, or physical science. In every case the claims of the recipient of a life peerage should be fully set out in the *London Gazette* containing the announcement of his appointment. The Bishops of the Established Church and the Lords of Appeal in Ordinary, should sit in the Upper House, as at present.

The prerogative of the Crown to create life peers should not extend farther than I have described. But it should have the power to confer a hereditary peerage on any such peer, and, as at present, to raise any hereditary peer from a lower to a higher grade : but not otherwise to create new hereditary peerages, except in the case of princes of the blood royal, and of the Lord Chancellor, who, however, if he preferred it, might receive a life peerage as a Lord of Appeal in Ordinary. And no peer, in whatever peerage, should be eligible for a seat in the House of Commons.

A House of Lords, reconstituted on these lines, would be lifted above the vulgar range of party

of eminent Colonists. I do not think that any other mode of representing the Colonies in the Upper House is practicable. Mr. Macpherson's interesting work, *The Baronage and Senate*, contains an elaborate scheme for converting that House into a sort of Imperial Legislative Council. The scheme appears to me to belong to the domain of what Milton calls, " Atlantic and Utopian politics which can never be drawn into use."

politics, and would be the most powerful Senate in the
world.   It would represent all those higher elements
of the national life which are already so much weakened in the House of Commons, and which must inevitably become weaker.   It would express " the
judgment as contrasted with the emotion " of the nation ; or, to use the words of the framers of the
American Constitution, it would act as a curb on
" the propensity of a single numerous assembly to
yield to the impulse of sudden and violent passions." [1]
It would bring to the service of the country what
Mill has described as those " better qualifications
for legislation than a fluent tongue and the faculty
of getting elected by a constituency " which he truly
asserts, " exist and may be found if sought for." [2]
It would represent the force of reason against the
force of numbers ; it would assert the sanctity of
right against the brutality of might.   It would do
much to safeguard that ethical sentiment of the
country which Hegel has called " the mainspring of
Democracy."   It would restore and preserve to us,
as perhaps nothing else could, the reality of self-
government.

[1] *The American Commonwealth*, vol. i., p. 164.
[2] *Considerations on Representative Government*, p. 100. Of course,
the ultimate power must reside somewhere. In case of the Lower
House insisting on a Bill sent up to the Lords in two successive Parliaments, and rejected by them, a conference of the two Houses
might be held in Westminter Hall, in which, without debate, a vote
might be taken on issues previously agreed upon, the decision of the
numerical majority of the two branches of the Legislature, thus
united, being final.

I am concerned in this volume with First Principles rather than with their application to practical
politics.   I trust, however, I may be pardoned, in
view of the debt which every man owes to his country, if occasionally—as just now—I have gone beyond my proper scope by indicating how certain of
those principles might be carried out.   The question
may be asked, Is there any prospect that any remedies or palliatives for False Democracy will be
adopted?   Do the signs of the times point in that
direction?   I think there is such a prospect, how
ever dim.   I think the signs of the times are beginning so to point.   Certainly, I find among the more
considerable publicists of Continental Europe a well-
nigh unanimous consent in the opinion expressed by
Bluntschli : "The radical vice of our constitutional
systems is that they take the individual vote as the
unique point of departure."   It is surely significant
that such strenuous Liberals as M. Desjardins in
France, and Herr Schäffle in Germany, insist upon
the representation of *interests* as necessary for the
rational organisation of Modern Democracy.   M.
Desjardins, indeed, who is addressing primarily
French readers, speaks, as it were, with bated breath.
He compares Democracy, as it is at present, to a
conqueror intoxicated with victory, and resting on
the field of battle ; watching with jealous eyes its
conquests, and apt to be alarmed by a word, a gest-
ure, that may seem to threaten them.   Still, he

thinks that the abuses of unlimited numerical force
must cause even the least clear-sighted to reflect;
that Democracy, *majeure et maîtresse d'elle-même*, may
set itself to organise its victory, may itself open the
door to some reforms; he thinks that the representation of interests may be regarded as " a desideratum
of the future." [1] Herr Schäffle, while justly regarding
the complete elementary representation of nations by
universal suffrage as a great step, not to be retraced,
in political progress, insists on the absolute necessity
of adding to it the representation of inequalities of
fact, of all those local and social interests of the body
politic which play so necessary and so important a
part in the co-ordination and subordination of civil
life.[2] Even in our own country it is at last beginning to be discerned that the qualities of insight,
knowledge, wisdom, not to say patriotism, are not
the necessary or even the probable product of universal and equal suffrage operating by ballot-boxes;
that, ever comparatively rare—*minora saniora*—they
are proportionately more difficult to find as the conditions of social life become more complicated; that

---

[1] Page 238. It is one of M. Desjardins's many pregnant observations, *Ce qui fait le principal obstacle à l'établissement de la liberté
politique dans les républiques modernes, c'est que la force du nombre
y tend à tout remplacer* (p. 227).

[2] *Ich die vollständige Elementarvertretung der Bevölkerung als einen
grossen, nicht mehr umzustossenden Fortschritt, als das eine und
hauptsächliche Stück ächt neuftzeitstaatlicher Volksvertretung ansehe,
welchen man das andere gliederungsmässige zur hinzuzufügen
braucht, um all' die grossen Gefahren einseitiger Geltung des allge-
meinen Stimmrechtes zu bannen.—Deutsche Kern- und Zeitfragen,*
p. 135.

they are indispensable for good government; and
that the gravest political problem of the present day
is how to render them available for the general benefit. The discredit which has overtaken the old
orthodox political economy is advancing surely—
though perhaps *pede claudo*—to claim as its own the
Rousseauan political philosophy, which is simply
another manifestation of spurious individualism. On
all sides I find indications that the cult of majorities
is losing its hold upon those who were once its most
enthusiastic votaries.[1]

[1] One of the most significant of such indications is supplied by the
following remarks of Mr. George Julian Harness, the last survivor of
the Chartist Convention of 1839. The occasion on which they were
made was a gathering at Newcastle, in February, 1897, of a number
of people to pay him a tribute of respect and esteem upon his attainment of his eightieth birthday—respect and esteem amply merited by
his entire sincerity of purpose, utter disinterestedness, ungrudging
self-sacrifice, and unswerving devotion to the faith that was in him.
"I know we are in the way of being congratulated on having obtained most of the points of the Charter. Well, we have vote by ballot, no property qualification, an approximation to equal electoral
districts, and a very wide extension of the suffrage. Whether we
have an equally wide extension of intelligence to make a right use of
the vote, is a matter I will not now discuss. Whether the present
Parliament, elected on a democratic basis, is much superior to,
or even compares favourably with, Parliaments elected on a restricted suffrage—Parliaments that contained such men as Bul-
ler, Molesworth, Roebuck, Leader, Wakley, Duncombe, Sadler,
and Lord Ashley—is doubtful. Indeed, Parliaments seem to me to
have fallen into discredit. In our case we have a mob of seven hundred gentlemen, most of whom are of no earthly use, except to vote
as they are directed by party leaders. . . . There is a feeling
abroad, not only in this country, but in others—France, Germany,
Italy, the United States, and our Colonies—that Parliaments are
played out, and that some better legislative machinery will have to
be devised. I shall not live to see it, but that question will have to
be seriously entertained by political philosophers and practical
politicians."

We may trust, then, that, in time, public opinion will recognise organic unity as better than atomistic uniformity; the force of reason as superior to the force of numbers. I say "in time"; for mere argument is not sufficient for these things. To determine great public issues by counting heads, is just as demonstrably absurd as to determine them by measuring stomachs. But mere logic goes only a short way in such matters. There is a wise observation of Mr. Herbert Spencer's: "A wave of opinion, reaching a certain height, cannot be stopped by evidence, but has gradually to spend itself." It does spend itself. Carlyle, looking out upon the world with old, sad eyes, pronounced it to be "fast rushing to total anarchy and self-government by the basest." The judgment would be true if things progressed in a straight line. But they do not. *Inest in humanis rebus quidam circulus.* The very greatness of the evil in False Democracy indicates a remedy. According to that word of ancient wisdom, the generations of men have been made *sanabiles*. There is a certain principle of recovery in human nature. The reasonableness of the universe is not less certain than the supremacy of duty. We may not believe that our race, of which reason is the most distinctive attribute, will permanently recede from rational principles in politics, or elsewhere. The stars above us, the graves below us, speak to us—the heirs of all the ages—of a nobler faith: they bid us trust, not

faintly, the larger hope, and admonish us to do what
in us lies for its realisation.

> " Yet yonder the presage
>   Of spirits is thrilling,
>   Of masters fulfilling
>   Our life with their message
>   Of just men made perfect.

> " They weave in the starland
>   Of silence, as ever,
>   For work, for endeavour,
>   The conqueror's garland,
>   And bid us ' Hope onward.' " [1]

[1] I am indebted to Mr. Walter Sichel for this admirable translation of Goethe's well-known verses.

> " Doch rufen von drüben
>   Die Stimmen der Geister,
>   Die Stimmen der Meister :
>   Versäumt nicht zu üben
>   Die Kräfte des Guten !

> " Hier winden sich Kronen
>   In ewiger Stille,
>   Die sollen mit Fülle
>   Die Thätigen lohnen !
>   Wir heissen euch hoffen."

CHAPTER VII

THE thought with which we ended the last
chapter may well serve to begin this. It is,
indeed, a thought which has been ever with us,
throughout the present work, and which may be
called the keynote of what I have written. Reason,
manifesting itself in ethics, is man's most distinctive
attribute. It is the first law of his being: the right
rule of the action, whether of the individual or of the
State. "The moral laws of nature and of nations,"
Shakespeare says, in one of his noblest lines. And so
Hooker: "Nature itself teacheth laws and statutes
to live by [which] do bind men absolutely, even as
they are men, although they have never any settled
fellowship, never any solemn agreement amongst
themselves what to do or not to do." "The law of a
commonwealth [is] the very soul of a politic body,
the parts whereof are by law animated, held together
and set on work in such actions as the common good
requireth." [1] But a law implies a sanction. That is a
necessary part of it, distinguishing it from a mere

---

[1] *Ecclesiastical Polity*, book i., § x.

counsel. What are the sanctions of "laws politic ordained for external order and regiment amongst men?" Or, to put it more shortly, What are the sanctions of the State? That is our topic in this chapter.

To answer that question, let us pass from the master just cited to a greater. The first sanction of the State is in the individual conscience. We should obey "for conscience' sake," as St. Paul teaches. And so Aquinas, amplifying this thought in words cited in the Third Chapter: "If laws are just, they gave a binding force in the court of conscience in virtue of the Eternal Law from which they are derived": and in which, as he elsewhere observes, the rational creature participates. But if, as must too frequently happen, the human race being what it is, a man through defect of will or nature, will not obey for conscience' sake, there is another argument to enforce his obedience: the argument from "wrath"—to quote St. Paul again. Let us hear Aristotle unfold it:

.

If mere reasons were sufficient to make men well-behaved, then, as Theognis says, "Many and great would their rewards have justly been." . . . But these seem to have no power to dispose the bulk of mankind to goodness. For it is not the nature of the bulk of mankind to obey from a sense of shame, but from fear; nor do they abstain from evil because it is wrong, but because of punishment. . . . The bulk of mankind live by feeling; they pursue the

pleasures they like, and the means thereunto, and shun the
contrary pains ; but they have no thought of, as they have
no taste for, what is right, and truly sweet. . . . The
man who lives by passion will not listen to the voice of
reason, nor can he understand it. And when this is a man's
state, how can any arguments effect a change in him ? It
would seem, indeed, as if passion were deaf to argument,
and yielded to force only. . . . Law has a coercive
sanction, although it is the reasoned conclusion of abstract
wisdom and intelligence.' [1]

"Laws politic, ordained for external order and
regiment amongst men," possess, then, a penal as
well as an ethical sanction. And—significant com-
mentary upon human nature—it is this penal sanction
which is almost always meant when the sanction of a
law is spoken of. There cannot be a "*societas sine
imperio.*" The civil magistrate, who is clothed with
the State's authority, beareth the sword, and beareth
it not in vain. He is "a revenger, to execute wrath
against him that doeth evil."

Such is the penal sanction of the State. The end
of the State, as we have seen, is to maintain its rights
and the rights of its subjects. Its courts of justice
attend continually upon this very thing. Rights
may be enforced there by actions arising from contract or quasi-contract; from delict or quasi-delict.
And certain gross infringements of right, violating
the public order, and branded as crimes, may there
be visited with punishment. Let us proceed to con-

---

[1] *Nicomachean Ethics*, x., 9.

sider this penal sanction of the State.   We will first
inquire what is the true conception of crime, and
next, what is the true rationale of punishment.

The conception of a crime universally prevailing
until quite lately, was—to quote the words of Kant
—"an act threatened by the law with punishment:"
of a criminal, one who wilfully commits such act,
and who, therefore, rightly incurs the punishment.
The primordial principle upon which the penal
legislation of the civilised world has hitherto rested
is that crime has its root in volition; that a man can
be held criminally responsible for a nefarious deed
only when he is at liberty to do or to abstain from
it.   Thus the German Penal Code (art. 51): "No
act is punishable when its author, at the time of its
perpetration, did not know what he was doing, or
was in a mental state which excluded the *free
exercise of his will*."   Similarly the Hungarian Penal
Code (art. 76): "An act is not imputable to one
who commits it in a state of unconsciousness, or
whose intellectual faculties were so disturbed that he
had no longer his *free will*."   To the like effect the
Italian Penal Code (art. 46): "No man may be
punished save for a *voluntary* action or omission."
That is the doctrine, too,—not to multiply quotations
—of the criminal law of England, France, and
Austria, and, we may say, of the whole world.   But
a school has arisen which insists that this first

principle of penal legislation, so universally accepted,
is wrong; which in the name of "science," offers us
an entirely new conception of crime, and proposes
an entirely new method of dealing with criminals.
It may not be a very numerous school, but it is a
very noisy one. And as shouting is certainly a
power in this age, its pretensions may be worth
examining.

We are told by this school that we are to study
crime scientifically; and, in fact, a new science, or
what purports to be such, has been invented for that
purpose, and christened " criminology," or " criminal
anthropology." Its votaries have expounded their
views in the numerous and diverse publications, of
which, perhaps, the most instructive are the Trans-
actions of the Congresses of Criminal Anthropology
held from time to time. First, then, what is criminal
anthropology? Professor van Hamel, a shining
light at these gatherings, defines it as the study of
the penal sciences by the Positivist method.[1] M.
Dimitri Drill tells us that " it makes a study of the
criminal himself in his very various types, the criminal real and concrete, as life, the court, and the
prison present him, analysing him according to *data*
purely scientific, and by the aid of exact methods of
all kinds which apply equally to the study of other
natural phenomena." [2] But what is crime in the

[1] *Actes du Troisième Congrès International d'Anthropologie Criminelle*, p. 339.
[2] *Ibid.*, p. 39.

17

new science? " It is impossible at this time of day,"
M. Danville insists, " to found the notion of crime
upon the hypothesis of responsibility, if one admits
that this hypothesis presupposes free will; for, besides that such a conception starts from a point of
view which is rather that of metaphysics, and unfit,
therefore, for any attempt at practical application
really scientific, such as is necessary in this matter, it
offers numerous and evident contradictions with the
observation of facts, which seems to exhibit to us, in
the place of this vague, ill-defined liberty, a rigorous
determinism more conformable with the general laws
of science." [1] M. Danville does but express in the
sentence, which thus drags its slow length along, the
views of the whole sect of criminal anthropologists,
who, however divided else, agree that crime is merely
the result of social and biological factors.

The new science, then, is frankly determinist, and
treats with small respect what its exponents term the
soi-disant sens moral.[2] Its founder, Signor Lombroso,
is, indeed, something more than a determinist. His
doctrine is that a criminal belongs to a special type
of humanity, and is absolutely and inevitably predestined to crime from the moment of his birth;
that the true account of the murderer, or the burglar,
as of the poet, is *nascitur non fit.* This dogma,
however, appears to be now out of fashion. *Il*

[1] *Actes du Troisième Congrès International d'Anthropologie Criminelle*, p. 303.
[2] *Ibid.*, p. 34.

semble que le type criminel de Lombroso ait vécu,
said one of the orators at the Brussels Congress.[1]
But it is an article of faith among criminal anthropologists that we must regard the delinquent as de-
humanised (*déshumanisé*), as abnormal, by which
they mean suffering from an anomaly unfitting him
for self-adaptation to social life[2]; that the common
idea, "no crime without moral responsibility," is incompatible with scientific facts.[3] Crime, indeed, in
the only sense the word has ever borne among men,
does not exist for the doctors of criminal anthropology: the malefactor is not really criminal at all.
He is to be regarded as a psycopath, a moral invalid,
the victim of a mind diseased, of an organisation
malformed, impoverished, or incomplete; of a temperament hallucinative or epileptic[4]; and of what
M. Drill calls "the peculiarities of external influences, whether of the climate and nature of his
country, or of his social environment."[5] And with
the notion of crime, the notion of punishment also
disappears. There are only two valid reasons, we
are told, why a psycopath, a moral invalid, an abnormal man, should be repressed: namely, for the protec-

[1] *Actes du Troisième Congrès International d'Anthroplogie Criminelle,* p. 278.
[2] *Ibid.,* p. 304.
[3] See *Abnormal Man,* by Arthur Macdonald, p. 45.
[4] According to some eminent criminal anthropologists, murderers,
burglars, and fraudulent persons are the victims of epilepsy, or of a
tendency to epilepsy.
[5] *Actes du Troisième Congrès International de Anthropologie Criminelle,* p. 40.

tion of society against those tendencies of his which
are dangerous or disagreeable, and for the cure of
his defective adaptability to the social environment.

Such, in brief outline, are the theoretical positions
of the new science.   Let us now glance at its practical application, first to the study, and secondly, to
the treatment of those whom it is still the fashion to
call criminals.   By way of a specimen of a "scientific" diagnosis of a malefactor, take the following
contribution by an eminent specialist, Signor Guido
Rossi, to the *Archivio di Psichiatria, Scienze Penale
ed Anthropologia Criminale:*

S. C., 38 years of age, born in Turin, a typefounder by
trade ; condemned twice : the first time, ten-year sentence
for cruelty to father.   While in prison he attempted suicide
twice.   Being unable to work, he wrote his history upon a
vessel.   Always suffered sensations of heat in the head ; was
subject to vertigo ; had an alcoholic attack and epileptic
prison insanity—*follia carceraria epilettica*—during which he
broke the glass in the window, for having been punished ex-
cessively ; did not think in such moments of the possibility
of being punished again ; had a true morbid epileptical
hypochondria.   His physical examination gave : Pallid skin,
thin chestnut hair, abundant beard, thin moustache, blue iris ;
nose long, and crooked teeth ; median incisors hypertrophied
the lateral decayed ; slightly projecting ears, squint in left
eye, paralysis of the eyebrows.   Craniometry : anterior-
posterior diameter, 182 millimetres ; transverse, 151 ; anterior-
posterior curve, 340 ; transverse, 317 ; total circumference,
540 ; cephalic index, 83 ; cranial capacity, 1530 ; a depression
at the union of the frontal and parietal, not evident whether
it is due to a wound or not ; lacks the ethnic type ; a scar on
right hand, arising out of a dispute after gambling.   Sensibility : with Faradaic current, the right hand feels at 32,
the left at 35 ; touch gives 3 millimetres for left and 2 for

the right. Meteorological sensibility is moderate ; two or three days before bad weather he is restless. He is credulous ; was made to see a bottle of black wine under a white paper. . . . The dynamometer gave 46 for left hand, 53 for the right. Motility : gait, awkward ; speech, stammering ; writing, good ; knee-jerk exaggerated ; had a simian agility since infancy. He walks often without consciousness of where he goes ; this is one form of propulsive epilepsy ; at certain moments there comes to him a desire to destroy everything, and often he does it. He does not believe in any religion. He sleeps uneasily ; commenced to like wine at 10 ; was forgetful ; smoked ; liked gambling ; is fond of striking ; knows the criminal slang. His father was 44 at the birth of S. C. ; his mother 50 ; his father drank much, but supported the wife, and was never in jail. The mother played much at lottery ; his sister was mother of thirteen sons, all healthy, except one who died, disease unknown. He was studious in his four elementary classes ; said he never had difficulty in learning. He reads the *Cronaca dei Tribunali.* He does not like the present system of government ; would like the republican form.[1]

The most perfect example of the treatment of malefactors according to the new science, is supplied by the famous Elmira Reformatory in the State of New York. In that institution there are some fifteen hundred male inmates—the word "prisoner" is tabooed—not known to have been previously imprisoned for high crimes, and of various ages between sixteen and thirty. They are committed to the institution indeterminately—that is, for no fixed period, but until its authorities are satisfied that they are "morally, intellectually, and physically capable of earning a living," and then they are discharged.

[1] Quoted by Macdonald, *Abnormal Man,* p. 58.

The plan pursued for their reformation has been described as "a gigantic system of coddling." The notion of retributive justice has, of course, no place in it. The efforts of the authorities are directed towards the improvement of the physical health of the inmates by abundance of fresh air and exercise, by pleasant and easy employment, and by a copious—we might, indeed, say a luxurious—diet. The elevation of their minds is pursued by instruction in various branches of knowledge, such as "Drawing, Designing, German, English and American History, Business Law, Arithmetic, Physical Geography, Economics, Political Science."[1] It is sought to compass their moral elevation by an appeal to self-interest through the medium of Utilitarian ethics. Classes of what is called "Practical Morality" are held for the discussion of such questions as "Is Honesty the Best Policy?" "The Ethics of Politics," "The Abolition of Poverty": and the inmates are encouraged to deal with these and similar topics in essays, which are occasionally printed in the weekly journal published in the Reformatory. A paper written by one of them on a cold snowy day in January, 1888, compassionately described the wretched homes, almost visible from the walls of the establishment, where ill-fed and ill-clad children, and wives of unemployed or weary men were crouching in the cold, and contrasted their lot with that of

[1] Tallack, *Penological and Preventive Principles*, p. 99.

the convicts, adding: "Here, at this prison, 'tis the
dinner hour; up from the great dining-hall below
rises the fragrant odour of good food, and the hum
of animated voices, with rippling laughter inter-
spersed. The food is hot, and sufficient as to quantity;
the apartments are warmed with steam, and after the
short day is passed the electric light brightens things
for the long evening: long, but not dreary, for books
are abundant."[1] The Reformatory library is vaunted
as containing "the best contemporary publications,
among which they specify the novels of Alexandre
Dumas, Eugène Sue, Ouida, Bulwer, Jules Verne,
and others. There is also a liberal supply of newspapers and periodicals."[2]

The inmates of Elmira are classified in three
grades: "On entry each prisoner is placed in the
middle stage. If he does not earn a sufficient number
of good marks by his labour, conduct, and studies,
he is put down into the lowest grade. But if he
obtains a good rank in marks, he is promoted in six
months to the highest one. If he remains for six
months in this, he may be be liberated on parole for
half a year, but he can remove into another State, or
out of reach, if he chooses to do so. If his conduct
during that period is clearly known to be unsatis-
factory, he is recalled to prison for the remainder of
his term, if he can be arrested; but if he has avoided
misbehaviour whilst on 'parole' he is absolutely re-

---

[1] Tallack, *Penological and Preventive Principles*, p. 99.   [2] *Ibid.*

leased from liability to undergo further detention."[1]
Before the prisoners are "parolled" it is in general
arranged, either by their own friends or by the cor-
respondents of the prison managers, that suitable
situations shall be secured for them. Mr. Z. R.
Brockway, the warden and governor of the institution,
states that "so-called indulgences are freely used
[there] for their value in promoting reformation."[2]
Asceticism appears to be discountenanced. Thus, at
p. 48 of the *Annual Report for* 1898, under the
head of "Practical Ethics," the convicts are exhorted :
"Let us not confuse the virtues and strength of
temperance with the vicious weakness of total
abstinence."[3]

Such is the new science as practically applied.
What are we to say of it? I would first observe
that its method of studying criminals, as exemplified
in the case so elaborately described by Signor Rossi,
would seem absolutely useless. What profiteth it
to know that S. C., or any other criminal, or number of criminals—assuming that their account of
themselves is true, which is a great assumption—
attempted to commit suicide, or had "alcoholic
attacks" and "epileptic prison insanity," that their
noses are long and crooked, and their median incisors
hypertrophied, that they do not believe in any re-

[1] Tallack. *Penological and Preventive Principles,* pp. 98–100.
[2] *Ibid.,* p. 101.
[3] *Ibid.,* p. 306.

ligion, and would like the republican form of government? Science means a knowledge of the causes of phenomena, and a reasoned exposition of those causes. What science can possibly underlie, or issue from, such a farrago of observations, even if multiplied to infinity? Equally unscientific appears the method pursued at Elmira. Sickly sentimentality seems a truer account of it. And, surely, judged by the standard of the criminal anthropologists themselves, it must be pronounced a ghastly failure. Its *modus operandi*, apparently, is this: to raise the standard of comfort in the minds of convicts, and to convince them that it will be more advantageous for them not to break the law, or, at all events, not to be found out in breaking it, for the future; it seeks to persuade them—to adapt a phrase of Professor Huxley's—that in seeking the laws of comfort they will find the laws of conduct. How far it really succeeds in indoctrinating them with this view, and in leading them to act upon it, is by no means certain. Major Griffiths well remarks: "Trustworthy statistics are not forthcoming. The reports made on those who have been enlarged extend over rather a brief space of time. The supervision is apparently continued for only six months, which is scarcely sufficient to prove permanent radical cure."[1] But even supposing, as the admirers of the system contend, that 80 per cent. of the Elmira men become

[1] *Secrets of the Prison House*, vol. i., p. 12.

"reformed," who does not see that their reformation—what is called reformation [1]—is achieved at
the cost of a frightful injury to the community? The
first object of penal repression, according to the
criminal anthropologists themselves—on this they
seem pretty well agreed—is the protection of society.
Now, the bond of society is obedience to law. And
the law is operative through its penal sanction.
But the Elmira system renders void that sanction.
Punishment, in the proper sense, and that moral dis-
approbation of which punishment is the evidence,
have no place in it.

What—taking human nature as it actually is—
what must be the effect upon society at large of
such a spectacle as that which the convicts of Elmira
present? Is murder or burglary likely to be diminished by the vision of well-fed and well-clothed murderers and burglars, spending their brief period of
seclusion from the world in apartments warmed by
steam, brightened by the electric light, and resound-
ing with "the hum of animated voices" and "rippling
laughter," their days an unbroken round of

> "Moderate tasks and moderate leisure,
> Quiet living, strict-kept measure,

(but not too "strict kept"), which Matthew Arnold
has commended as "The Second Best"—amusement
and instruction going hand in hand? Is this just—

[1] Improperly, as I shall show later on.

even as Utilitarian morality accounts of justice
—towards the millions of poor who are taxed for it?
Poor who by arduous effort just manage to keep
themselves out of the police-court, scantily fed,
thinly clothed, filthily lodged, and assuredly unable
to beguile their too often enforced idleness, and the
cold and hunger which accompany it, by "the novels
of Alexandre Dumas, Eugène Sue, Ouida, Bulwer,
Jules Verne, and others," and "a liberal supply
of newspapers and periodicals"? Surely Major
Griffiths is well warranted when he observes that
" the Elmira system, if generally adopted, might be
followed by unexpected consequences. Much less
favoured but more honest persons might be induced
to take up crime as a profitable career, the avenue to
a comfortable future, with well-stored mind and the
means of acquiring a competence."[1] A significant
comment upon these observations is supplied by the
fact that in ten years the population of the Elmira
Reformatory nearly trebled.

This fact may suffice to show how the dangerous
classes have received the gospel preached unto them
by the new school of criminal anthropologists—a
school chiefly of account, perhaps, as a sign of the
times in which we live. It is, in truth, a manifestation of that tendency (of which I spoke in the first
chapter) so observable everywhere and in every
department of human thought and action, to bring

[1] *The Secrets of the Prison House*, vol. i., p.14.

everything within the boundaries of physical science
—the only science, we are told: to subject everything to the laws of matter. One of the most
favourite accusations hurled by differing criminal
anthropologists at one another in their congresses is,
"You are talking metaphysics." It seemed to be
assumed as certain, whatever else might be doubtful,
that metaphysics has no right to exist. For my
own part, I must take leave to hold that the whole
subject of crime, scientifically considered, falls under
the domain of moral philosophy, and that moral
philosophy is based upon metaphysics, and can have
no other basis. Moral philosophy treats *de actibus
humanis*, of acts properly called *human;* that is,
acts which are voluntary as proceeding from a man's
will, with a knowledge of the end to which they
tend, and free as so proceeding that under the same
antecedent conditions they might or might not have
proceeded. And the criterion whereby it judges of
such acts is their conformity with, or opposition to,
man's rational nature. Those which conform with
that nature are morally good; those which oppose
it are morally bad. It is man's princely and perilous
prerogative, as "man and master of his fate," to
choose between them. For that choice he is morally
responsible. We praise or blame him—and the oracle
within his own breast confirms the exterior judgment—according as his choice is rightly or wrongly
made. Of such praise and blame an ethical element

is the essence. This is the common teaching of the great masters of morals in all ages. [1]

So much must suffice to indicate what appears to me the only real foundation of moral science. The doctrine of Kant as to the identity of liberty and morality seems profoundly true. It is sometimes said that the doctrine of free will is of small practical consequence. And so Mr. Sidgwick observes that it has little or no bearing on systematic ethics. [2] But, surely, systematic ethics must deal with the grounds of moral obligation; it must rest on the philosophy of morals. A simple string of precepts, a mere manual of rules, cannot claim to be systematic ethics. And is not the question whether or no a man can comply with these precepts or rules, in the highest degree practical? I am altogether aware, and cheerfully concede, that many who hold a rigid Determinism are blameless, nay, beautiful in their lives. But for myself, I must agree with Fichte's well-known observation: "If any one adopting the dogma of necessity should remain virtuous, we must seek the cause of his goodness elsewhere than in the innocuousness of his doctrine: upon the supposition of free will alone can duty, virtue, and morality have any existence."

To pursue this subject at length would be

---

[1] Aristotle has summed it up in a pregnant sentence : Πάντας ἐπαινοῦμεν καὶ ψέγομεν εἰς τὴν προαίρεσιν βλέποντες μᾶλλον ἢ εἰς τὰ ἔργα (Eth. Eud., ii., 11).

[2] Methods of Ethics, bk. i., c. v., §§ 4 and 5.

impossible here. I may, however, be permitted, before
I pass on, to make two observations concerning it.
And first I would remark how much the controversy is darkened by the habit of many who deal
with it to use words without knowledge. No doubt
this comes from want of metaphysical training in
many cases, but not in all. Such an excuse, whatever it is worth, may validly be urged for Mr. Herbert Spencer. But it can hardly be pleaded for Dr.
Bain. And when we find that learned man describing free will as " a power that comes from nothing,
has no beginning, follows no rule, respects no known
time or occasion, operates without impartiality,"[1] it
is difficult to acquit him of consciously caricaturing
a doctrine which he dislikes. What we mean by

---

[1] *The Emotions and the Will*, p. 500, 3rd edition. M. van Hamel,
represented, I dare say rightly, as a "savant of the first order,"
sought, at the Brussels Congress of Criminal Anthropologists, to
demolish liberty of volition by the following argument : "If you are
in a restaurant, and choose between two *plats*, it is not your free
will, but your stomach which speaks" (*Actes*, etc., p. 272). The
argument seems to me most unfortunate for M. van Hamel's purpose. No doubt in a mere animal the stomach would ordinarily
decide whether he should or should not devour food that came in his
way. I say "ordinarily," for a well-trained dog, in which, we may
observe what Aristotle calls μιμήματα τῆς ἀνθρωπίνης ζωῆς, would
often be influenced by the recollection that his master had forbidden
him to eat this or that. But when a man orders dinner at a restaurant, other voices besides that of the stomach are wont to make themselves heard—the voice of his physician, for example, if he is
dyspeptic or gouty ; of his religion, if he practises one into which
dietary prescriptions enter ; of his purse, unless he is prepared to
dine regardless of expense. In making up his mind (as the significant phrase is) what *plats* he will select, he will choose between the
motives which thus speak to him ; and such choice is what we mean
by free will.

freedom of volition is the power of acting from a
motive intelligible to, and chosen by, a self-conscious
being, in virtue of the property of his will to be a
law unto itself, or, in the oft-quoted words of Kant,
"a faculty of choosing that which reason independently of natural inclination declares to be practically
necessary, or good." And in treating *de actibus
humanis* we distinguish between different kinds of
freedom. A deed may be free and therefore deliberate, we say *actu, habitu, virtute,* or *interpretative.*
We fully allow "that every man, during by far the
greater part of his life, is solicited by conflicting
attractions, and that, in the very large majority of
such instances, a certain definite or decisive inclination or impulse of the will spontaneously ensues[1];"
but it does not follow from this, as determinists
maintain, that the term "will" really signifies no
more than a certain amount of reflex action, accom-
panied by a certain degree of sensation.

My second observation is, that the objections
urged at the present day against freedom of volition
are no new discovery. They come before us decked
in the garb of modern science. But there is not one
of them, of any real weight, which was not met and
sufficiently answered by the Schoolmen centuries
ago. For example, Hume's doctrine on free will is
simply the translation into non-theological language

---

[1] *The Philosophy of Theism,* by William George Ward, vol. i., p.
246.

of the old error revived by Jansenius, that the power
of delectation—whether of vice or virtue—which is
stronger at the moment, draws the will by an
irresistible necessity, as by its own weight. "Among
conflicting motives the strongest must prevail."
But how are we to judge of the strength of the
various motives? What common measure is there
for determining it? There is none. Dr. Martineau
well observes : " If, as Bain admits, the only test of
greatest strength is the victory, we are simply
landed in the tautology that the prevailing motive
prevails." [1]

What is commonly accounted the most formidable
argument for determinism is derived from the doctrine of evolution now so generally accepted. I confess I do not understand why it is thus accounted.
The question whether, and in what sense, a consciousness of right has been evolved, seems to me to
present no special difficulties. Evolution of the organism is required, up to a certain degree, for the
senses to act. But we do not call the organism the
efficient cause either of sense or perception. Another
kind of material and social evolution may be indispensable for the exercise of the hitherto dormant
moral faculty. But how does it follow that such
evolution is the true *cause*, and not merely a *conditio
sine qua non ?* The truth is that these disputants
have not the least notion of the nature of intellect.

[1] *A Study of Religion*, vol. ii., p. 233.

Here we come to the real issue. The school of which I am speaking will have it that the intellect is nothing more than a bundle of associations; "the aggregate of feelings and ideas, active and nascent, which there exists,"[1] as Mr. Spencer puts it. And so Dr. Bain: "The collective 'I' or 'self' can be nothing different from the feelings, actions, and intelligence of the individual."[2] "*Can* be nothing different!" It is an admirable example of "affirmativeness in negation."

I venture, nevertheless, to maintain that it can be, and is, something very different. I maintain that the intellect is, in fact, a power of perception and judgment *sui generis;* that the unity of consciousness, the *Ichheit* of the Ego, the selfhood of the Me, is the original and ultimate fact of man's existence: and that the will is *egoagens.* I quite understand the disinclination of this school of philosophers to allow that man is anything more than a sequence of physical action and reaction; that there is in him an activity superior to matter. To admit that would be to lay the axe to the root of their most cherished speculations. But I demur when they appeal to us in the name of science. Must we not then build upon science? they ask. Yes, assuredly; but what science? Not the science of matter only, but a science which embraces the whole man; which observes and weighs everything about him;

---

[1] *Principles of Psychology,* § 219.   [2] *Mental Science,* p. 402.

which ignores and puts aside nothing. *Humani nihil a me alienum puto* is the true scientific principle. But the scientists shut the eyes of their understanding to those facts of human nature—a vast array—which will not square with their theories. And the inadequacy of their doctrine to life is its sufficient condemnation. Thus, to give an instance pertinent to the subject now specially before us, if the province of physics is to " become coextensive with knowledge, with feeling, with action," conterminous with all regions of human thought, if physical and mathematical laws are everywhere supreme, and men are mere automata, then the only power left in the world is brute force, and " unawares morality expires." But Professor Huxley will have it—to quote his words in controversy with me some years ago—that " the safety of morality lies neither in the adoption of this or that philosophical speculation, or this or that theological creed, but in a real and living belief in that fixed order of nature which sends social disorganisation upon the track of immorality as surely as it sends physical disease after physical trespasses." [1] I will take leave to cite a portion of what I said in reply, because it has not been answered, and I venture to think it unanswerable :

Physical science, as such, can do nothing, good or bad, about morality : *il n'y a rien de sale ni d'impudique pour la*

[1] See my work *On Right and Wrong*, p. 241 (3rd edition).

science, writes Diderot in the *Rêve d'Alembert,* correctly enough. . . . The morality of an act, we must surely all admit, is not a physical quality ; it resides in the motive, and, again, in the nature of the act : whether, namely, the latter is conformable to a standard of perfection which the mind alone apprehends. The outward effects of two actions may be precisely similar, as when an assassin slays his victim and an executioner hangs a convicted criminal. But one of these acts will be foul murder ; the other a righteous ministration of retributive justice. Will Professor Huxley point out any science which is not a part of philosophy or theology and is yet competent to discriminate between the two ? What can " science " affirm about them unless it becomes philosophy or theology ? Nothing whatever. Physical science perceives only what the senses grasp, and the senses know nothing of justice and injustice. Is it by physics that we know when social disorganisation is the consequence of immorality ? I trow not. To physics the deeds of a Wellington and of a Genghiz Khan are " molecular changes," and no more. Physical science may predict that, if certain physical actions take place, certain physical structures will be injured or broken up. But it can never tell what is the moral quality of those physical actions. Physical science may, indeed, mark the difference which in time becomes outward and visible between those who cultivate morality and those who trample it under foot. But there its competency stops ; its powers of interpretation are exhausted. What lies at the root of the difference it can never tell. It has no means of discerning virtue and vice, which are of the will and of the intellect. And when it proceeds, unscientifically, to formulate its ignorance into a creed, it is doing its best not to subserve morality, but to ruin it.[1]

It appears to me, then, that the world will have to adhere to the old paths in ethics, since the new ones so manifestly lead nowhither—a sufficient *reductio ad absurdum.* The universe is rational, not

[1] *On Right and Wrong,* pp. 243–264.

irrational; reason is at the heart of things. And if the school of physical philosophers will not agree with us in this, we may at all events fairly ask them to refrain from using our ethical terminology, which, in their system, is absolutely unmeaning. They may tell a man of whose doings they disapprove that he is foolish, ill-advised, short-sighted; that he is preferring lower pleasures to higher; that his conduct would be viewed by Mr. Spencer as "imperfectly evolved," and not adjusted to achieve "totality of life in self, in offspring, and in fellow-men." They cannot tell him that he is *wrong*, for right and wrong, in the old and only intelligible sense, do not enter into their doctrine. The distinction between pleasure (*bonum delectabile*) and virtue (*bonum honestum*) does not exist for them. They recognise only one kind of goodness, the test of which is a balance, on the whole, of agreeable feelings over disagreeable. And when they proclaim that "the welfare of society in general must be put in the foreground," they have no answer to give to the question, Why must it? The sufficient reply to their exhortations is that no principle causally determining a man's welfare can be cited which should lead him to sacrifice himself to the social organism; that no man can be more highly evolved than he actually is evolved, according to Mr. Spencer's own showing; that the quality of pleasure is a matter of taste; that the true folly is to postpone the certainty of a

present and pungent gratification to the possibility
of a future and feeble one.   To which may be added
that since we all follow necessarily the impulses of
our organism, it is useless to admonish any man to
do or to abstain from doing any act.   Nor, according
to Mr. Herbert Spencer, is this matter for regret.
Have we not his assurance that "freedom of the will
would be at variance with the beneficent necessity
displayed in the evolution of the correspondence
between the organism and the environment"?[1]

It is satisfactory to observe that these considerations were, to some extent, urged upon the criminal
anthropologists assembled at their Brussels Congress, and received a certain amount of recognition.
M. Meyers, a magistrate of distinction, descended
among them and deemed it his duty to testify that
by denying free will they were ruining the fundamental principles of penal law and of repression.
He continued, in a passage which is well worth
quoting:

You do not admit free will, and yet you have just naïvely
told us that a man can do what he wishes.   What a contradiction!   You maintain that you do not know how to resist
the least of your tendencies; and, on the other hand, you
affirm, not only that you can modify yourselves, but that
you can modify others!   Please be logical.   If you are victims of your defective organisation, if you are urged towards
crime, be victims to the end, and don't say that you can
change that fatal tendency by something which is not volition, which is not free will—for you don't admit that—but

---

[1] *Principles of Psychology*, § 220.

which still exists within you, in spite of all your denials.   In your system there is no justification for repression : for why should the tendency of the murderer, which is to kill, yield to the tendency of the rest, which is to protect life ?   Your theory of social defence is that of force ; for if you admit neither right, nor the moral law, I see nothing else except number and force, to justify repression.   But are you quite sure that the interest of the greater number is always on the side of repression ? [1]

M. Meyers' vigorous remarks seem to have made a certain impression upon his hearers.   One of the most accomplished and influential of them, M. Tarde, went so far as to express a doubt of their vocation.   He began his very significant speech by suggesting that the question, *Sommes-nous encore des anthropologistes criminels?* might possibly receive a negative answer.   Lombrosoism, with its fatalistic doctrine that the human machine is inevitably impelled to a predestined goal, that the will is " a negligible quantity," he pronounced to be dead. It was incompatible, he judged, with the application of any penal law whatever.   He thought it a grave misfortune that criminologists had had to seek for recruits chiefly among physicists, anthropologists, and *aliénistes* (I preserve the French word lest I should give offence by speaking of mad doctors)— persons who, however distinguished in their own way, were little prepared by the nature of their occupations to bend their minds to the social *data*

---

[1] *Actes du Troisième Congrès d'Anthropologie Criminelle*, p. 260.

of the penal problem. He expressed satisfaction that the new current of their studies was turning towards the jurists. And he insisted emphatically, *Il faut reconnaître les caractères de la volonté qui n' ont assurément rien d'inconciliable avec le déterminisme scientifique.*[1]

These are the words of truth and soberness. A scientific determinism is not in the least incompatible with a rational doctrine of free will. Determinism is the postulate of the physical and physiological sciences. Liberty of volition—a relative liberty, of course—is, as certainly, the postulate of the psychological and moral sciences. *Kein Mensch muss müssen*, said Lessing. "The will," writes Schiller, commenting upon the dictum, "is the distinctive feature of man, and reason itself is only its eternal rule. All nature acts rationally. Man's prerogative is only that he acts with consciousness and will. All other things must. Man is the being who wills."[2] This is what Coleridge has called "the sacred distinction between person and thing, which is the light and life of all law, human and divine." No doubt the power of volition varies indefinitely. No doubt there are malefactors in whom it is practically inoperative; and these are the proper subjects, not of punishment, but of seclusion from human society, as unable to exercise the distinctive faculty

[1] *Actes du Troisième Congrès d' Anthropologie Criminelle.* p. 336.
[2] "Ueber das Erhabene" (*Werke*, vol. xii., p. 245).

which qualifies them for taking part in it. No
doubt, too, the view of criminality taken by the
existing penal legislation of the civilised world—I
have indicated it in a previous page—is substantially
correct, although some of its authoritative expositions may be lacking in scientific precision. As
such must we account the dicta of not a few
distinguished English lawyers that the true test of
criminality is knowledge. This is not so. It is not
enough that the perpetrator of the noxious deed
should have known what he was doing, and should
have known, moreover, that it was wrong and
against the law. To make a man really culpable
there must be the *mens rea*, the criminous intention.
And by "intention" I mean, as the Schoolmen
define it, " the free tendency of the will toward some
end through some means." Our law, indeed, to
quote Lord Mansfield's well-known words, "judges
not only of the act itself, but also of the intention
with which it is done." Obviously, the law is right
in so judging. It cannot divine the workings of the
mind, or explore the penetralia of conscience, but it
presumes that a man intends the necessary, nay, even
the probable or natural consequences of his own
acts. The presumption is indeed rebuttable. It
may be rebutted by showing that the man's volition
was paralysed, that he could not help himself. The
plea is rightly regarded by the courts with extreme
suspicion. Some of our best criminal judges have

expressed their "alarm at the admission of irresponsible impulse as an excuse for crime." On one
occasion Mr. Justice Byles was trying a case of
theft, and counsel for the prisoner, in setting up the
defence of kleptomania—the word appears to have
just then come in — observed, "Your Lordship
knows of that particular disease." To which the
Judge replied, " Yes, and I have been sent here to
cure it." We have advanced since then in our
knowledge of maladies of the will. Kleptomania
and homicidal mania are as much facts as dipso-
mania and nymphomania.[1] They are facts which it
is peculiarly difficult to establish. And, unquestionably, the evidence of specialists, by which it is
usually sought to establish them, should be accepted
with great reserve. Whatever criminal anthropologists may achieve—and I am far from denying that
in this direction they may achieve much—cases will
probably always occur in which persons really irresponsible are punished as if they had been capable
of willing, and had willed, to do the prohibited act
laid to their charge. It is lamentable, but it is
inevitable. We judge not with all-seeing eyes,
but *ex humano die.* There is a " border-land of

---

[1] On this subject see a painfully interesting paper by Dr. Magne
in the *Actes du Troisième Congrès International d'Anthropologie
Criminelle*, p. 153. The latest of the world's Penal Codes—the Italian
—has the following very judicious section : " *47. Non e punibile colui
che nel momento in cui ha commesso il fatto, era in tale stato di
deficienza ò di morbosa alterazione di mente da togliergli la con-
scienza dei proprii atti ò la possibilità di operare altrimenti.*"

injustice" into which the wisest and most cautious cannot help straying from time to time.[1]

We must say, then, with the old Greeks, that only τὰ κατὰ προαίρεσιν ἀδικήματα, wrongful acts intentionally done, can be accounted crimes. Such is the right account of culpability. Let us go on to the next point, and inquire, What is the true *rationale* of punishment? The criminal law is unquestionably designed for the protection of society and the prevention of further crime. But is this the whole account of it? Is it only a regulation of police? That seems to me a very inadequate conception of it, perverting it in its theory, robbing it of its dignity in the life of men, and emptying it of its vivifying idea. The proper conception of punishment is that it is the correlative of culpability. The penalty which human law threatens for a specific act is either just or unjust. If just, it presupposes a moral obligation in respect of the act, as in the case of culpable homicide: "Thou shalt do no murder." If there is no such moral obligation, there is no culpability, and therefore the threatened punishment is unjust. So it was when the decree was made that all men who would not fall down and worship the golden image that Nebuchadnezzar

---

[1] But, perhaps, we need not stray into it quite so frequently as we do. The English Prison Commissioners in their Sixteenth Report, give a communication from their medical inspector, Dr. Grover, in which it is stated that in the year 1893 eighty-one persons were tried and sentenced while insane (p. 44).

the king had set up, should be cast into the midst of
a burning fiery furnace. Justice—let me again insist upon this: such insistence is not superfluous—is
of the very essence of human law:

> "there 's on earth a yet auguster thing,
> Veil'd though it be, than parliament and king."

And that thing is Justice, from which all our enactments derive their binding force on conscience, so
far as they are binding. Legal justice is but one
aspect of what metaphysicians call general justice,
which is, as Ulpian defines it, "the constant and
perpetual will to render to every one his due."
Now, crime is the forcible negation of right, the
violent disturbance of the rational order of society.
And punishment—"the other half of crime," Hegel
calls it—is something due to the reasonable part of
the criminal. By his criminous act the criminal has
subjected himself to it. *Ipse te pœnæ subdidisti*, the
maxim of Roman jurisprudence says. It is his right
to reap what he has sown. There is in our nature a
deep-rooted instinct which testifies to the connection
between punishment and crime. It is finely remarked by Dr. Martineau: "The conscience of mankind refuses to believe in the ultimate impunity of
guilt, and looks upon the flying criminal as only
taking a circuit to his doom."[1] There is a human
debt of crime as well as a divine debt; retribution

[1] *A Study of Religion*, vol. ii., p. 46.

is due for the breach of the social order; the community is rightly avenged upon the disturber of the public peace. The International Prison Congress, held in London in 1872, very properly insisted, in one of their resolutions, "the prisoner must be taught that he has sinned against society, and owes reparation."

It is well to insist on this verity in an age like the present, which shrinks from the sterner realities of existence, and delights in "mealy-mouthed philanthropies." One of the primary instincts of human nature is the desire for retribution. Nor is it confined to man. We find it, like the instinct of self-defence, throughout the whole realm of animate existence. *Dem Schwachen ist sein Stachel auch gegeben.* There can be no question that these instincts are at the root of criminal law. As a matter of historical fact, we discern, as human society is evolved, three stages in the evolution of the idea of punishment. First, the right of vengeance is restricted to the injured person or to his next of kin (*ultio proximi*). Then comes the notion of pecuniary compensation (*Wehrgeld*). And lastly, the idea of public punishment is developed, and public authority is recognised as the proper and the sole "avenger to execute wrath upon him that doeth evil." But from the beginning it was discerned that this retribution was righteous; that it was in conformity with the divine law which primitive humanity believed to be

in man, and around man, and above man. Nor was
this simple faith at fault. Neither the physical
world nor the moral gives any support to the notion
that unmixed "benevolence" is at the heart of
things. The Infinite and Eternal, in whom all ideals
are realised, is not only Truth, Purity, Love, but
Justice. He is *Deus Ultionum*—the God to whom
vengeance belongeth. Cardinal Newman has pointed
out, in a powerful passage of the *Grammar of
Assent*, that conscience primarily reveals Him under
this Attribute of Retributive Justice.[1] And it is as
the representative of the Supreme Moral Governor
of the universe that St. Paul contemplates the civil
ruler. "He is God's minister; he beareth not the
sword in vain." The cry, "Avenge me of mine
adversary," is the expression of a divinely implanted
instinct of humanity. Like all instincts, it has to be
brought under the control and discipline of reason.
And when so controlled and disciplined, it becomes
criminal justice.

Punishment, then, must be just; it must be
rightly proportioned to the offence, so that, as Kant

---

[1] "Conscience suggests to us many things about that Master, whom
by means of it we perceive, but its most prominent teaching, and its
cardinal and distinguishing truth, is that He is our Judge. In consequence, the special Attribute under which it brings Him before us,
to which it subordinates all other Attributes, is that of justice—
retributive justice. We learn from its information to conceive of the
Almighty, primarily, not as a God of Wisdom, of Knowledge, of
Power, of Benevolence, but as a God of Judgment and Justice; as
One, who, not simply for the good of the offender, but as an end
good in itself, and as a principle of government, ordains that the
offender should suffer for his offence" (p. 390, 5th ed.).

says, "the punished person, when he looks thereon, must himself confess that right is done to him, and that his lot is entirely commensurate with his conduct.[1] But what is the proper measure of penality? How graduate it to crime? The question is one of exceeding difficulty, and can be only approximately solved by us who know in part, who investigate not with "those pure eyes and perfect witness of all-judging Jove," but with the dim vision of the "purblind race of miserable men," trusting to testimony alike fallible and incomplete. The underlying principle of a just sentence is the *lex talionis*, in virtue of which his wrongful deed is returned on the offender.[2] The crude jurisprudence of primitive ages applied the principle literally: "an eye for an eye; a tooth for a tooth." In our deeper apprehension of the sacredness of human personality, we reject this severity as barbarous. *Misericordiam et judicium cantabo*, sang the Hebrew bard: "My song shall be of mercy and judgment." But the rest of his canticle hardly corresponds with this exordium. "Implacable, unmerciful," is St. Paul's account of the Gentiles to whom he was sent. And what scholar can deny its correctness? It was reserved for Him whose gospel St. Paul preached, Him by

---

[1] *Kritik der prak. Vernunft*, Part I., book i., § 8.

[2] M. Zakrewsky told the Criminal Anthropologists at their Brussels Conference: *En ce qui concerne la loi du talion je ferai observer que nous ne sommes pas ici pour réfuter Moïse* (*Actes*, p. 258). This savant apparently believes that the *lex talionis* is an invention of Moses.

whom, in the fulness of the time, grace and truth
came, to manifest the Divine Attribute of pity,
"unlimited in its self-sacrifice." "*Misericordiam et
judicium*": it is the explanation of the crucifix;
and the lesson has sunk slowly—how slowly!—into
the hearts and consciences of the nations that bear
the Christian name.   "*Moses lapidat ut judex;
Christus indulget ut rex*," says St. Augustine.

> "And earthly power doth then show likest God's,
>   When mercy seasons justice."

Again, who can say that circumstances are irrele-
vant in the judgment which right reason pronounces
on each misdeed? They may gravely aggravate,
they may largely extenuate, the offence.   One stands
aghast not less at the undoubting sincerity, the un-
hesitating good faith, with which our forefathers
assumed the full responsibility of every malefactor
for his noxious act, than at the inexorable and unintelligent severity with which they chastised him.
Thanks to the growth of a milder and more rational
spirit in penality, behind the delict we now see the
delinquent : still, in all his degradation and dishonour,
a *person*, with claims upon, and rights against society,
springing from the essential ground of human nature.

Still, however softened the application of the rule
of retaliation, by it and by it alone, are the true kind
and measure of punishment indicated.[1]   The canon

[1] One great blot upon the administration of English criminal law is
the absence of any uniform standard of punishment. I have myself
heard men sentenced by different judges to six months' imprisonment

of Rhadamanthus: "If a man has done to him what
he has done to others, that is the straight course of
justice," expresses a deep and universal instinct of
human nature; and instinct never deceives; there is
always a reality correspondent with it. Offences in-
volving cruelty, whether to men or animals, merit
the infliction of sharp bodily pain, the most obvious
and appropriate instrument of which is the lash.
Crimes merely against property, when the motive
has been to acquire ease or enjoyment by the violation of another's possessory right, properly subject
the wrong-doer to the deprivation of ease and enjoyment by the hard labour and scanty fare of prison
life. Again, there is one crime—the supreme crime
—for which nature herself exactly prescribes the
just chastisement. Only the punishment of death is
commensurate with the offence of wilful murder.
" Ye shall take no satisfaction," enjoined the Hebrew
legislator, " for the life of a murderer which is guilty
of death, but he shall be surely put to death, for the

and to six years' penal servitude for precisely the same offence, committed in circumstances which were practically identical ; by which
I mean that there was no element of extenuation in the one case,
and no element of aggravation in the other. I may note, too, with
what irrational severity offences against property are often punished,
and what equally irrational lenity is displayed by many judges in respect to offences against the person. I remember the case of an old
woman tried a few years ago at York before Lord Coleridge for stealing a piece of cloth. She had just undergone a sentence of ten
years' penal servitude for stealing a door-mat. The Lord Chief Justice sentenced her to three months' hard labour, remarking : " I do
not know what is to become of punishment. If people are to be sent
to ten years' servitude for stealing a door-mat, what is to become of
them for half-killing their wives ? "

land cannot be cleansed of the blood that is shed therein, but by the blood of him that shed it." The precept is true for all time, and for all stages of political evolution, not because it was laid down for the guidance of a small tribe of Western Semites, in the infancy of civilisation, but because it is founded on the nature of things,[1] and is in accordance with

---

[1] I am, of course, writing from the point of view of Libertarianism. But it is interesting to observe that Criminal Anthropologists, regarding man as an automatic organism, as a machine, with no more rights —in the proper sense of the word—than any other machine, arrive at the same conclusion. Baron Garofalo, a shining light of the school, expressly lays down that "murderers who act in the absence of grave injury on the part of their victims," must be regarded "as beings morally degenerated and perpetually unsociable"; that "the impossibility of adaptation of such individuals being recognised, it is necessary to eliminate them absolutely from society." "Nor," he argues, "if imprisonment for life were one means of elimination, should it be given the preference. For why should beings who no longer form part of a society be preserved for life? It is hard to understand why citizens, and even the families of the victims themselves, should be obliged to pay a tax in order to feed and clothe the perpetual enemy of society." I quote from the full and correct summary of Garofalo's teachings given by MacDonald, *Abnormal Man*, p. 90. It may be noted that in Italy, where the death penalty has been abolished, there are now between three and four thousand convicts undergoing sentences of life imprisonment for murder : sentences which are never commuted. Mr. Tallack, in his work on *Penological and Preventive Principles*, well points out that "death may be mercy itself compared with the prolonged injury inflicted upon the spiritual and mental powers, by means of the hopeless misery of the solitary cell, on the one hand, or by the corruptions of filthy and blaspheming convict gangs on the other. A process thus continued may ultimately be as *real* an execution, but by slow operation, as the more visible and instantaneous deprivation of life. . . . The Italians in their hatred for capital punishment, have substituted for it a worse penalty" (p. 238). This is perfectly true. A sentence of such life imprisonment is simply a more cruel and more cowardly mode of inflicting the death penalty. Hence, perhaps, the favour it has found with the baser kind of Italians, as pandering to their two characteristic vices.

19

the everlasting laws of human society and of eternal justice. *Homo res sacra homini.* And he who violates that sacrosanct bond of human fellowship by wilful murder, forfeits his right to human fellowship: he dooms himself, by his own act, to be cut off from the " kindly race of men," and to expiate, by his own life, the shedding of innocent blood.

The first function, then, of punishment, is to punish, to vindicate the majesty of outraged justice, to dissolve that *vinculum juris* to which crime gives rise, by meting out to the transgressor his due. Its second function is to deter the offender from repeating his offence, and others from imitating it. This is so generally admitted that I need but touch upon it here. I may, however, remark that corporal pain is not only the appropriate penalty for deeds of violence, but the best deterrent from them. The most unscrupulous in inflicting it are, usually, the most cowardly in shrinking from it.[1] To which I would add that the objections commonly urged to the penalty of whipping, that it is disgraceful and that it brutalises, are, to speak plainly, mere sentimental claptrap. Sir Henry Maine, in one of his best speeches, has briefly indicated the true answer to them. With regard to the first he admirably observes: " The difficulty is that ordinary punishments are not felt by criminals to be disgraceful, and if

---

[1] Such was my experience in India. While exercising the powers of a District Magistrate in that country I passed some fifty or sixty sentences of flogging, almost all of which I saw executed.

therefore a punishment can be discovered which
raises under all circumstances the sense of shame,
that punishment will have a value of its own." His
reply to the second is just as conclusive : " What is
intended when it is said that whipping brutalises ?
Is it that it appeals to the offender's animal nature
as distinguished from his moral nature ? Why, every
punishment deserving the name inflicts physical
pain. . . . When you sentence a criminal to punishment you deliberately make up your mind to render
him extremely uncomfortable ; and for my part, I cannot in the least understand why one form or degree
of physical pain should brutalise more than another."[1]

But the chastisement of criminals is also intended
to act as a warning to others. Aristotle's words,
"The bulk of mankind obey from fear, nor do they
abstain from evil because it is wrong, but because of
punishment," are, I suppose, as true of our times as
of his. Hence the example of the punished person
is of general utility ; nor is it any real hardship to
him that it should be so. No man liveth to himself. We are members one of another, knit together
by a necessity arising out of the nature of things,
which is rational, in the social organism whose law
is reason. And a man who will not obey that law,
but abandons himself to mere animal impulse, divests
himself, so far as in him lies, of · his dignity as a

[1] *Life and Speeches of Sir Henry Maine*, p. 122. I translate my
quotations out of the *obliqua oratio* in which this speech is unfortunately reported.

person: he approximates to the level of irrational existence: he is made like unto horse and mule which have no understanding, and may be used like them, not as an end to himself, but as an instrument for benefiting others. It is on this consideration that Aquinas founds his justification of capital punishment. "Man by wrong-doing withdraws from the order of reason, and thereby falls from human dignity, so far as that consists in man being naturally free and existent for his own sake. . . . And there-fore, though to kill a man while he abides in his native dignity be a thing of itself evil, yet to kill a man who is a wrong-doer, may be as good as to kill a wild beast. For worse is an evil man than a wild beast, and more noxious as the Philosopher says."[1] I may add that the death penalty is the supreme terror of men of blood. "I don't care what I get, so long as I don't swing," was the expression of one of them, tried not long ago for the capital offence, and, unfortunately, found guilty only of manslaughter. The sentiment is common to the class.

But there is a third end of punishment. It is, first, vindictive, and, secondly, deterrent. It should also be, if possible, reformatory. To deter a criminal from further crime is not, necessarily, to reform him. Reformation means a great deal more than deterrence. It means deterrence *from a moral motive.* It means the conversion of the will from

[1] *Summa Theologica*, 2, 2, q. 64, a. 2 ad. 3.

bad to good. And so the admirable inscription, which greatly impressed John Howard, placed by Clement XI. over the gate of St. Michele, the first of the model prisons and the pattern of the rest: *Parum est improbos coercere pœna nisi probos efficias disciplina.* We are told that we may reasonably expect punishment to prick the conscience, to bring crime before the criminal's mental vision in true colours and right proportions, to lead him to desire his own spiritual and moral amendment, and to work with those who are striving to change him from a bad man to a good. Is it reasonable to expect this from punishment?

It seems eminently reasonable to expect it from the supreme punishment—the punishment of death. Green well observes: " The just punishment of crime is for the moral good of the criminal himself . . . even if a true social necessity requires that he be punished with death. The fact that society is obliged so to deal with him, affords the best chances of bringing home to him the anti-social nature of his act." [1] Experience amply proves that the most hopeful means of working the reformation of a murderer—by reformation, let me remind my readers, I mean the conversion of his will from bad to good—is supplied by the certainty of his impending execution. However seared his conscience, however atrophied his moral sense, however blurred his

[1] *Works,* vol. i., p. 510.

vision of judgment to come, this certainty often quickens him into new spiritual life, and works, as Schopenhauer expresses it, "a great and rapid change in his inmost being." "When [condemned criminals] have entirely lost hope," this keen observer of human nature adds, "they show actual goodness and purity of disposition, true abhorrence of committing any deed in the least degree bad or unkind; they forgive their enemies, . . . and die gladly, peaceably and happily. To them, in the extremity of their anguish, the last secret of life has revealed itself."[1] They obtain "a purification through suffering."

What has just been said of the efficacy of capital punishment as a reformatory instrument, applies in some, though a much less degree, to the punishment of flogging. The lash is eminently fitted to bring home—say—to the garroter the anti-social nature of garroting. The experience of physical pain by those who have barbarously inflicted it, whether on men or animals, for the gratification of lawless passions, affords the best chance of enabling them to realise the hideousness of cruelty, and of awaking them to new spiritual life. Concerning imprisonment as a reformatory agency, we must speak much less hopefully. If we weigh the matter well, a gaol is ill adapted for the purposes of an ethical seminary. To borrow words from a recent most powerful and

_____
[1] *Die Welt als Wille, etc.*, vol. i., bk. 4, p. 465.

pathetic novel, prison life with its manifold degradation, eating into a man's flesh, becoming infused
into his blood, and running for ever through his
veins,[1] seems fitted rather to quench all sense of
personality, and so to destroy the very foundation
upon which character must be built up.   The
thought of the venerable Pontiff, cited just now,
which fired the zeal of John Howard, is, in itself,
beautiful and true.   The practical application, or
rather perversion, of it in our own day, by sentimental faddists, is neither beautiful nor true.   Their
spurious humanitarianism, ignoring the true idea of
crime, the true *rationale* of punishment, amply merits
the scorn poured upon it by Carlyle in the *Latter
Day Pamphlets*, and by Dickens in *David Copper-
field*.   A very different authority, Sir Henry Maine,
has well observed: "The theory that all punishment
should be directed towards the reformation of the
criminal has been thoroughly tested. . . . What is
the result? Twenty or thirty years of costly ex-
periments have simply brought out the fact that, by
looking too exclusively to the reformatory side of
punishment, you have not only not reformed your
criminals, but have actually increased the criminal
class."[2]   I believe I am warranted in saying that
eighty per cent. of those who have been in prison
commit crime again.

   This is certainly a gigantic failure. One reason

<hr />

[1] *Derelicts*, by William J. Locke.   [2] *Life and Speeches*, p. 123.

of it is excellently indicated in certain words of the late Archbishop Ullathorne, himself most successful in dealing with the worst criminals: "Many advocates of political and social reform are admirable in inventing expedients for regenerating human nature, if it were not that the nature to be regenerated is missed out of the calculation."[1] One of the common errors of the present day is to take an optimist view of humanity, flatly opposed to facts. It is the delusion to which the *philosophes* of the last century gave such wide currency, and which their principal English admirer and exponent has succinctly formulated, and blessed as a "cheerful doctrine": that "human nature is good": that "the evil in the world is the result of bad education and bad institutions."[2] I certainly do not incline to underrate the mischievous effects of "bad education and bad institutions." But assuredly it is a gross delusion to attribute to them exclusively, or even principally, the evil of the world. No; the ultimate source of the evil of the world is far deeper than defective social mechanism. If anything is absolutely certain it is that there is innate in every human being a propensity which renders him prone to evil and averse from good. *Nitimur in vetitum semper cupimusque negata*, said the Roman poet. It is invariably true. You may get rid of the name of original

---

[1] *The Management of Criminals*, p. 24.
[2] Morley, *Diderot*, vol. i., p. 5.

sin; but the thing which the name represents is a primordial permanent ingredient of human nature, explain it how you will. It is aboriginal, not adventitious; congenital, not the product of bad education and bad institutions. It is more in one, and less in another. But, in whatever proportion, it is always there, a taint transmitted by heredity. It is this taint which vitiates the will, and that vitiation breeds evil deeds. To hinder a man from such deeds by fear of consequences—let me once more insist upon this—is not to reform him. Every real reform must rest upon the cure of the vitiated volition. It must be moral, not mechanical; psychical, not physical; it must start from within, not from without. Its motive power must be something which acts directly and powerfully upon the will. Where shall we find such an agent?

In good education, we are often told. But education is a question-begging word. If mere intellectual instruction is meant by it—as is generally the case—experience is conclusive that such instruction is not in itself moralising. Mere knowledge does not convert the will from bad to good. How should it? Lombroso, in his *L'Uomo Delinquente*, testifies that the number of malefactors is greatest, relatively, in the liberal professions. An English expert, who speaks on the subject with an authority possessed by few, tells us that "some of the worst thieves are those who have previously had a training in Board

Schools, and that the most depraved girls and women
are amongst the more educated ones."[1] No; mere
knowledge is one thing. Virtue is quite another.
Experience confirms the assertion that, taking mankind as a whole, the effectual reform of human
nature can be achieved only by an agent above
nature. *Philosophia dux vitæ*, said the ancients.
But what is philosophy? It is a theory of being, of
speculative thought; its proper object to contemplate
the world as a manifestation of spirit. A mere system of speculative physics such as, for example, Mr.
Herbert Spencer's, however ingenious and interesting,
is not philosophy at all. It is a true observation of
Eduard von Hartmann: "Philosophy is essentially
concerned with the one feeling only to be mystically
apprehended, namely, the relation of the individual
with the Absolute." The very function of philosophy is to raise man above the self of the senses and
animal nature, and to approximate him to the Divine.
I am far from denying, indeed I strenuously maintain,
that in discharging that function, it may present a
clear perception of ethical truth. Nay, I firmly hold
that the human reason, rightly exercised, is adequate
to the deduction of moral rules which shall indicate
the limits of right action. But how many of us are
capable of laying hold of a system of abstract
thought and of translating it into deed? For the

---

[1] Mr. Neame, "a Chief Superintendent of discharged convicts in
London," quoted by Tallack, *Penological and Preventive Principles*,
p. 217.

vast multitude of men the only effective teacher of morality is religion, which affords it a sanction and reward, which incarnates it in august symbolism, and works upon volition by touching the heart. This is, and always must be, true of the over-whelming majority of mankind. It is pre-eminently true of the criminal classes with their domineering passions and debilitated wills. And here again I am glad to find myself in agreement with Sir Henry Maine. "The great agent of reformatory discipline in English gaols is the chaplain."[1] It was a saying of Dr. Colin Browning, a veritable apostle of the worst convicts, and that amid the enormous diffi-culties and discouragements of the old transporta-tion times, "We hear much of various systems of prison discipline, as the Separate, the Silent, and the Congregate systems; but unless the Christian system be brought to bear with divine power on the understanding and consciences of criminals, every other system, professedly contemplating their refor-mation, must prove an entire failure."[2]

Again. A great obstacle to the reformation of criminals arises from forgetting that there are two distinct kinds of offenders, requiring very different treatment. There are those whose past lives were blameless until they succumbed to strong temptation, and fell into crime; we may call them occasional

[1] *Life and Speeches*, p. 124.
[2] Quoted by Tallack, *Penological and Preventive Principles*, p. 285.

offenders. There are habitual offenders, whose lives are a perpetual warfare against society. Of course, with regard to certain of the gravest crimes, such as murder or rape, it is hardly possible to discriminate between delinquents of these very different categories. But in cases of less serious offences, whether against the person or against property, we may and should discriminate. In such cases, the punishment of a first transgression should be short and sharp; and that for two reasons. Experience shows that a brief term of imprisonment often induces reflection, remorse, and resolution to amend— resolutions which, in fact, are not unfrequently carried out; whereas a long one almost always hardens the novice in crime, who, moreover, when it has expired, finds his home broken up and his friends forgetful of him—serious obstacles to his return to the path of rectitude. A third conviction at the assizes, or a quarter sessions, should stamp a man as a habitual criminal, who, for the rest of his life, should forfeit his personal liberty, and should be reduced to a state of industrial serfdom. Nor would there be any real hardship in this. On the contrary, it would be a positive benefit to habitual offenders. If they reform at all, they reform while under penal restraint. When left to themselves, they, almost invariably, fall away. One of the Reports of the Prison Commissioners quotes the testimony of a very experienced Protestant chaplain: "The majority of habitual criminals make excellent prisoners; it is only when restored to their liberty that they fail." It would be a little short of a miracle if they did not. In spite of philanthropists, the difficulties in the way of their finding honest employment are, naturally enough, immense. On the other hand, the temptation to relapse, from force of old habit, and from the influence of former associates, is such as might well overmaster a stronger power of volition than that which they can, as a rule, oppose to it. I remember when visiting, some years ago, the great prison at Dartmoor, how much I was impressed by what the excellent Catholic chaplain there—now dead—told me of his painful experience in this matter. He observed: "It is a happiness to me when any of these poor fellows die here; they make a good end; if they went back to the world, they would, almost for certain, live badly and die badly." I add that the perpetual seclusion of habitual offenders is justly due to the community. It has been remarked, "We pay immense sums for a police to watch men and women perfectly well known to be criminals, lying in wait to rob and murder, and other immense sums to catch and try, *over and over again*, these criminals, who are shut up for short terms, well cared for, physically rehabilitated, and then sent out to continue their prowling warfare against society."[1]

[1] Mr. C. Dudley Warner, a well-known American writer, quoted by Tallack, *Penological and Preventive Principles*, p. 104.

So much as to the true principles of penality.
But there is still something to be said regarding the
criminal. We cannot consider him as an isolated
being apart from the society in which he struggled,
and sinned, and suffered. Its responsibility for
crime is as grave a question as his. I do not know
who has more powerfully stated the question than
Victor Hugo in *Claude Gueux*—that wonderful book
which came as a revelation to the heart and conscience
of the civilised world. Claude Gueux is a poor
artisan in Paris; naturally intelligent, dexterous at
his work, quite uneducated. He lives with a girl to
whom he is not married, and has a child by her.
One winter he finds himself out of work. There is
no fire in the grate of his poor lodging, no food on
the table. The man steals. His theft results in
three days' nourishment and warmth for the woman
and her baby, and in five years' imprisonment for
himself. He is sent to the central prison of Clair-
vaux. There, the stupid tyranny of an official drives
him to desperation, and he kills his tormentor. In
due time he is brought to trial for the murder before
the assizes at Troyes. When sending the jury into
their room to consider their verdict, the presiding
judge asks him if he has anything to say. He
replies, "Very little. Only this: I am a thief and
an assassin; I have stolen and killed; but *why* have
I stolen? *why* have I killed?" I take the case as
Victor Hugo states it. And so taking it, can society

be acquitted? "A fair day's wage for a fair day's work is as just a demand as governed men ever made of governing: it is the everlasting right of man," said Carlyle, in words quoted in a previous chapter, and worth quoting a second time. Again, a prison should be a purgatory. Those who are confined in it are wronged if it be made a hell. Claude Gueux might well arraign society as accessory, by its injustice, to his crimes. In England, at all events, we may congratulate ourselves that our poor-laws, whatever may be justly said against them—and I know too well how much may be justly said—leave no one to starve; and that the grave defects in the management of our prisons are due rather to the congenital stupidity than to the intentional cruelty of officials.

But there is much more than this to be considered with regard to the responsibility of society for crime. That huge menacing fact of the criminal classes, as they are called, may well send us to an examination of conscience. To speak of London alone, "the number of the *residuum* of habitual offenders and vicious loafers," in that great city, is estimated, by a very careful and competent authority,[1] "at scores of thousands." What has caused this *residuum?* The answer must be, To a large extent, poverty. But what is the cause of poverty? No doubt, in many cases, vice, of which it is the

[1] Mr. Neame, quoted by Tallack, *Penological and Preventive Principles*, p. 216.

proper punishment; but, assuredly, in many more, injustice. The criminal classes are largely the outcome of English pauperism. Now, certain it is, as we saw in the Fourth Chapter, that the era of English pauperism began with the plunder, three centuries ago, of the religious houses which were, in the strictest sense, the patrimony of the poor, and of the thirty thousand religious guilds, which were the great institutions of thrift and mutual help. No less certain is it, that the giant growth of pauperism in these latter days is largely due to the iniquitous individualism which, under the specious formulas of "supply and demand," "freedom of contract," and "the course of trade," has withheld from the labourer, skilled and unskilled, his fair share of the fruits of his labour. The labourer has sunk into a pauper: the pauper into a vagrant, a loafer, a confirmed offender; and the class of habitual criminals has been formed as an element of modern society. The law of human progress is—

> "Move upward, working out the beast,
> And let the ape and tiger die."

But these unfortunates have retrogressed : they have moved downward, working out the man; and their faces have, more or less completely, lost the human expression : their lineaments irresistibly remind us of the wild animals to whose level they have well-nigh sunk—the wolf, the jackal, the panther, the hyena. And these degraded beings increase and multiply, giving the world a more vitiated progeny: children born with special pre-dispositions for crime.

What, then, are the remedies? They would seem to be chiefly three. First, what a distinguished Austrian jurist has called " the transformation of the existing order of rights (*Rechtsordnung*) in the interest of the suffering working classes"[1]—a transformation which is even now in progress, as every one that has eyes must surely see—will doubtless do much to diminish pauperism. Secondly, that addiction of adult habitual offenders to industrial servitude, which I have recommended in a previous page, is unquestionably the only effective way of dealing with them. Thirdly, the modification—nay, to a great extent, the eradication—of the terrible tendencies transmitted by them to their offspring, if possible. There is in human nature a principle of recovery, which, if rightly cultivated in childhood and youth, before habit has fatally developed the germs of evil, may largely transform the vitiated character transmitted by heredity. And the instrument of that cultivation is a system of ethical discipline, of training of the will—this alone is education in the true sense—which, as experience demonstrates, will, in many cases, make of these unhappy children men fitted for their appointed place in the

---

[1] *Das Recht auf den vollen Arbeitsertrag in geschichtlicher Darstellung*, von Anton Menger: *Vorrede*, p. 2.

social order: ready, patiently and profitably, to fulfil their allotted tasks in it.

The poor in this world's goods we have always with us. And we may say the same of the poor in virtue. But only in a society which has lost, or largely forgotten, " the mighty hopes that make us men," does poverty degenerate into pauperism, and vice grow rankly into crime. Without those hopes —our special heritage among the tribes of animate existence—to lift us above the self of the appetites and the passions, we do not rise to the true level of *human* life, whether individually or collectively. This is not, indeed, a first principle in politics. But it is a first principle underlying all politics. The known and natural do not suffice for human society. It requires supersensuous, superhuman, spiritual ideals : ideals which point to a life beyond the phenomenal, where justice shall at length triumph, where its rewards and penalties shall be adequately realised : ideals which therefore witness to a Supreme Moral Governor who shall bring about that triumph and realisation. This is the central thought, the direct teaching, of the parable of Dives and Lazarus. It declares, in terms, that beyond the grave, the relative conditions of rich and poor will be completely inverted : that in the life of the world to come, restitution shall be made to those who have been disinherited in this life. On that teaching the poor lived throughout those ages which, whatever

else they were or were not, most assuredly were
" Ages of Faith." St. Edmund of Canterbury, in
his *Mirror*, one of the most popular books in mediæval England, lays it down, with startling plainness,
that the rich can be saved only by the poor; for
the poor are they of whom it is said, "Theirs is the
Kingdom of Heaven," and only through them can
the rich enter it. Dives has had his consolation
here : the hereafter belongs to Lazarus ; the rich
man must share with the beggar in this world if he
would have fellowship and portion with him in the
next. Such was the contribution of Christianity to
" the social problem," as we now speak. I know
well that this teaching has been perverted, or, rather,
has been blasphemously prostituted, to an argument
for retaining the masses in material and economical
degradation, by representing the All Just as an ac-
complice in human wrong and robbery. Certainly,
I do not so employ it. And the abuse of a truth
does not vitiate its proper use. The question which
I invite my readers to consider is : Can the social
problem be—I do not say solved, it will never be
solved, but—rationally treated without that belief in
the Divine Law of Righteousness, expressed in the
teaching of Christ concerning poverty and riches ?
It is a question worth pondering. I shall leave my
readers to ponder it, placing before them certain
words of a great master—whose inimitable beauty
and pathos, as I know too well, no translation can

more than dimly adumbrate—which may perhaps
aid them in the task, and which may fitly serve as
the epilogue to this volume.

"A disaster—I might almost call it the disaster
of our time "—Victor Hugo is reported to have said [1]
—" is a certain tendency to bring everything within
the limits of this life. Give to man, as his sole end
and object, this earthly and material existence, and
you aggravate all his miseries by the inherent negation : you lay upon wretches already crushed to the
ground the unsupportable burden of Nothingness :
you convert mere suffering, which is the law of God,
into despair, which is the law of hell. Hence con-
vulsions which shake society to its base. Assuredly,
I am one of those who desire,—no one in this place
doubts it—I am one of those who desire, I do not
say sincerely, the word is all too weak, I desire
with an ardour that no words can express, and by
every possible means, to ameliorate in this life the
material lot of those who suffer. But the first of all
ameliorations is to give them hope. How little do
our finite miseries become, when an infinite hope is
mingled with them. The duty of us all, be we who
we may, whether we be legislators or writers, is to
diffuse, to spread abroad, to expend, to lavish, under
every form, the whole energy of society in warring
against and destroying misery : and, at the same
time, to lead all to lift their heads towards heaven,

---

[1] In the debate on the Falloux Law (1850).

to direct all souls, to turn all expectations, towards
a life beyond this, where justice shall be done, where
justice shall be requited.   Let us proclaim it aloud :
No one shall have suffered unjustly or in vain.
Death is a restitution.   The law of the material
world is equilibrium : the law of the moral world is
equity.   God is recovered at the end of all.   Let us
not forget it : let us teach it to all : there would be
no dignity in living—it would not be worth the
trouble—if we were destined wholly to die.   What
lightens labour, what sanctifies toil, what makes
man strong, good, wise, patient, benevolent, just, at
once humble and great, worthy of intellect, worthy
of liberty, is to have ever before him the vision of a
better world, shining athwart the darkness of this
life."

INDEX.

Abelard,
on language and intellect, 26
Abortion,
new duty of, 71
the fruit of the old "orthodox"
political economy, 93
Althorp, Lord,
on the first Reform Act, 214
Animals, the lower,
differences between, and man,
20–28
function of the State regarding, 85, 86
have, in strictness, no rights,
85, 86
cruelty to, should be severely
punished, 86, 288
Anne, Queen,
her plan of government, 151
Aquinas, St. Thomas,
his account of law, 4
on human law, 34
on royalty, 36
on almsgiving, 43
on resistance to the civil
power, 50
on the principal end of the
ruler, 62
on the punishment of heresy, 62
on the true justification of private property in land, 117
on the first and essential qualification for a ruler, 165
his justification of capital punishment, 292
Argyll, the Duke of,
a judicious observation of, 130
Aristocracy,
none in England, 119
Aristotle,
on the extra-social man, 18
his definition of man, 24
on the nature of a thing, 29
his definition of freedom, 32
on the reason for the existence
of the State, 35
his division of the powers of
the State, 133

on the perversion of the State,
169
on absolute equality, 222
on the coercive sanction of law,
254
on the ethical element in praise
or blame, 269
Arnold, Dr.,
on the bond of a Church, 66
Art, animal, 23
Augustine, St.,
on language and thought, 25
on courtesans, 81
Austria,
representative government in,
144

Babeuf,
as Socialist, 126
Bagehot, Mr.,
on the Unreformed Parliament,
142
his caution regarding Parliamentary reform, 215
on the *structure* in English
political society, 218
Bain, Dr.,
his account of free will, 270
on the "I" or self, 273
Ballot, the,
a foolish and mischievous institution, 47, 48
Barnett, Canon,
on a practical result of the corruption of American public
life, 208
Basil, St.,
his account of freedom, 147
Bax, Mr. Belfort,
on marriage and chastity, 72, 78
Beaconsfield, Lord,
on the House of Commons, 160
Belgian Constitution, the,
provision of, on the right of
public meeting, 40
Belgium,
representative government in,
145, 146

311

Index

Economics.

Hadley's Economics.

An Account of the Relations between Private Property
and Public Welfare. By ARTHUR TWINING HAD-
LEY, Professor of Political Economy, in Yale University. 8°, $2.50 *net*.

The work is now used in classes in Yale, Princeton, Harvard, Amherst, Dart-
mouth, Bowdoin, Vanderbilt, Bucknell, Bates, Leland Stanford, University of
Oregon, University of California, etc.

"The author has done his work splendidly. He is clear, precise, and
thorough. . . . No other book has given an equally compact and intelligent
interpretation."—*American Journal of Sociology*.

The Bargain Theory of Wages.

By JOHN DAVIDSON, M A., D Phil. (Edin.), Professor of
Political Economy in the University of New Bruns-
wick. 12mo, $1.50.

A Critical Development from the Historic Theories, together with an examination of Certain Wages Factors: the Mobility of Labor, Trades Unionism, and
the Methods of Industrial Remuneration.

"This able volume is the most satisfactory work on Distribution that has yet
appeared. Prof. Davidson's theory appeals to our common sense as in harmony
with actual conditions, and he has worked it out with convincing logic in accordance with the principles of economic science We recommend it all students of
economics as the most important contribution to the science of Political Economy
that has recently appeared."—*Interior*.

Sociology.

A Treatise. By JOHN BASCOM, author of "Æsthetics,"
"Comparative Psychology," etc. 12°, $1.50.

"Gives a wholesome and inspiring word on all the living social questions of
the day ; and its suggestions as to how the social life of man may be made purer
and truer are rich with the finer wisdom of the time. The author is always
liberal in spirit, generous in his sympathies, and wise in his knowledge."—*Critic*.

A General Freight and Passenger Post.

A Practical Solution of the Railroad Problem. By
JAMES L. COWLES. Third revised edition, with additional material. 12°, cloth, $1.25 ; paper, 50 cts.

"The book gives the best account which has thus far been given in English of
the movement for a reform in our freight and passenger tariff policy, and the
best arguments in favor of such reform."—EDMUND J. JAMES, in the *Annals of
Political and Social Science*.

"The book treats in a very interesting and somewhat novel way of an extremely difficult subject and is well worth careful reading by all students of
the transportation question." — From letter of EDW. A. MOSELEY, Secretary of
the Interstate Commerce Commission, Washington, D.C.

G. P. PUTNAM'S SONS, New York & London.

Sociology.

Social Facts and Forces.

The Factory—The Labor Union—The Corporation— The Railway—The City—The Church. By WASH- INGTON GLADDEN, author of "Applied Christianity," "Tools and the Man," etc. 12°, $1.25.

"The book is full of invigorating thought, and is to be recommended to every one who feels the growing importance of public duties."—*The Outlook.*

Socialism and the Social Movement in the Nineteenth Century.

By WERNER SOMBART, University of Breslau. Germany. Translated by ANSON P. ATTERBURY. With Intro- duction by JOHN B. CLARK, Professor of Political Economy in Columbia University. 12°, $1.25.

"Sombart's treatise on socialism impresses me as admirable ; and the translation is certainly an excellent piece of work."—J. B. CLARK, Professor of Political Economy in Columbia University.

The Sphere of the State,

or, The People as a Body Politic. By FRANK S. HOFF- MAN, A.M., Professor of Philosophy, Union College. Second edition. 12°, $1.50.

" Professor Hoffman has done an excellent piece of work. He has furnished the student with a capital text-book and the general reader, who is interested in political science, with much that is suggestive, much that is worthy of his careful attention."

Anarchism.

A Criticism and History of the Anarchist Theory. By E. V. ZENKER. 12°, $1.50.

" The fullest and best account of anarchism ever published. . . . A most powerful and trenchant criticism."—*London Book Gazette.*

Suggestions Toward an Applied Science of Sociology.

By EDWARD P. PAYSON, 12°. $1.25.

" Mr. Payson has given us a valuable little volume on a very large and most important subject."—*Portland (Me.) Press.*

G. P. PUTNAM'S SONS, New York & London.